NONPROFIT MARKETING BEST PRACTICES

NONPROFIT
MARKETING BEST
PRACTICES

JOHN J. BURNETT

BICENTENNIAL
1807
WILEY
2007
BICENTENNIAL

JOHN WILEY & SONS, INC.

Library of Congress Cataloging-in-Publication Data:

ISBN 13: 978-0-471-79189-8

Printed in the United States of America.

10 9 8 7 6 5 4 3 2 1

I dedicate this book to my daughter, Laura, who despite her disabilities, lives a courageous and joyful life.

CONTENTS

ACKNOWLEDGMENTS

Typically, an author can identify a handful of individuals who profoundly contributed to the successful completion of his or her book. In this instance, however, literally thousands of people have influenced this book and its content. Therefore, I thank all those working in the nonprofit sector who have shared their wisdom, affirmation, and criticisms about the topics covered. Still, this book has been a 15-year process, and the one person who has offered the greatest support and enthusiasm throughout has been my wife Nancy.

About the Author

Dr. John Burnett is a Professor of Marketing and Director of the DU Marketing Roundtable at the Daniels College of Business, the University of Denver. During his 37-year career as a university professor and tenure at six universities, he has always been involved with nonprofit organizations, including The Boys Club of America, The American Red Cross, Lubbock General Hospital, the National Parks Service, the Denver Zoo, and Easter Seals, to name just a few. He has also consulted with companies and organizations that assist and market to nonprofits, such as Johnson & Johnson, AT&T, IBM, and Scott & White Clinics. Since 1988, prompted by the severe brain injury suffered by his daughter, he has focused most of his energy on the disabled community. As such, he was appointed to President Clinton's Commission on Disability and Employment, as well as playing a prominent role as president of the Brain Injury Association of Colorado (BIAC) and the National Brain Injury Association.

Dr. Burnett has authored/co-authored 16 books, including the number one textbook in advertising called Advertising: Principles and Practices (Upper Saddle River, NJ: Prentice Hall). He has also authored/co-authored over 50 academic and trade articles, which have appeared in the leading marketing journals. Of particular importance is the fact that he is one of a handful of authors who has conducted primary research on the disabled consumer.

The impetus for this book is the one-half day workshop he developed 15 years ago and has presented numerous times to nonprofit marketers entitled, "Marketing for Nonprofits: A Strategic Approach." Encouragement from the participants in these workshops, along with hundreds of suggestions, prompted Dr. Burnett to pursue this project.

PREFACE

The challenges faced by twenty-first century nonprofits are severe and getting worse. Despite the historical aversion nonprofits have had toward marketing, these new challenges mean that nonprofits must embrace marketing completely and master the principles and practices that work for them. Determining and satisfying the needs of customers through products that have value and accessibility and whose features are clearly communicated is the general purpose of any business, including nonprofits. It is also a fundamental definition of marketing. This book introduces the nonprofit marketer to the marketing strategies and tools that he or she can use to satisfy customer needs and sustain the success of the organization.

To emphasize how various marketing elements work together to create strategy, I define and explain the various marketing areas and their competitive strengths and weaknesses, as well as stress how to best mix marketing tools in a strategic, integrated plan. The book begins with an overview of the nonprofit sector, along with a discussion of challenges faced. It continues with a discussion of the marketing planning process, the preliminary tasks of developing a plan, and concludes with the tactics available to the marketing planner. This complete coverage ensures that the reader will learn how to plan, execute, and evaluate a marketing program that is effective and efficient from start to finish.

An important difference in this book is the inclusion of "services" marketing as a bridge from traditional marketing to nonprofit marketing. Services marketing, which represents 65 percent of our gross domestic product (GDP), demonstrates the adjustments that are needed when marketing intangible products rather than tangibles. Nonprofit organizations clearly fall into the services category and this book identifies and demonstrates how this sector should approach marketing differently than their for-profit counterparts. This translation is the key to marketing success in a nonprofit.

This book shows how nonprofit organizations should use marketing. It acknowledges that most nonprofits devote limited resources to marketing. Specific examples appear not only in the text discussion, but also serve as chapter openers. Examples and stories bring theory to life, demonstrating the relevance of the recommended principles and practices. This text focuses on U.S.-based nonprofits, since international nonprofits operate under very different parameters.

Time is a precious commodity to those working for nonprofits. My twenty years of working with nonprofits has revealed that there is a clear need for a basic, introductory text that omits unnecessary details. While some professionals working in nonprofit marketing may assess their understanding of marketing as high, I have discovered that this knowledge tends to focus on tactics such as fundraising and event management. Few have a thorough understanding of strategic marketing. Consequently, the topics herein have been carefully selected to impart essential, nonprofit-specific information while still providing adequate depth. It is my hope that you will find these 12 chapters of relevant information extremely useful and comprehensive.

1

NONPROFITS: YESTERDAY, TODAY, AND TOMORROW

"Because the purpose of a business is to create a customer, the business enterprise has two–and only two–basic functions: marketing and innovation. Marketing and innovation produce results. All the rest are costs."

—Peter Drucker

According to the experts who keep track of these things, Hurricane Katrina is the worst catastrophe to befall the contiguous United States since the Civil War. While all the numbers are not yet final, we do know that over one million residents of the Gulf Coast region were displaced. Over 1,100 died. And, nearly 275,000 have sought jobless benefits.

Sadly, a term long used in family counseling, the fractured family, has now been applied to the more than 4,000 kids who have been separated from their families. Fortunately, several experienced investigators have volunteered to find and reunite these children via organizations such as www.missingkids.com and The National Center for Missing & Exploited Children. As usual, there are a handful of evil individuals who have illegally taken some children as their own or perpetrated other scams and frauds.

Katrina also brought out the basic humanity of Americans and individuals worldwide. Over $1 billion was donated by people rich and poor. In addition, thousands of hours have been donated by volunteers who distributed food and water, drove buses, offered their homes, and gave comfort, both professional and personal.

Many corporations have also weighed in to help. Most notably, Wal-Mart had 45 truckloads of relief supplies ready to ship before Katrina made landfall. Wal-Mart ultimately shipped 1,900 trailer loads of emergency supplies to the affected areas. It also pledged more than $22 million in contributions to relief efforts and was operating free stores in several evacuation centers, where it also donated 150 Internet-ready computers to help reunite loved ones separated by the disaster. Many other companies such as Home Depot, General Electric, Anheuser-Busch, and Whole Foods Market played a prominent role. Over 150 companies pledged at least $1 million each.[1]

Clearly, Katrina will impact us all for decades do come. We are left with many unanswered questions. How are we going to pay the estimated $200 billion required to put the Gulf Coast back on its feet? Will Congress raise taxes or cut programs? If the latter, which social programs will be reduced and by how much? How will other parts of the country provide the social services needed for former residents who will never return to the Gulf Coast? If taxes are raised, or existing cuts are not reinstated, will that mean people will be less willing to contribute to nonprofits? Will they be less likely to volunteer? What would be the result if one or more other natural disasters struck the United States or other parts of the world? Does a U.S. crisis mean that tsunami relief donations in the future will not be forthcoming? Nonprofits tend to deal with tough questions such as these.

Ultimately, Katrina highlighted the many areas where our government and the various help agencies were unable to forecast accurately or in time. Yet the Louisiana State University Hurricane Center predicted the disaster years earlier. Even a few days before Katrina hit, the Center warned that the levees would not hold, the pumps were not adequate, and that immediate evacuation was needed. Did the various governments not know that the affected parishes were primarily populated by minorities who did not have the capacity to evacuate? Thus, it comes down to the historical debate of whether the problem was poor information or bad implementation or both.

INTRODUCTION

The point of this discussion is not to resolve this debate but to indicate that traditionally nonprofits have often been caught in the middle. Quite simply, nonprofits meet the needs of the world's inhabitants (animal, vegetable, and mineral) that governments and private industries cannot or will not meet. Hurricane Katrina illustrates that the gap between the observed social needs and satisfied social needs is vast and that the role played by nonprofits worldwide will increase for reasons noted later in this chapter.

The intention of this book is to offer nonprofit marketing managers a set of principles and practices that will make them more effective, competitive, and successful. After working with nonprofits for twenty years, it is clear to me that an answer for many of their problems lies in marketing. In addition, marketing can offer a more reliable forecasting system while also providing an implementation process that will work for nonprofits of all sizes and missions. Moreover, this book offers an important advantage. Unlike existing books, which provide an overview of basic marketing with nonprofit examples thrown in where appropriate, this book incorporates primary data collected from a cross-section of practicing nonprofit marketing managers. It also incorporates the strategic division of products into two categories—goods products and service products. The latter reflects the nonprofit sector. Fortunately, services marketing is a facet of marketing that has produced a unique set of principles and practices that tend to work better within service (nonprofit) organizations. These principles and practices are integrated throughout this book to ensure that it represents nonprofit marketing as it should be practiced.

THE PURPOSES OF NONPROFIT ORGANIZATIONS

Early in the history of America, nonprofit institutions served marginal roles. We then believed that the government could and should discharge all major social tasks, and that the role of business and nonprofits was to supplement governmental programs where necessary. Today, nonprofits support far more initiatives in support of specific needs. Nonprofits are now America's largest employer and facilitate the fundamental American commitment to responsible citizenship. They represent the most important human change agent, bringing education to the unlearned, cures to the unhealthy, and integrity to the shameful.

Religious institutions were the first voluntary associations having evolved out of a religious tradition of serving community needs building on teachings from the Torah, New Testament, Koran, and other holy books written thousands of years ago. Historically, the activities associated with nonprofit organizations such as healthcare, religion, the arts, and social welfare activities were organized and administered by nonsecular bodies.

Tax exemption laws in the United States had their roots in the laws passed by the British Parliament in 1601. These laws set out a list of legitimate objects of charity and established a procedure for accountability for charitable fraud. The earliest charitable organization in the New World was Harvard College, established in 1863, which was free to attend. Following the American

Revolution, the established governments in the former colonies, now states, adopted a new doctrine of not funding religious institutions. Private organizations were created to provide services funded through donations and purchases of services rather than through direct and indirect grants from government.

The number of nonprofit organizations grew dramatically between the end of the Civil War and 1920 as corporate America and private wealth, along with religious congregations, financed the growth of universities, libraries, hospitals, professional organizations, and private clubs. In 1894, the Congress enacted the first federal income tax and provided an exemption for corporations, companies, or associations organized and conducted solely for charitable, religious, or educational purposes.

More recently, research conducted in the late 1990s indicated that the nonprofit sector did undergo rapid expansion during the 1977–1996 period, but that this expansion was not fueled by increases in charitable donations. Rather, the increase in revenues by social service organizations came from commercial income, such as from fees, investment income, and sales of products. Despite the changing character of nonprofits during this period, this sector increased at a rate much faster than the economy.

Today, the modern charitable organization bears little resemblance to the typical charity of the nineteenth century. The challenges for funds are immense, as is the growth of new competitors. Technology has allowed nonprofits to compete worldwide, partnered with a wide variety of government regulations. Yet, nonprofits remain the touchstone for a society's moral agenda. And, yes, there is a reason to be optimistic. Peter Drucker, the father of management and grandfather of marketing, posits that nonprofits remain the most successful business format, given their inherent disadvantages. He notes two success keys in this new environment. First, nonprofits must "convert donors into contributors." Relationships must be formed. Second, nonprofits must "give communities a common purpose."[2]

What Is a Nonprofit Organization?

Few categorical concepts have such a vast array of synonyms and extensions as that of nonprofits or not-for-profits (NFP). Partly this may be a result of the range of organizations that call themselves nonprofits. A nonprofit can be as small as a one-person organization that wants to save a corner park, to the behemoth of the Bill & Melinda Gates Foundation with a budget of billions and a staff of hundreds. A quick review of the definitions of the word "nonprofit" found on Google show a common range of elements:

- A term describing the Internal Revenue Service's designation of an organization whose income is not used for the benefit or private gain of stockholders, directors, or any other persons with an interest in the company. A nonprofit organization's income must be used solely to support its operations and stated purpose. (www.indianagrantmakers. org/give/glossery.html)
- Means any corporation, trust, foundation, or institution which is entitled to exemption under section 501(c)(3) of the Internal Revenue Code, or which is not organized for profit and no part of the net earnings of which insure to the benefit of any private shareholder or individual (except that the definition of "nonprofit organization" at 48 CFR 28.30 shall apply to the use of the patent clause at Section 600.27). (www.1.pr.doe.gov/f600a3.html)
- An organization can be organized with the Internal Revenue determination under several categories of nonprofit status (cannot pay individuals, do not pay taxes on income). (www.delewarecountrybrc.com/ glossaryterms.html)
- A nonprofit organization (often called "non-profit org" or imply "nonprofit" or "not-for-profit") can be seen as an organization that doesn't have a goal to make a profit. It may be entirely funded by voluntary donation.
- Nonprofit institutions exist to benefit society(i.e, serve the public interest),
- regardless of whether profits are achieved.

Salamon and Anheir (1992) posit that the nonprofit sector is a set of organizations that are:

- formally constituted;
- nongovernmental in basic structure;
- self-governing;
- non-profit-distributing;
- voluntary to some meaningful extent[3]

As we move from one country to another, complexity and purpose vary. In Japan, for instance, the nonprofit corporate system, as written in the Japanese civil law, has a complicated divisional structure. Within the civil code, public interest corporations are separated among their fields, with categories such as school corporation, social welfare corporation, religious corporation, and so forth. Accordingly, the NPO Law specifies an organization can become a "specified nonprofit corporation" if it:

- is formed principally to implement one of the specified activities like: art, culture community safety, etc.
- is not formed for generating profit
- has paid staff members less than one-third of the total staff
- is not involved in religious teaching or preaching, or in performing religious ceremonies
- is not for promoting, supporting, or opposing a political ideology, political party, a person holding a public office, or candidate for a public office
- is not operated for the interest of a specified individual or corporation
- is not used for a specified political party
- has provisions of acquisition and loss of membership, which are not unreasonable

It is evident that many of the U.S. nonprofits would not qualify in Japan.

- Australia defines nonprofit institutions (NPIs) in the following way:

> NPIs are legal or social entities created for the purpose of producing goods and services whose status does not permit them to be a source of income, profit, or other financial gain for the units that establish, control, or finance them. In practice, their productive activities are bound to generate either surpluses or deficits but any surpluses they happen to make cannot be appropriated by other institutional units. The articles of association by which they are established are drawn up in such a way that the institutional units which control or manage them are not entitled to a share in any profits or other income which they receive. (SNA 93, para. 4.5-4)

Clearly, the concern in Australia is the management of "profits." Given the varied definitions, what are the characteristics shared by all nonprofits operating worldwide? They are as follows:

- The primary motive of a nonprofit organization is not financial gain.
- If profits are achieved they cannot be paid to any private shareholders or individuals.
- Sources of revenue may be obtained from donations, grants, fund balances, and perhaps sales.
- Taxes are not paid as long as the organization is approved by the governmental guidelines and continues to meet governmental guidelines.
- Accountability and success are determined by the Board vis-à-vis the mission statement, as well as the senior staff (who may or may not also serve on the board).

In sum, a nonprofit organization is not prohibited from making a profit, but there are limitations on what it can do with its profits. There are also limitations on how it can make money – and it must make money in accordance with its nonprofit purposes. Thus, the agenda (mission) for the National Rifle Association is the antithesis of the Brady Campaign to Prevent Gun Violence. Yet, they are both legitimate nonprofits.

In general, U.S. nonprofit organizations receive two primary benefits. First, all organizations can receive tax-deductible contributions from businesses and individuals. Second, most organizations are exempt from income tax and property tax, and some are exempt from sales tax.

To receive these benefits, nonprofit organizations must: (1) obtain a license from the Internal Revenue Service, and (2) file a tax return if their annual revenue is greater than $25,000.

CLASSIFYING NONPROFITS

Definitions and classification are, in a sense, two parts of a related process. The first specifies what the entities in a group have in common, and the second spells out the ways in which they nevertheless differ. Broadly speaking, two basic issues have to be settled in the design of any classification system. The first of these is the unit of analysis to be used; and the second is the basis of the classification, the central variable, or variables, in terms of which entities are to be differentiated from each other. In the case of Japan, for example, the classification is a legal designation known as Charitable Trusts (koeki shintaku), and there is no need to create nonprofit classifications.

At the macro level we can consider three kinds of organizations: the government sector, the private sector, and the voluntary sector. The voluntary sector and nonprofit organizations are synonymous terms. The distinction is somewhat obvious and is illustrated in Exhibit 1.1, which shows how each participated in the Hurricane Katrina disaster.

There are a number of general classification schemas that are available for differentiating the types of organizations that comprise the nonprofit sector: the United Nations International Standard Industrial Classification (ISIC) of all economic activities, the General Industrial Classification of Economic Activities (NACE) developed by the European Statistical Office, and the National Taxonomy of Exempt Entities (NTEE) developed by the National Center for Charitable Statistics in the United States. Essentially, none of these systems are completely aligned, and a system that is precise enough to demarcate an organization in a particular country may not apply to another country. Making comparative work of nonprofits across countries remains difficult.

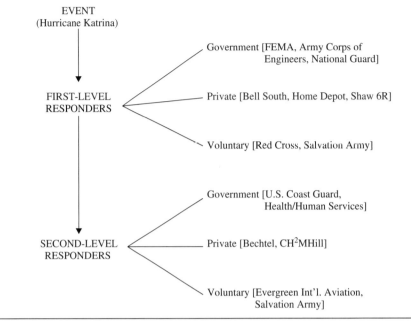

EXHIBIT 1.1   KATRINA RELIEF EFFORT: GOVERNMENT, PRIVATE, AND VOLUNTARY SECTOR PARTICIPATION

THE SIZE AND SHAPE OF NONPROFITS

Because of the differences in nonprofit laws country-to-country, as well as the variety in classifications, there is no accurate count of nonprofits nationwide. However, by focusing on the United States, we can get a fairly accurate snapshot of that nonprofit sector. As shown in Exhibit 1.2, there were 1,397,263 nonprofits registered with the IRS in 2004, with 58.9 percent categorized as 501(c)(3) Public Charities. The overall category has grown 28.8 percent since 1996, while Public Charities have grown 53.5 percent during that same period of time. These numbers do not represent the organizations with less than $25,000 gross receipts, of which there are over a half-million.

If we examine growth, it is apparent that religious organizations are the clear winner, increasing by over 50,000 since 1999, or a 180 percent growth. Coming in second and third are new educational organizations followed by human-service groups. In general, most of this recent growth is attributed to organizations reporting less than $25,000 gross receipts. The growth of charitable organizations in recent years has been fairly consistent. The number of groups increased by 6.1 percent from 2003 to 2004, 6 percent from 2002 to 2003, 5.1 percent from 2001 to 2002, and 5.6 percent from 2000 to 2001.

	1996		2004		
	Number of Orgs.	Percent of All Orgs.	Number of Orgs.	Percent of All Orgs.	Pct. Change
All Nonprofit Organizations	1,084,897	100.0%	1,397,263	100.0%	28.8%
501(c)(3) Public Charities	535,888	49.4%	822,817	58.9%	53.5%
501(c)(3) Private Foundations	58,774	5.4%	102,881	7.4%	75.0%
Other 501(c) Nonprofit Organizations	490,235	45.2%	471,565	33.7%	-3.8%
Small Community Groups and Partnerships, etc.	Unknown	NA	Unknown	NA	NA
501(c)(3) Public Charities	535,888	49.4%	822,817	58.9%	53.5%
501(c)(3) Public Charities Registered with the IRS (Including Registered Congregations)	535,888	49.4%	822,817	58.9%	53.5%
Reporting Public Charities	297,691	27.4%	317,689	22.7%	6.7%
Operating Public Charities	261,640	24.1%	272,236	19.5%	4.0%
Supporting Public Charities	36,051	3.3%	45,453	3.3%	26.1%
Non-Reporting, or with Less than $25,000 in Gross Receipts	238,197	22.0%	505,128	36.2%	112.1%
Congregations (About Half Are Registered with IRS)*	—	0.0%	385,874	27.6%	NA
501(c)(3) Private Foundations	58,774	5.4%	102,881	7.4%	75.0%
Private Grantmaking (Non-Operating) Foundations	56,377	5.2%	98,529	7.1%	74.8%
Private Operating Foundations	2,397	0.2%	4,352	0.3%	81.6%
Other 501(c) Nonprofit Organizations	490,235	45.2%	471,565	33.7%	-3.8%
Civic Leagues Social Welfare Orgs, etc.	127,567	11.8%	119,515	8.6%	-6.3%
Fraternal Beneficiary Societies	102,592	9.5%	87,833	6.3%	-14.4%
Business Leagues, Chambers of Commerce, etc.	68,575	6.3%	71,470	5.1%	4.2%
Labor, Agricultural Horticultural Orgs	61,729	5.7%	58,362	4.2%	-5.5%
Social and Recreational Clubs	57,090	5.3%	56,494	4.0%	-1.0%
Post or Organization of War Veterans	30,578	2.8%	35,097	2.5%	14.8%
All Other Nonprofit Organizations	42,104	3.9%	42,794	3.1%	1.6%

Note: Excludes out-of-scope organizations.

*The number of congregations is from the website of American Church Lists (http://list.infousa.com/acl.htm), 2004. These numbers are excluded from the the totals for the state since approximately half of the congregations are included under registered public charities.

Sources: IRS Business Master File 12/2004 (with modifications by the National Center for Charitable Statistics at the Urban Institute to exclude foreign and governmental organizations).

EXHIBIT 1.2 NUMBER OF NONPROFIT ORGANIZATIONS IN THE UNITED STATES, 1996–2004

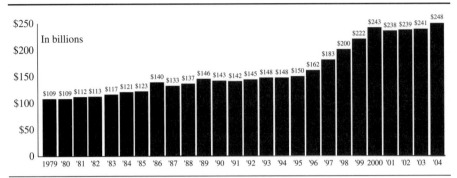

EXHIBIT 1.3 DONATIONS TO NONPROFIT GROUPS OVER THE PAST 25 YEARS
Source: AAFRC Trust for Philanthropy

The IRS has acknowledged that an unknown number of the organizations classified under Section 501(c)(3) are still on the government books even though they have shut down.

The other key statistic that has a direct bearing on nonprofits is the level and target of giving. Exhibit 1.3 shows the trend in U.S. giving since 1979 to 2004, when giving rose 2.3 percent since 2003 to $248.5 billion. Moreover, until Hurricane Katrina hit, many fund raisers were predicting a very promising 2005. This catastrophe, combined with the country's perceived somewhat diminished economic well being financial health, high fuel prices, and possible legislation restricting some types of non-cash gifts has made charities more wary.

The "Giving USA" annual report on philanthropy points to several less obvious worrisome trends. For example, the gains reported have not been evenly realized among the nation's nonprofit groups. Many small and medium-sized charities are still struggling to raise as much as they did in 2001. Social-services groups have faced an especially difficult time. Donations to them fell 1.1 percent last year, which marks the third consecutive year of declines. International groups, which faced a 1.8 percent decline, were the only other type of organizations where giving dropped.[4]

Several explanations have been offered to explain this divergence between groups of different sizes and missions. Fairly obvious is the fact that small charities tend to receive donations from a broad mix of individuals, while bigger groups receive most of their money from foundations, corporations, and wealthier people. A vibrant stock market has helped the latter groups, while a high jobless rate and stagnant economy has been deleterious for the former.

Among other key findings from the report:

- Gifts by living individuals grew by 1.4 percent in 2004, while bequests rose by 6.4 percent.
- Businesses and foundations both increased their giving by 4.5 percent.
- Wealthy Americans put a lot of their money into philanthropic foundations. Gifts to foundations grew by 8 percent, a bigger percentage gain than any other type of nonprofit organization.

FACTORS AND TRENDS AFFECTING NONPROFITS

There are many events that have occurred during the last three decades that have had, and will continue to have, a bearing on the future of the nonprofit sector. They include a growth of new diseases and the possibilities of the return of old ones; the dissolution of the Soviet Union and its emergence as a second-rate power; global terrorism and the shift of resources to protection and mitigation; a succession of armed conflicts, especially Iraq; the development of China and India as potential economic leaders; climate changes such as global warming and pollution; and political instability, especially in Third World nations.

Aside from these general trends, there are several that have ramifications for nonprofits more directly.

The World Is Flat

In his recent bestseller, Thomas Friedman proclaims, *The World Is Flat*. This declaration was based on his travels through Bangalore where he observed the convergence of technology and software, along with reduced costs, allowing every corner of the world to compete for global knowledge work. Essentially, the global competitive playing field was being leveled. "It is now possible for more people than ever to collaborate and compete in real time with more other people on more different kinds of work from different corners of the planet and on a more equal footing than any previous time in the history of the world—using computers, e-mail, networks, teleconferencing, and dynamic new software." We have arrived at a period in history where individuals can collaborate and compete globally.

Many nonprofits will become a major element in this flattening phenomenon. The support of the tsunami relief effort exemplifies one such example. The funding and dissemination of international aid was accomplished through this convergence. Requests for donations originated with phone banks in India, Australia, Los Angeles, and Brussels to name but a few locations. Until Hurricane Katrina, the tsunami spawned the largest e-mail campaign to date.

There are possible risks to globalizing a nonprofit. For one, it could mean that the inherent identity of a local, regional, or even national cause could be lost in the maze of cultural cross-over. Similarly, individual giving and volunteering might diminish as people seek global solutions to what might better be regarded as national or even local issues.

Irrespective of locale, individuals can now identify and fund worthy projects in countries all over the world. Furthermore, these individuals can receive immediate feedback along with suggestions as to how they might contribute in other ways such as lobbying and campaigning.

Even corporate donors will be affected. Those that operate globally will surely support nonprofits that provide them with recognition in the countries in which they operate. Procter&Gamble, for example, is a major supporter of UNICEF. In turn, UNICEF works with P&G to create programs that benefit both parties.

An Era of Accountability

Although corruption has always been part of the world, the last decade has witnessed a plethora of corporate scandals. New laws, such as the Federal Sarbanes-Oxley, State-level versions of Sarbanes-Oxley, various congressional actions, and the Tax Relief Act of 2005 in the United States, have emerged as a way of holding organizations accountable. While trust has always been an underlying trait of nonprofits, it has become even more salient as scandals with nonprofits such as Easter Seals and their questionable allocation practices have become known. While the public has always had the right to know how their money is being spent and to what extent objectives have been achieved, the amount and quality of information has changed.

Changes in the rules of accounting have flowed over into the nonprofit sector. The list of financial data required of nonprofits is now much longer and more detailed. Clearly, the auditing process will continue to change and nonprofits will have to collect additional financial information well beyond that found on the current Form 990. Creative accounting is a thing of the past.

Accountability is also part of the due diligence assigned to nonprofit organizations. A major challenge of all nonprofits is to meet their objectives while remaining financially viable. An operating deficit might indicate to donors that an organization that may be worthy of additional support or that it is wasting money on fundraising or administration. Conversely, a nonprofit with a large surplus could indicate that an organization is good at raising money but bad at meeting the needs of its constituents.

Historically, nonprofits have not had good measures of operational efficiency. This gap has begun to change through the creation of benchmarks of performance. For example, the Council of Better Business Bureaus and the Philanthropic Advisory Service (both located in the United States) currently specify a 35 percent limit on fund-raising costs. The National Charities Bureau specifies a minimum of 60 percent of annual expenses should be spent on programs. These numbers remain somewhat arbitrary, and it is expected that future guidelines will be more scientific.

Finally, the nonprofit sector has exhibited a greater interest in self-regulation. Examples include the Better Business Bureau's "Wise Giving Alliance" program and the State of Maryland's Association of Nonprofits "Standards for Excellence." This trend toward self-monitoring will definitely continue.

Boomers and Beyond

The baby boomers include all U.S. citizens born between 1946 and 1964. During that period, 76.4 million people were born in the United States, of whom approximately 67 million are still alive. They represent over one-fourth of the total U.S. population. The majority of baby boomers are in blue-collar occupations and they have fallen short of reaching the modern American Dream. Theoretically they will begin retiring in 2011, although only 11 percent of the U.S. workforce actually retires at age 65. The impetus for the Baby Boom segment of the population was the end of World War II and the simultaneous return of soldiers who all began new families around the same time. All the countries involved in World War II have the equivalent of a Baby Boom segment.

The significance of the Baby Boomers to the nonprofit sector is profound. Obviously, since they will soon begin to retire they will become major recipients of the services offered by both the government and nonprofit sectors. What is unknown is the extent to which they will be able to sustain themselves financially, medically, and socially. Current statistics indicate that as many as 40 percent of Boomers expect to live off of Social Security only. Experts suggest that this is dangerously optimistic. Moreover, mortality tables suggest many Boomers will live into their 90s and beyond, requiring medical support from a Medicare system that is already strained.

The Catch-22 is that while Boomers will require more support services from a cross-section of nonprofits, they will be unable to pay for them.

Because of their low income base, their proportion of taxes paid will be low as well. Moreover, their two younger cohorts, Generation X (born between 1965 and 1972) and Generation Y (born between 1973 and 1984), are unlikely to vote for programs that increase the benefits to the Boomers because they already will be paying for the Boomers' Social Security benefits. In the end, the Boomers will likely be a tremendous burden on society and will prompt a growth in nonprofit organizations that focus on social services. This may come at the expense of the more esoteric nonprofits such as the arts and education. This trend will likely be mirrored throughout the world.

There is one piece of good news associated with the Baby Boomers. The pool of volunteers will be huge. Many retired Boomers with a great deal of spare time will look for opportunities to fill that time and/or give back. However, nonprofits should not expect these Boomers to volunteer cash. Rather, nonprofits should provide opportunities to volunteer time, expertise, and ideas.

MARKETING'S BENEFITS TO NONPROFITS

We have already provided a bit of history as to the partnership between nonprofits and the discipline of marketing. Most agree that marketing now plays a prominent role in the success of nonprofits. What are those benefits?

A prerequisite to this discussion is to offer a basic definition of marketing. Marketing is often simply described as "finding, attracting, satisfying, and keeping customers." As will become evident throughout this book, marketing is much more than that and includes many possible strategies and useful tools. Still, this simple definition will suffice for now. Now, onto the benefits.

- Marketing offers a paradigm that is more appropriate for the environment in which nonprofits must operate. Essentially, the traditional exchange model employed by nonprofits, where individuals and institutions donate with no expectations, is no longer valid. Instead, nonprofits now reflect a commercial exchange where all the parties expect to benefit. This is the realm of marketing.
- In conjunction with the notion of exchange is the premise that marketing plays a major role in influencing the behavior of others. In the nonprofit sector, however, the behavior requests are often more difficult. Examples are trying to persuade a junkie in need of a fix to carry clean needles or to persuade a teenager to always use a condom when having sex. People are reluctant to give their time, money, and bodily fluids to causes that are vague and difficult to hold accountable.

Therefore, employing a marketing mindset is a necessary requisite to facilitating nonprofit exchanges.

- Good marketing introduces measures of performance into the nonprofit sector that are more appropriate for nonprofits. In addition to metrics of social responsibility, marketing performance measures such as market share, incremental sales, and return on investment (ROI) can be applied consistently to nonprofits and allow nonprofits to gauge success in a more salient manner. These marketing measures have been tested in many settings, and although modifications may be necessary, they are superior to the current metrics used by nonprofits.

- Marketing introduces a terminology into the nonprofit sector that better aligns the tasks performed by nonprofits with the reality of the marketplace. Thinking of the homeless person or blood donors, for example, as "customers" seems to be alien in nonprofit sectors. However, the term becomes meaningful when a nonprofit organization reformulates its thinking to position their service users as individuals who are giving up something of value, just as a customer gives up dollars for a new car. Similarly, clustering survivors of Katrina into market segments with respect to their needs for goods and services will resonate as a meaningful marketing strategy that will lead to better solutions. One of the benefits of this book is to introduce the reader to this terminology and way of thinking.

- Marketing is a business function that transitions smoothly from one culture to another. Nonprofits are now operating in a global arena, as noted earlier. All the marketing strategies and tactics discussed in this book are employed wherever a business exists. Marketing provides a bridge for nonprofits that wish to move to other cultures and/or countries. Nonprofits need to know how to operate in a country quite different than their own, while still understanding the inherent elements of the exchange process, good product design, appropriate pricing, effective communication, and efficient distribution systems.

- Marketing has an impact on society as a whole, and nonprofits certainly deal with the problems of society. Concepts such as trade deficits, embargoes, devaluation of foreign currency, price fixing, deceptive advertising, product safety, and unethical selling take on new meaning when viewed from a marketing standpoint. This knowledge should make for a more enlightened nonprofit marketer who understands what such social and political issues mean to you, your organization, and society.

PROBLEMS IN APPLYING MARKETING

While the benefits of employing marketing as part of the operation of non-profits is somewhat obvious, there are inherent problems with nonprofits that make implementation of marketing difficult.

- *A restrictive business model.* The notion that nonprofits are not supposed to make a profit makes operating a successful organization a hit-or-miss proposition. This model is particularly deleterious to marketing planning, which often requires an investment of cash or other resources before a measurable result is noted. This lag phenomenon is not possible where the goal is to break even at the end of the year. Advertising, for example, is a marketing tactic that requires a long-term horizon to build the necessary momentum to achieve its objectives. Likewise, most nonprofits consistently operate at the financial margin and investing in the unknown benefits of marketing is looked upon with a degree of fear.
- *The traditional view of marketing.* Until the last three decades, marketing and all its facets were not viewed as proper for nonprofits. It was believed that individuals should volunteer to work in nonprofits for altruistic reasons and give their dollars from the goodness of their hearts. The notion that nonprofits would *trick* people to volunteer or donate through a variety of marketing gimmicks was unacceptable. Unfortunately, that premise is still alive and well with many nonprofit staffs, boards, volunteers, and donors. As a result, marketing is often totally rejected or minimally employed as a strategic option. This means that marketing is disjointed and is forced to consider strategic alternatives that are both ineffective and costly.
- *Intangible benefits.* When a person donates $100 to the Red Cross for the victims of Hurricane Katrina, he is not exactly sure what he expects to gain or how to measure it. If the statistics hold true, 30 to 40 percent of those who pledged will not honor that pledge. For many nonprofits, the benefits offered to all their constituents are, for the most part, intangible. People make a sacrifice that accrues to others and may feel good initially, but grow resentful after a few hours or days. Somehow the nonprofit marketer must "tangibilize" all these elements, including unconscious feelings, so that all the constituents will feel satisfied and become loyal customers. A premise of this book is that the way to do this is to consider nonprofit marketing as a part of "service marketing," a topic that will be discussed in a later chapter.

- *A static product.* For companies such as Microsoft, it is relatively easy to modify the many elements that constitute one of their software products. Such changes might make the product less expensive, perform better, or simply be more attractive. In any case, changes are possible. For many nonprofits, the elements of the product offering are strictly dictated by the Mission Statement. The Red Cross is mandated to rescue all known survivors regardless of the cost or benefits derived. They are not allowed to make modifications in order to make the operation more profitable. Many social services offer a wide range of products, even though many are used infrequently. In addition, nonprofit marketers often sell products that no one wants or where the level of engagement is small. People don't want to be tested for AIDS, students don't want to take physics, and the home-bound don't want to be cared for by strangers. Because the basic offering cannot be changed, marketers must be clever in creating a marketing strategy that engages the other marketing tactics. Much of this book will deal with the various ways of accomplishing this objective.

- *Limited research opportunities.* Despite the fact that the exchange process is more complex and intangible in nonprofits, there is very little concrete data available to better understand the decision-making process and how the various marketing tactics affect it. For many, gathering market behavior data from the various constituents of nonprofits is essentially considered the ultimate invasion of privacy. Consequently, either data is not collected or the quality is suspect. And, much of the information that is gathered comes from secondary sources and is not necessarily applicable to that specific nonprofit. A fundamental understanding of marketing research is provided in a later chapter.

- *Poor control of employees, volunteers, and board.* Historically, individuals who seek employment with a nonprofit have a personal desire to help others, regardless of the low pay or poor working conditions. This often correlates with limited education and/or skill sets. It is unlikely that they will have a background in marketing. Even if they are assigned to do marketing, they will wear several other hats. Volunteers will be even more diverse, and perhaps severely limited in their marketing expertise. Board members may be more experienced, but not necessarily in marketing. Because of factors such as these, plus a predilection against marketing and inadequate time to do marketing tasks, marketing is often poorly controlled in nonprofits.

GUIDELINES FOR MARKETING SUCCESS IN NONPROFITS

The social environment in which nonprofits now operate is dynamic and variable. Strategies that are effective in one community fail in another. Understanding, adaptability, and execution are critical attributes to organizational success. The following are guidelines applicable to twenty-first century nonprofit marketing:

- Marketing decisions must be carefully crafted based on relevant information. There must always be enough time for strategic marketing, and intuition and guesswork should be kept to a minimum.
- Marketing is a long-term process. While meeting short-term objectives is often important, marketing is a marathon not a sprint.
- Although monitoring competition is important, marketers must focus on their unique mission and objectives.
- Marketers must solve real customer problems. Resolving only superficial problems or those defined only by the marketer will always lead to failure.
- Everything a marketer does should be held accountable—there are no free rides or implied promises.
- The ultimate success of marketing is based on excellent implementation.

ORGANIZATION OF THIS BOOK

As indicated at the outset of this chapter, it is critical that nonprofit marketing managers have a clear and accurate understanding of the marketing planning process. Therefore, the organization of this book mirrors that process. It begins in Chapter 2 with a discussion of marketing and the planning process employed. In Chapter 3, the various approaches to the marketplace are explained. Marketing research and its various tools are delineated in Chapter 4. Chapter 5 considers the environmental elements outside the control of the organization. Chapter 6 begins the transition to another form of marketing, referred to as services marketing. Nonprofits operate in the service sector and this transition makes the tactical chapters of this book more relevant. In Chapter 7 the decision making process employed by the consumer is investigated, along with the variables that influence this process. Chapter 8 discusses the facets of creating and managing service (nonprofit) products. Chapter 9 does the same for the many tools of marketing communications. Chapter 10 considers the pricing channels of distribution decisions related to service products. Chapter 11 examines the new marketing-related technologies available to nonprofits. In Chapter 12 we consider all this new information and how it facilitates fundraising and attracting volunteers.

REFERENCES

1. Lewis, Nicole and Nicole Wallace, "Donations to Help Victims of Hurricane Katrina Surpass $585 Million", *The Chronicle of Philanthropy*, (September 15, 2005), pp. 17–18; "Kindness of Strangers", *The Chronicle of Philanthropy*, (September 15, 2005) p. 6; Jones, Del, "Corporate Giving Reaches $547 Million", *USA Today*, (September 13, 2005), p. 48; Neff, Jack, "Katrina Brings Out WalMart's Inner Good Guy", *Advertising Age*, (September 12, 2005); pp. 1, 55.

2. Drucker, Peter F., *Managing the Nonprofit Organization*, Harper Collins, (1990), p. xvii.

3. Blum, Debra E. (2005), "Giving Ticks Upward", *The Chronicle of Philanthropy*, www.philanthropy.com/premiums/articles.

2

THE ESSENCE OF MARKETING: TERMS AND PROCESSES NONPROFITS NEED TO KNOW

> Marketing is the distinguishing, unique function of the business....The aim of marketing is to make selling unnecessary."
>
> —*Peter Drucker*

Chicago's Field Museum faces the same challenges of most nonprofit institutions. Most notably, they need to identify opportunities to supplement the revenues they receive from grants, donations, and admissions. One particular success is the safari led by William Stanley, a long-time zoologist at the museum. Every winter, for two weeks, Stanley leads a group of tourists on a safari through Tanzania and provides a depth of information that travelers on other tours rarely get. At campfires each night, he talks about his childhood growing up in Kenya. Stanley, collection manager of the museum's division of mammals, says he enjoys sharing his experiences: "I love to see the expression on people's faces when they first go to the Ngorongoro Crater," a 102-square-mile crater filled with rhinos, cheetahs, and lions. This field trip is one of eight led by Field Museum scientists.

While this sort of tourism is not new, it is growing in popularity due to the approaching retirement of the Baby Boomer generation; those Americans born between 1946 and 1964. Part of the baby boomer sector is particularly appealing to exotic travel marketers. "They are educated, they are healthy, and they have been life-long learners," notes Amy Kotken, director of Smithsonian Journeys. Smithsonian Journeys is part of the great Smithsonian

Institution and runs about 250 trips a year. There is a vast variety in these trips, including expeditions to remote locations such as Siberia, city-based excursions, hiking or biking tours, and cruises. Typically, these opportunities are only available to members.

Such trips tend to be pricier, but are usually worth it. They include at least one full-time expert, a tour manager, educational materials, high-end accommodations, local guides, and private receptions. In some instances they may target certain audiences. For example, a safari offered by the Denver Zoo focused on educators and included visits to several schools in Kenya. Participants were encouraged to bring various school supplies to donate. On the American Museum of Natural History's family trip to China, participants had an opportunity to tour a panda breeding facility and make Chinese kites.[1]

It is evident that creating these tours is marketing, even though nonprofits may not like to admit that fact. Smithsonian Journeys employs a comprehensive marketing plan that compares well with the best for-profit organizations. In contrast, the Denver Zoo considers their safari to be just one of several potential money-making endeavors, somewhat detached from a rather limited planning document.

INTRODUCTION

The value of engaging in strategic marketing will become clear in this chapter and those that follow. Smithsonian Journeys has consistently increased their profits from these programs, and their marketing plan has a five-year horizon. The Denver Zoo isn't sure about future tours until they assess the return on the current one.

Regis McKenna (1991) suggested that "Marketing today is not a function; it is a way of doing business." (p. 69).[2] This statement concurred with an earlier comment by Schonberger (1990, p. 16), a world-renowned production and manufacturing authority: "The marketing message doesn't belong just to the marketing people. We all must assume part of the job of presenting our products, services, talents, and capacity to the customers."[3] Therefore, if firms are truly to become market-oriented, the marketing function itself must become more strategic in its orientation.

Marketing constitutes just one of the functions available to every business. Along with personnel, research, production, finance, accounting, and a myriad of other functions, marketing contributes to the ability of a business to succeed. In many businesses, marketing may be deemed of highest importance; in others, it may be relegated to a lesser role. The very existence of business depends upon successful products and services, which in turn rely on successful marketing. For this reason, every businessperson will benefit from a basic marketing knowledge. Moreover, marketing principles have been effectively applied to several nonbusiness institutions for more than 30 years. Bankers, physicians, accounting firms, investment analysts, politicians, churches, architectural firms, universities, and the United Way have all come to appreciate the benefits of marketing.

MARKETING: DEFINITION AND JUSTIFICATION

Defining Marketing

Noted Harvard Professor of Business Theodore Levitt states that the purpose of all business is to "find and keep customers." Furthermore, the only way you can achieve this objective is to create a *competitive advantage*. That is, you must convince buyers (potential customers) that what you have to offer them comes closest to meeting their particular need or want at that point in time. Hopefully, you will be able to provide this advantage consistently, so that eventually the customer will no longer consider other alternatives and will purchase your product out of habit. This loyal behavior is exhibited by people who drive only Fords, brush their teeth with only Crest, buy only Dell computers, and have been season ticket holders to the San Francisco Ballet for 20 years. Creating this blind commitment—without consideration of alternatives—to a particular brand, store, person, or idea is the dream of all businesses. It is unlikely to occur, however, without the support of an effective marketing program. In fact, the specific role of marketing is to *provide assistance in identifying, satisfying, and retaining customers*.

While the general tasks of marketing are somewhat straightforward, attaching an acceptable definition to the concept has been difficult. A textbook writer once noted, "Marketing is not easy to define. No one has yet been able to formulate a clear, concise definition that finds universal acceptance." Yet a definition of some sort is necessary of we are to lay out the boundaries of what is properly to be considered "marketing." How do marketing activities differ from nonmarketing activities? What activities should one refer to as marketing activities? What institutions should one refer to as marketing institutions?

Marketing is advertising to advertising agencies, events to event marketers, knocking on doors to salespeople, direct mail to direct mailers. In other words, to a person with a hammer, everything looks like a nail. In reality, marketing is a way of thinking about business, rather than a bundle of techniques. It's much more than just selling stuff and collecting money. It's the connection between people and products, customers and companies. Like organic tissue, this kind of connection—or relationship—is always growing or dying. It can never be in a steady state. And like tissue paper, this kind of connection is fragile. Customer relationships, even long-standing ones, are contingent on the last thing that happened.

Tracing the evolution of the various definitions of marketing proposed during the last 30 years reveals two trends: 1. expansion of the application of marketing to nonprofit and nonbusiness institutions such as charities, education, or healthcare; and 2. expansion of the responsibilities of marketing beyond the personal survival of the individual firm, to include the betterment of society as a whole. These two factors are reflected in the official American Marketing Association definition published in 2004.

> Marketing is an organizational function and a set of processes for creating, communicating, and delivering value to customers and for managing customer relationships in ways that benefit the organization and its stakeholders. (*Marketing News*, September 15, 2004)

This new definition denotes some significant changes. Most notably, it suggests that marketing is an organizational activity, and is the responsibility of everyone in an organization, not just a group of self-defined marketing experts. Likewise, marketing is a revenue-generator and is responsible for providing adequate returns to all stakeholders. Finally, marketing should meet a specific need or want for a particular customer. It is not about producing irrelevant goods and services.

While this definition can help us better comprehend the parameters of marketing, it does not provide a full picture. Definitions of marketing cannot flesh out specific transactions and other relationships among these elements. Nor can they assess the inefficiencies of having too few or too many marketers operating in a particular market or assume that every product or service is worthy of consumption for everyone. The following five propositions are offered to supplement this definition and better position marketing within the firm:

1. The overall directive of any organization is the mission statement or some equivalent supplement of organizational goals. It reflects the inherent business philosophy of the organization. Today it is appropriate that this direct major societal and public policy issues.

2. Every organization has a set of functional areas (e.g., accounting, production, finance, human resources, marketing) that are necessary for the success of the organization. These functional areas must be managed if they are to achieve maximum performance.

3. Every functional area is guided by the philosophy (derived from the mission statement or company goals) that governs its approach toward its ultimate set of tasks.
4. Marketing differs from the other functional areas in that its primary concern is with exchanges that take place in markets, outside the organization (called a *transaction*).
5. Marketing is most successful when the philosophy, tasks, and manner of implementation are coordinated and complementary.

Perhaps an example will clarify these propositions: L.L. Bean is an extremely successful mail order company. The organization bases much of its success on its longstanding and straightforward mission statement: "Customer Satisfaction: An L.L. Bean Tradition" (Proposition 1). The philosophy permeates every level of the organization and is reflected in high quality products, fair pricing, convenience, a 100 percent satisfaction policy and—above all—dedication to customer service (Proposition 2). This philosophy has necessitated a very high standard of production, efficient billing systems, extensive and responsive communication networks, computerization, innovative cost controls, and so forth. Moreover, it has meant that all of these functional areas have been in constant communication, must be totally coordinated, and must exhibit a level of harmony and mutual respect that creates a positive environment in order to reach shared goals (Proposition 3). The L.L. Bean marketing philosophy is in close harmony with its mission statement. Everything the marketing department does must reinforce and make real the abstract concept of "consumer satisfaction" (Proposition 4). The price-product-quality relationship must be fair. The product must advertise in media that reflects this high quality. Consequently, L.L. Bean advertises through its direct-mail catalog and through print ads in prestigious magazines (for instance, *National Geographic*). It also has one of the most highly regarded websites (see Ad 1.1). Product selection and design are based upon extensive research indicating the preferences of their customers. Since product delivery and possible product return is critical, marketing must be absolutely sure that both these tasks are performed in accordance with customers' wishes (Proposition 5). While one might argue that the marketing function must be the most important function at L.L. Bean, this is not the case. L.L. Bean is just as likely to lose a customer because of incorrect billing (an accounting function) or a flawed hunting boot (a production function) as it is from a misleading ad (a marketing function).

Admittedly, marketing is often a critical part of a firm's success. Nevertheless, the importance of marketing must be kept in perspective. For many large manufacturers such as Procter & Gamble, Microsoft, Toyota, and Sanyo, marketing represents a major expenditure, and these businesses depend on the effectiveness of their marketing effort. Conversely, for regulated industries (such as utilities, social services, or medical care) or small businesses providing a one-of-a-kind product, marketing may be little more than a few informative brochures. There are literally thousands of examples of businesses—many quite small, many nonprofits—that have neither the resources nor the inclination to support an elaborate marketing organization and strategy. These businesses rely less on research than on common sense. In all these cases, the marketing program is only worth the costs if it fits the organization and facilitates its ability to reach its goals.

CHARACTERISTICS OF A MARKETING ORGANIZATION

The application of marketing in a particular organization varies tremendously, ranging from common-sense marketing to marketing departments with thousands of staff members and multimillion dollar budgets. Yet, both may have a great deal in common with respect to how they view the activity called marketing. We refer to these common characteristics as the *Cs of Marketing*. They are your clues that a business understands marketing.

Consumer Content

What makes the existence of any organization possible is that there are a significant number of people who need the product or service offered by that organization. As soon as that group becomes too small, or the need no longer exists, or some other organization can satisfy that need better, the organization will be eliminated. That is the way of a free economy. Thus, a politician doesn't get reelected, an inner-city church closes its doors, the money needed to cure AIDS is not allocated, and the Vail Ski Resort files for bankruptcy.

In the case of business organizations, and marketing organizations in particular, the people with the need are called *consumers* or *customers*. For nonprofits, customers are clients or recipients. In marketing, the act of obtaining a desired object from someone by offering something of value in return is called the *exchange process*. Moreover, the exchange between the person with the need (one who gives money or some other personal resource) and the organization offering this need-satisfying thing (a product, service, or idea) is inherently economic, and is called a *transaction*. There tends to be some negotiation between the parties. Individuals on both sides attempt to maximize rewards and minimize costs in their transactions so as to obtain the most profitable outcomes. Ideally, all parties achieve a satisfactory level of reward.

In each transaction, there is an underlying philosophy in respect to how the parties perceive the exchange. Sometimes deception and lying permeate the exchange. Other exchanges may be characterized as equitable, where each party receives about the same as the other—the customer's need is satisfied and the business makes a reasonable profit. With the emergence of the Internet and e-commerce during the 1990s, the nature of the exchange for many businesses and customers has changed dramatically. Today's customers have access to far more and far better information. They also have many more choices. Businesses must provide a similar level of information and must deal with new competitors that are quicker, smarter, and open 24/7.

An organization that employs marketing correctly knows that keeping customers informed is easier if they keep in constant contact with the customer. This does not necessarily mean that they write and call regularly, although it could. Rather, it more likely means that a marketing organization knows a great deal about the characteristics, values, interests, and behaviors of its customers, and monitors how these factors change over time. Although the process is not an exact science, there is sufficient evidence that marketers who do this well tend to succeed.

When this attempt to know as much about the consumer as possible is coupled with a decision to base all marketing on this information, it is said that the organization is *consumer-oriented* or has adopted the *marketing concept*. It means working back from the customers' needs, rather than forward from the marketer's capabilities.

Both historically and currently, many businesses do not follow the marketing concept. Companies such as Texas Instruments and Otis Elevator followed what has been labeled as *production orientation*, where the focus is on technology, innovation, and low production costs. Such companies assume that a technically superior or less expensive product sells itself. There are also companies, such as Amway, where sales and marketing are essentially the same thing. This *sales orientation* assumes that a good salesperson has a capability to sell anything. Often, this focus on the selling process may ignore the consumer or view the consumer as someone to be manipulated. Insightful businesses acknowledge the importance of production and sales, but realize that a three-step process is most effective: 1. continuously collect information about customers' needs and competitors' capabilities; 2. share the information across departments; and 3. use the information to create a competitive advantage by increasing value for customers. However, the identification of multiple potential customers as well as satisfying their many needs is not easy. This was evidenced by a nonprofit organization whose goal was to stop domestic violence. Funding was their most serious problem. The executive director and founder of this nonprofit organization wondered, "Who is my customer? I need to get information about our services to the people who need it most: victims of domestic violence. Yet, I also need to market my ideas to people who don't need it, in order to obtain funding for resources and education." Nonprofits are especially challenged by the fact that they always have dual markets that have different needs and desires.

Company Capabilities

All marketing organizations try to objectively compare their existing capabilities with their ability to meet the consumer's needs now and in the future. Moreover, when deficiencies are found, a good marketing organization must be willing to make changes as quickly as possible. When Toyota realized that their products were not connecting with consumers aged 35 and younger, it decided to take direct action. In 1999, it gathered eight people in their 20s and 30s from around the company into a new, ethnically diverse marketing group called Genesis. Their first assignment was to launch three cars meant to pull in younger buyers: the entry-level ECHO subcompact, a sporty new two-door Celica, and the MR2 Spyder, a racy convertible roadster.

Although assessing company capabilities often begins in the marketing area, all the business functions must be assessed. Do we have the technical know-how to produce a competitive product? Do we have the plant capacity? Do we have the necessary capital? Do we have good top management? A "no" to any of these questions may stymie the marketing effort. Conversely, a strong advantage in cost control or dynamic leadership may provide the company with a competitive marketing advantage that has little to do with marketing, but everything to do with the business succeeding.

For nonprofits, which often have very scarce resources, assessing capabilities is even more critical. A simple rule-of-thumb for nonprofits is to "focus only on those things you are competent to do." If you run a hospital, you had better not try to do what you are not competent to do. For clinical neurology, you need a certain critical mass—forty beds, fifty beds—to do a decent job. If you are the only hospital in Ulin, Illinois, and there's not another hospital around for fifty miles, you have to do what has to be done. Many liberal arts colleges think they can do everything, without an objective consideration of their strengths and weaknesses. This leads us to the second rule for effective nonprofit marketing: "Don't put your scarce resources where they aren't going to have results."

Communication

Few doubt that the secret of success in any relationship is communication. This is especially true in a marketing relationship, where the attitude of both parties is frequently skeptical, the nature of the contact is hardly intimate, and the message delivery system tends to be impersonal and imprecise. It's because of these factors that communication plays such an important role in a marketing organization.

Marketers know that consumers are constantly picking up cues put out by the organization, or about the organization, that they use to form attitudes and beliefs about the organization. Many of these message-laden cues are controlled by the organization, including factors such as product design, product quality, price, packaging, outlet selection, advertising, and the availability of coupons. In this case, marketers follow basic communication principles that are discussed throughout this book. Most notably, there is a constant attempt to make sure that all of these elements deliver a consistent message and that this message is understood and interpreted in the same way by the various consumers.

On the other hand, there are many message-laden cues that are not under the control of the marketer, yet may be more powerful in the minds of consumers, and that must be anticipated and dealt with by the marketers. A recent report that United Air Lines had the worst customer satisfaction scores created a downturn in both United's stock and customer reservations. Although there are many sources delivering such information, the three most prominent are employees, competitors, and the media.

Employees from the president on down are all considered representatives of the organization for which they work. Consumers often assume that the behavior, language, or dress of an employee is an accurate reflection of the entire organization. Making employees—and possibly even former employees—positive ambassadors of the organization has become so important that a new term has emerged—*internal marketing*.

Competitors say a great deal about one another, some truths, some bold-faced lies. A marketing organization must be cognizant of the possibility and be prepared to respond. The automobile industry has used *comparison messaging* for over thirty years. Coke and Pepsi have been attacking and counter-attacking for about the same length of time. Negative political messages appear to be very effective, even though few politicians admit to the strategy.

Finally, the media (editors and reporters working for newspapers, TV and radio stations, and magazines) looms as one of the greatest communication hurdles faced by marketers. In a large marketing organization, the responsibility of communicating with the media is assigned to a public relations staff. Public relations people write press releases about their organization that they hope the media will use. If the press releases are not used, the marketer attempts to ensure that whatever the media says about the organization is accurate and as complimentary as possible. For smaller companies, dealing with the media becomes everyone's responsibility. Many businesses now face a new media, the Internet: chat rooms, Web sites, blogs, podcasts, and propaganda campaigns intended to destroy a business have become commonplace. Companies that are willing to focus on communication as a means of doing business engage in *relationship marketing* —a type of marketing that builds long-standing positive relationships with customers and other important stakeholder groups. Relationship marketing identifies "high value" customers and prospects and bonds them to the brand through personal attention.

Competition

We have already mentioned the importance that competition plays in a marketing organization. At a minimum, marketing companies must thoroughly understand their competitors' strengths and weaknesses. This means more than making sweeping generalizations about the competitors. It means basing intelligent marketing decisions on facts about how competitors operate and determining how best to respond.

This somewhat simplistic approach toward competition has all changed in the last fifteen years. Most notably, the worldwide web has made it imperative for even the local nonprofit to develop strategies for competing with companies locally, nationally, and internationally. The Internet has opened the door for a matching of customers and companies which goes beyond marketing's traditional approaches to product and market development. The competitive landscape in today's business environment mandates that businesses move with the swiftness that almost defies velocity.

Marketing expert Theodore Levitt coined the term "marketing myopia" several years ago to describe companies that mis-identify their competition. Levitt argued, for example, that the mistake made by the passenger train industry was to restrict their competition to other railroads instead of all mass transit transportation alternatives, including automobiles, airlines, and busses.[4] Today we see the same mistake being made by companies in the entertainment industry (movie theaters, restaurants, and resorts), who assume that their only competition is like-titled organizations.

This tendency to be myopic is particularly prevalent with nonprofits. In addition, nonprofits tend to be very uncomfortable with the notion of competition per se. Since all nonprofits assume they are engaged in societally-beneficial works, nonprofits conclude that there are no competitors. In fact, nothing could be further from the truth. Existing competitors are still after the donors' limited dollars, and new competitors (including for-profit businesses) are appearing daily.

Research on identifying competitors should start as broadly as possible. For example, we might start with the notion that consumers spend their income on fixed expenses, unplanned expenses, and discretionary expenses.

Marketers, such as utility companies or automobile manufacturers, likely fall under the fixed expense category. As such, their primary competitors are like-titled. The exception might be a Ford SUV owner who decides to sell his or her vehicle and opt for public transportation.

Unplanned expenses include the many unknowns that appear in all our lives. A car accident can create a domino effect that forces us to prioritize our limited extra dollars. Do we get the car repaired and pay the deductible? Do we skip the car repair so that we can pay for the physical therapy our spouse (the driver) requires? Do we not replace our furnace because we selected a vacation? Ultimately, if we are a marketer of furnaces we would need to research our customers so thoroughly that we are familiar with their personal situation and how the buyers make such decisions. However, doing such research would likely not be cost-effective. However, we would be wise to assume our competitors are well beyond like-titled companies. Think about product purchases that can be delayed.

Directionary expenses and the related competitors are the most difficult to understand. Mostly, this is because the decision process is irrational and unpredictable. Vacations, buying art, building a swimming pool, and donating to a charity most likely employ discretionary dollars. The personal benefits tend to be intrinsic rather than extrinsic, and consumers may not be in touch with the real reasons for their decisions. For most consumers the discretionary pie is limited, but the range of choices is unlimited. As such, the possible competitors are vast and not like-titled. Thus, it may not be a choice between giving $500 to the Red Cross or Easter Seals, but rather between Easter Seals and a weekend getaway. As will be discussed in a later chapter, donation behavior is learned and it is possible to do research to better understand this phenomenon.

Competition is a much more important marketing concept than ever before. Approaching it from the consumer's point-of-view is the most optimal alternative.

Cross-Functional Contacts

One of the first mistakes an organization might make is to allow the various functional areas to become proprietary. Whenever a marketing department considers itself most important to the success of the organization and self-sufficient without the need for accounting, manufacturing, or human resources, it ceases to be a reliable marketing group. True marketers know that they cannot be any better than their weakest link. Lack of understanding and trust between marketing and manufacturing, for instance, could mean that a product sold by marketing is not delivered when promised or with the right features. Marketers should consider their peers in engineering, who might not be able to produce an ambitious product requested by marketing at the cost desired. Likewise, human resources might not be able to locate the individual "with ten years of experience in package goods marketing" requested by the marketing manager.

The point is that marketing is far more likely to be successful if its staff relate intelligently and honestly with members of the other functional areas. In some organizations, the walls of parochialism have been standing so long that tearing them down is almost impossible. Nevertheless, creating interdepartmental connection is critical.

With downsizing and other cost-cutting activities prevalent during the last decade, the need for interrelated and harmonious business functions has become even more important. In the field of marketing, the term *integrated marketing* has been coined, suggesting that individuals working in traditional marketing departments are no longer specialists, but must become knowledgeable about all the elements of the business that currently and potentially have an impact on the success of marketing. At the corporate level, all managers should share a corporate vision, and there should be an organizational structure that makes it possible for departments or divisions to share information and participate in joint planning.

This approach represents the direction in which many companies are moving, including giants like Kraft and Disney. To be truly integrated, though, every decision at each level of the business should support decisions made at all the other levels. To illustrate, let's say that the corporate goal is to maximize profit. A marketing plan's objective is to increase sales by marketing new products matches the goal.

As companies highlight their ability to work together cross-functionally, there is also the need to collaborate across organizational boundaries. An example of external collaborators is the supply chain employed in most marketing. The supply chain extends from suppliers to consumer and organizational end users, and the players in this supply chain include manufacturers, agents, distributors, wholesalers, dealers, and retailers. Partnering with external distributors is a recognized method of getting a company's product to market, and requires considerable collaboration both within and outside the company for marketplace success.

Nonprofit marketers are beginning to understand the importance of internal and external collaboration. Examples abounded during the Katrina disaster and even more so with Hurricane Wilma that followed.

Community Contact

Most marketers are curious; they enjoy observing and noting what's happening in their community. Although the word community usually denotes a city, town, or neighborhood, we use the word here in a much broader sense. Community refers to the environment in which the marketer operates. For Esther and Jim Williams, who operate an A&W drive-in in Mattoon, Illinois, community is quite small. For Verizon Communication, community encompasses practically the entire world, extending even to outer space.

Regardless of the scope of the marketer's community, maintaining contact with it is essential. Contact could mean reading the local newspaper and listening to the local gossip. Or it could mean subscribing to information releases of several marketing research firms that monitor world events 24 hours a day, every day. Either might do the job, although the differences in financial costs would be great. Esther and Jim would find this discussion interesting, but not very useful.

Ultimately, to be considered a responsible citizen in the environments in which it operates, marketers have the ongoing task of engaging in only pro-societal activities and conducting business in an ethical manner. There are many marketing companies that donate millions of dollars or land to communities, clean up lakes and rivers, revamp deteriorating neighborhoods, give free product to the needy, manage recycling activities, and so forth. There is no doubt that the need for marketing to continue such activities will increase.

It is noteworthy that this facet of effective marketing is where the interface between for-profit and nonprofit organizations normally occurs. Nonprofit organizations offer many opportunities for for-profit companies to express their community involvement. Traditionally, the latter have created processes and internal organizations that give resources to selected nonprofits. Advertising agencies have a long history of doing pro bono creative work for nonprofits. Various mediums usually partner in these efforts. Companies such as Dell, Ford, and Coors have established internal foundations that offer large amounts of money to various nonprofits. More recently, many for-profits have implemented more strategic connections with nonprofits. *Cause marketing* has emerged as a way for a for-profit organization to appear more altruistic by serving as a conduit for raising money in partnerships with a nonprofit. Similarly, many for-profits have established formal programs that encourage employees to volunteer, facilitate placement, and may even offer some reward.

STRATEGIC COMPONENTS OF MARKETING

A necessary and useful starting point for the study of marketing is the consideration of the management process. The management of marketing serves as the framework for the process of marketing. Marketing management also serves as a central link between marketing and the societal level and everyday consumption by the general public. Although there are many variations of the marketing process, the one shown in Exhibit 2.1 will be employed in this book. Our process begins with corporate-level considerations, which dictate the direction the entire organization will take. The three corporate-level considerations listed here (mission, objectives, and strategy) are basic management topics, but are addressed in passing in the following sections.

Next come functional-level considerations. If a marketing firm is to adopt the customer-centered orientation discussed earlier, it must also extend this philosophy to the other functions/institutions with which it must interact. These functions, and the institutions that perform the functions, can be categorized as nonmarketing institutions and marketing institutions.

Nonmarketing functions can exist within the organization or outside the organization. The former include accounting, financial planning, human resources, engineering, manufacturing, research and development, and so on. Marketing must be familiar with the capabilities of each of these functions and plan accordingly. Establishing and maintaining rapport with leaders in these other functional areas is a challenge for every marketer. Nonmarketing

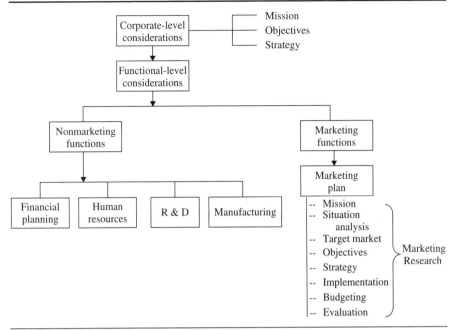

EXHIBIT 2.1   THE MARKETING PROCESS

institutions outside the firm facilitate the marketing process by providing expertise in areas not directly related to marketing. Examples include financial institutions that lend marketers necessary funds; regulatory institutions that pass laws to allow marketers to perform an activity; and the press, which tells the public about the activities of the marketer.

Marketing functions are all the activities that directly affect the exchange between the marketer and the consumer. Often they interact with some of the other nonmarketing functions. For example, as part of the marketing department's effort to create a new product, they would likely meet with design, engineering, and manufacturing. Similarly, everything marketing does must be cleared by legal.

The primary marketing functions include product development, pricing strategy, marketing communications, and supply chain management. Each of these functions are supported by a set of sub-functions or vendors. Marketing communications, for instance, includes personal selling (often organizationally separate from marketing), advertising, public relations, and sales promotion. Sales promotion, in turn, would work with vendors that create packaging, point-of-purchase displays, signage, and sampling systems.

Corporate-Level Considerations

All organizations should have a business plan. It is the starting point for all strategic planning and produces a sequence of decisions as shown in Exhibit 2.2. The first three stages are referred to as corporate-level considerations. Each will be discussed briefly.

Mission

Creating the mission statement for the organization is the initial challenge of every leader. It does not matter whether it is beautifully written or profound. All that matters is that it leads to right action. The mission of the Salvation Army is quite simple: "To make citizens out of the rejected." Yet it reflects the most important characteristic of a good mission statement—it is operational. It defines what the organization needs to do and suggests how each employee can contribute to that goal. Consider the mission statement of the Girl Scouts of the U.S.A.: "To help girls grow into proud, self-confident, and

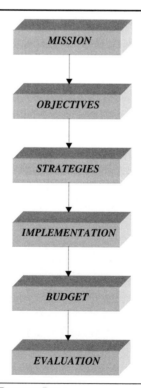

EXHIBIT 2.2   THE TRADITIONAL BUSINESS PLAN

self-respecting young women." Each scout master knows exactly what she is trying to accomplish. The organization must then give her the necessary ideas (strategy) and tools (tactics) to accomplish these goals. Ultimately, the task of the nonprofit manager is to try to convert the organization's mission statement into specifics.

A second characteristic of an effective mission statement is to make it clear and simple. It is wise to restrict it to no more than four elements. And as you add new tasks, you get rid of old ones. Consider universities that list dozens of goals as part of their mission statement. Bethel College follows the other extreme and "imparts Christian values to its students." Everyone knows the purpose of the organization—even though some would argue it is too restrictive.

A third consideration is to identify the organization's areas of expertise and do them well. In the context of nonprofits, specialties should be things that can really make a difference, really set a new standard. In the 1960s, hospitals entered the realm of health education. After decades of limited success, most hospitals realized that hospitals are not good at prevention, but they are good at curing existing physical problems. Today, many hospitals have created a reputation for excellence in an area of specialization—muscular dystrophy, cancer, or neonatal.

Finally, a mission statement should reflect goals that the organization and its staff can really believe in—a true commitment. There are thousands of examples of organizations that failed simply because people did not have a passion for the cause. This is particularly true for nonprofits where staff and volunteers have an emotional attachment to the mission. Changing the mission or minimizing it in any way may have serious negative consequences.

In the end, a mission statement should be revisited regularly. An annual assessment makes sense. Environments change and keeping up with change is always a good idea.

Objectives

Once the mission statement is formulated, a set of goals and objectives are created to reflect that mission. Although there is some ambiguity between the two terms, goals tend to be more general and less quantitative than objectives. For example, a goal might be to increase stockholder value. The corresponding objective is to increase stockholder value by eight percent during the next fiscal year. There is also a perspective on the two terms that suggests that goals describe objectives that are specific with respect to magnitude and time. We will employ the former interpretation.

There are several standard guidelines that apply to create viable objectives:

- *Objectives should be stated quantitatively wherever possible.* These numerical applications reflect a variety of elements including time, dollars, percentages, and ratios. An example for a charitable nonprofit might look like the following: We wish to increase our giving levels from the Southeast United States by $100,000, or 12 percent, during the next six months, which is twice as much as our nearest competitors.
- *Objectives should be challenging, yet realistic.* An overarching goal of many small colleges and universities is to be the "Harvard of the West (or East or South)." While this is a noble aspiration, it is highly unlikely. However, it is just as dangerous to low-ball your organization's objective. Both can lead to failure. The way to positioning objectives fairly and correctly is to consider the opportunities and strengths that pertain to their current situation. Research should lead the way.
- *Objectives should be consistent across the organization.* Although it may sound logical to assume that objectives at the corporate level should determine all other objectives, this is not always the case. The former may not translate well at the functional level. The grand objectives created by top management may be impossible to accomplish at the functional level. Consequently, objective setting should be interactive and consistency should exist across all levels.
- *Objectives should be arranged according to importance and sequence.* "Saving a business in trouble" will always be a primary objective. Similarly, some objectives are contingent on other objectives being accomplished first. Profitability, for example, may depend on the ability of the organization to generate additional revenue and/or decrease costs.
- *Long-term objectives and short-term objectives should be considered both separately and jointly.* Long-term objectives normally reflect a time horizon of 1 to 5 years. Short-term objectives consider a time frame of a year or less. Ideally, short-term objectives should contribute to long-term objectives. For example, short-term objectives might refer to saving costs or generating additional revenue, while the long-term objectives deal with market growth or mergers and acquisitions. However, these two sets of objectives may have little to do with each other. Short-term objectives may reflect immediate issues and problems, such as changing product features or entering a new market. Conversely,

long-term objectives deal with much larger issues, such as changing the direction of the company.

It is very important to create objectives for your organizations that meet the criteria discussed here. Nonprofits are notorious at either not having objectives or stopping at grand goals.

Strategy

The blueprint for achieving a company's objectives is its strategy. Strategies parallel the list of objectives the company is responding to at that point in time. In a nonprofit organization, the mission and the objectives—if there are any—are the good intentions. Strategies convert what you want to do into action. They are particularly important in nonprofit organizations since nonprofits are often better at dreaming and bad at implementation (work).

Strategies that tend to be appropriate at the corporate level include the following: 1. cost leadership, 2. differentiation, 3. segmentation, and 4. alliances. A company seeking cost leadership seeks the lowest production and distribution cost so it can either price competitors out of the market or simply keep the company operating. This was the popular strategy following the dot.com bubble of the late 1990s and continues today. Virtually every auto manufacturer has employed this strategy recently. Of course, there are serious risks. Most notably, costs can only be reduced so low. There is also the possibility that the quality of services may be reduced below an acceptable level. Many nonprofits have followed this path often eliminating staff, deleting programs, yet still unable to fulfill their mission.

Differentiation suggests the old "build a better mousetrap" business model. Companies that find their strength in technology and research development believe that a product breakthrough will appeal to a wide range of potential customers. Sometimes these technical advantages are profound and create a competitive advantage for months or even years. However, the lead time before a competitor matches or exceeds new technology is getting shorter and shorter. Even major hardware developers, such as Microsoft, or game developers, such as Sony, are finding that a market approach based on differentiation is both expensive and questionable. Nonprofits are rarely successful in differentiating their products since the features are often standardized and innovation is too costly.

Focusing on a particular group of customers (segments) is the most popular strategic approach used by businesses. It recognizes the observed conclusion that people are all different, yet they do share common characteristics or behavior that are meaningful to the organization. If these similarities create a group of consumers that are large enough, profitable enough, and respond favorably to one or more of our marketing strategies, we can think of segmentation marketing as an optimal strategy. Much more will be said about segmentation in Chapter 3.

Forming alliances through mergers and acquisitions only makes sense if there are obvious benefits to the organizations who participate. There are many reasons that prompt alliances. Perhaps most common is a strength one of the organizations brings to the partnership. Patents, technology, contacts, cash, inventory, and ownership of a particular market segment are all possible reasons for alliances. Alliances have been particularly prevalent in the telecommunications and consumer electronic sectors, where the high cost of technology and customer acquisition have forced companies such as Verizon, Disney, and Time Warner to seek partners. Alliances may offer strategic benefits to many nonprofits, as well.

Strategies convert the organization's plan into results. How do we get our service to the customer, that is, to the community we exist to serve? How do we market it? And how do we get the money we need to provide the service? For nonprofits, it is much more than creating products and selling them. It begins with a strong focus on knowing your market (through market research), segmenting customers, and viewing the market from the recipient's point of view. It is acknowledging that nonprofits are selling concepts. Finally, although marketing for a nonprofit uses many of the same tools as for-profit businesses; it is really quite different because the nonprofit is selling intangible service products. This last distinction is discussed in Chapter 6.

While the benefits of strategic planning for nonprofits are somewhat obvious, there are serious risks. First, to do it right, strategic planning requires a substantial investment of both time and money. Creating the strategy often involves the hiring of an outside consultant, commitments from staff, board members, volunteers, and other stakeholders for an extended period of time. Second, there is always the possibility that the resulting strategies will not align with the personal agendas of the director, board members, and other key supporters. In the case of one regional hospital, five different strategies for delivering excellent health care were derived. A final problem addresses the problem of assignment. In a for-profit setting, the outcomes are easily measurable—net profit and growth are statistics easily compiled. In the nonprofit sector, customer satisfaction, community benefit, and betterment of society often are considered more important than bottom-line results, and are difficult to measure satisfactorily.

Functional-Level Strategies

In addition to the four corporate-level strategies, there are also functional-level strategies. The primary examples include finance, accounting, human resources, research and development, technology, and marketing. All these functions can play a prominent role in meeting corporate objectives. Marketing, however, is the driver of an organization's ultimate success, and is the focus of this book. Still, marketers must have an understanding and appreciation of the other business functions.

The Marketing Plan

To a great extent, the same sequence of activities performed at the corporate level is repeated at the marketing level. The primary difference is that the marketing plan is directly influenced by the corporate plan as well as the role of the other functions within the organization. Consequently, the marketing plan must always involve monitoring and reacting to changes in the corporate plan (see Exhibit 2.3)

Apart from this need to be flexible to accommodate the corporate plan, the marketing plan follows a fairly standardized sequence. In addition, the marketing plan is supported by marketing research. *Marketing research* (a topic covered in chapter 4) is the process of gathering primary and secondary data in order to enhance decisions related to marketing. Virtually every facet of the marketing plan can be aided through marketing research. Unfortunately, nonprofits often have neither the dollars nor the expertise to conduct quality marketing research. It is a glaring weakness of many nonprofits.

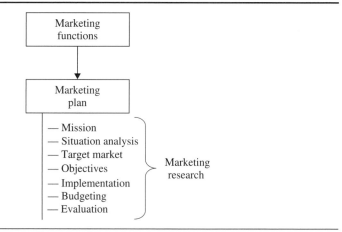

EXHIBIT 2.3   THE MARKETING PLANNING PROCESS

The marketing plan begins with a mission. A *mission* reflects the general values of the organization. What does it stand for? How does it define integrity? How does it view the people it serves? Every organization has an explicit or implicit mission. The corporate mission might contain words such as "quality," "global," "profitability," and "sacrifice." The marketing-level mission should extend the corporate mission by translating the latter into a marketing context. For example, a corporate mission that focuses on technology might be accompanied by a production-oriented marketing mission. A corporation mission that concentrates on value or quality reflects a consumer-oriented marketing mission. Once the mission is established, the situation analysis follows.

A marketing plan's *situation analysis* (background search) identifies factors, behaviors, and trends that have a direct bearing on the marketing plan. Much of this information is usually collected simultaneously with the corporate information. However, collecting information about potential and actual customers tends to be the concern of marketers. This is an ongoing activity and represents a great deal of the marketer's time and money.

The situation analysis investigates both the organization's external and internal environment. Elements of the *external environment* include the economic trends, technological trends, competition, social trends, ethical and legal factors, and the market situation. The market situation for a nonprofit might include the funding climate. The *internal environment* considers the organization's financial conditions, personnel conditions, technical expertise, legal protection, company history, past marketing efforts, and so forth. A good staff offers a wealth of information about what is going on in the organization.

The situation analysis serves as the basis for conducting the *SWOT (Strengths, Weaknesses, Opportunities, Threats)* analysis. A company's strengths are where the company has either a competitive advantage or is at least equal to competitors. Weaknesses are those areas where the company exhibits a competitive disadvantage. An opportunity is a consumer need not currently satisfied, that we have the marketing capability to satisfy. A threat is a trend or development in the marketing environment that will erode the business position of the company unless purposeful marketing action is taken. A SWOT is a result of a series of meetings with the key individuals within the organization (and perhaps an outside consultant).

The next step in the marketing planning process is to identify potential *target markets* and select the one(s) that will be the focus of this particular marketing plan. To properly identify the appropriate target markets, marketing managers need detailed information about the product and the market, who produces and sells the product, who uses the product and how it is used, who influences purchase decisions, and the perceptions of customers.

The launch of a new product, for example, demands a complex list of target market characteristics. Overall the marketer must provide a central message about the value the new product offers. Shareholders may want to know about the research and development costs and progress, and how the new product will affect shareholder returns. The local community will be interested in whether the new product means more jobs and plant expansion. Employees may be targeted because some will help with production, so their understanding and buy-in will enhance desired product quality. Suppliers and vendors will want to know what opportunities they will have for providing new resources and services to the company. Retailers will need to be motivated to provide space in their stores.

Ultimately, the notion of target market is both stable, in the context of end-user, and situational, in the sense that a variety of other individuals must be marketed to in order to reach the ultimate target market. Marketing managers must be cognizant of both types of target markets to ensure success. A list of typical target markets for a variety of nonprofit organizations is given in Exhibit 2.4. Further discussion is provided in the Chapter 3.

Category of Organization	Key Customer Groups
Charities	Volunteers
	Individual Donors
	Corporate Donors
	Charitable Trusts
	Recipients of Goods/Services
Arts Organizations	Visitors
	Audiences
	Corporate Sponsors
	Arts Funding Bodies
Healthcare Trusts	Patients
	Visitors/Relatives of Patients
	General Practitioners
	Insurance Companies
	Government Funders
Education	Students
	Alumni
	Industry
	Research Funders
	Local Communities
	Local/National Government

EXHIBIT 2.4 NONPROFITS AND KEY CUSTOMER GROUPS

The SWOT, along with the selection of a target market, helps produce a relevant set of *marketing objectives*. Marketing objectives help focus the organization on the purpose of marketing—whether to increase funds, membership, or participation. At the corporate level, typical objectives include profitability, cost savings, growth, market share improvement, risk containment, reputation, and so on. All these corporate objectives can imply specific marketing objectives. Introducing a certain number of new products may lead marketers to profitability, increased market share, and movement into new markets. Desire to increase profit margins might dictate the level of product innovation, quality of materials, and price charged. It is best to identify/create the measures you will use for each objective at this point in the planning process.

Once the objectives are established, the marketer must decide how to achieve these objectives. This produces a set of general marketing strategies that must be refined into actionable and achievable activities. Market strategies are the comprehensive approach an organization takes to engage its target markets. This includes not just what an organization says, but more importantly, what it does in everything, in every way. Strategies include how the organization designs and delivers programs and services; how it positions itself on issues; how it designs campaigns; and where it locates or places its programs or information. These operational tools are referred to as the marketing mix. The *marketing mix*—product, price, promotion, and distribution—represents the ways in which an organization's broad marketing strategies are translated into marketing programs for action.

- *Product*. Products (and services) are the primary marketing mix element that satisfies customer wants and needs and provides the main link between the organization and its customers. Marketing organizations must be ready to alter products as dictated by changes in competitive strategies or changes in other elements of the organization's environment. Many organizations have a vast array of products in their mix. Ideally, each of the products is profitable. But this is often not the case, so some tough decisions must be made concerning the length of time an unsuccessful product is kept on the market.
- *Distribution (Supply Chain)*. The organization's distribution system moves the product to the final consumer. Because there are many alternatives when selecting a distribution channel, marketing management must have a clear understanding of the types of distributors, of the trends influencing those distributors, and of how those distributors are perceived by customers.

- *Communication (Promotion).* The product's benefits must be communicated to the distributors and to the final customers. Therefore, the marketing organization must provide marketing information that is received favorably by distributors and final customers. Marketing organizations, through promotion, provide information by way of advertising, sales promotions, salespeople, public relations, and packaging.
- *Price.* Finally, marketers must price their products in such a way that customers believe they are receiving fair value. Price is the primary means by which customers judge the attractiveness of a product or service. Moreover, price is a reflection of all the activities of an organization. Finally, price is a competitive tool, in that it is used as a basis for comparison of product and perceived value across different organizations.

Decisions about the marketing mix variables are interrelated. Each of the marketing mix variables must be coordinated with the other elements of the marketing program. Consider, for a moment, a situation in which a firm has two product alternatives (deluxe and economy), two price alternatives ($6.00 and $3.00), two promotion alternatives (advertising and couponing), and two distribution alternatives (department stores and specialty stores). Taken together, the firm has a total of 16 possible marketing mix combinations. Naturally, some of these appear to be in conflict, such as the deluxe product/low price combination. Nevertheless, the organization must consider many of the possible alternative marketing programs. The problem is magnified by the existence of competitors. The organization must find the right combination of product, price, promotion, and distribution so that it can gain a differential advantage over its competitors. (All the marketing mix elements will be discussed in more detail in Chapter 8 of this book.)

Even a well-designed marketing program that has undergone a thorough evaluation of alternatives will fail if its implementation is poor. *Implementation* involves such things as determining where to promote the product, getting the product to the ultimate consumer, putting a price on the product, and setting a commission rate for the salespeople. Once a decision is made, a marketing manager must decide how to best implement the terms of the plan.

Scandinavian Airlines (SAS) provides a good example of an organization that has successfully implemented their marketing strategy. SAS has good on-time performance, a good safety record, and many services designed to make flying easier for its customers. However, these were not enough to improve SAS revenue. Other things had to be done to attract business-class customers. The approach taken by SAS was largely symbolic in nature. They put everyone who bought a full-price ticket in "Euroclass," which entitled them to use a special boarding card, an executive waiting lounge, designer steel cutlery, and a small napkin clip that could be taken as a collector's item. These and other values are provided at virtually no extra cost to the customer. The approach was very successful; business class passengers flocked to SAS, since they appreciated the perceived increase in value for the price of a ticket.

Marketing mix components must be evaluated as part of an overall marketing strategy. Therefore, the organization must establish a marketing budget based on the required marketing effort to influence customers. The *marketing budget* represents a plan to allocate expenditures to each of the components of the marketing mix. For example, the firm must establish an advertising budget as part of the marketing budget and allocate expenditures to various types of advertising media—television, newspapers, magazines. A sales promotion budget should also be determined, allocating money for coupons, product samples, and trade promotions. Similarly, budgets are required for personal selling, distribution, and product development.

How much should be spent? Consider the following example. A common question that marketers frequently ask is, "Are we spending enough (or too much) to promote the sales of our products?" A reasonable answer would revolve around another consideration: "What do we want to accomplish? or What are our goals?" The decision should next turn to the methods of achievement of goals and the removal of obstacles to these goals. This step is often avoided or skipped altogether.

Usually, when the question is asked, "Are we spending enough?" an automatic answer is given, in terms of what others spend. Knowing what others in the same industry spend can be important to an organization whose performance lags behind the competition or to an organization that suspects that its expenditures are higher than they need to be. But generally, knowing what others spend leads to an unproductive "keeping-up-with-the-Joneses" attitude. It also assumes that the others know what they are doing.

No marketing program is planned and implemented perfectly. Marketing managers will tell you that they experience many surprises during the course of their activities. In an effort to ensure that performance goes according to plans, marketing managers establish controls that allow marketers to evaluate results and identify needs for modifications in marketing strategies and programs. Surprises occur, but marketing managers who have established sound control procedures can react to surprises quickly and effectively.

Marketing control involves a number of decisions. One decision is what functions to monitor. Some organizations monitor their entire marketing program, while others choose to monitor only a part of it, such as their sales force or their advertising program. A second set of decisions concerns the establishment of standards for performance, for example, market share, profitability, or sales. A third set of decisions concerns how to collect information for making comparisons between actual performance and standards. Finally, to the extent that discrepancies exist between actual and planned performance, adjustments in the marketing program or the strategic plan must be made.

Once a plan is put into action, a marketing manager must still gather information related to the effectiveness with which the plan was implemented. Information on sales, profits, reactions of consumers, and reactions of competitors must be collected and analyzed so that a marketing manager can identify new problems and opportunities.

KEYS TO MARKETING SUCCESS

A primary guideline for marketing success is to realize that establishing customer satisfaction should be the company's number-one priority. The only people who really know what customers want are the customers themselves. A company that realizes this will develop a marketing mentality that facilitates information gathering and maintains effective communication with the primary reason for the company's existence: the customer.

A second guideline is to establish a company image that clearly reflects the values and aspirations of the company to employees, customers, intermediaries, and the general public. Easter Seals has done this for years with their advertising campaign that focuses on how their company benefits society.

Third, while marketing requires work that is clearly distinct from other business activities, it should be central to the entire organization. Marketing is the aspect of the business that customers see. If they see something they do not like, they look elsewhere.

Fourth, the business should develop a unique strategy that is consistent with the circumstances that it faces. The marketer must adapt basic marketing principles to the unique product being sold. This means that what General Foods does may not work for GTE because one is inherently a goods product and the other a service product. And neither will work for the State of Kentucky's Parks and Recreation Department, because that is a public, nonprofit organization. In other words, imitating what other organizations do without fully understanding one's own situation is a dangerous strategy.

Finally, technological progress dictates how marketing will perform in the future. Because of computer technology, both consumers and businesses are better informed. Knowledge is the most important competitive advantage. The world is one market, and information is changing it at light-speed.

To quote Peter Drucker once more: "To run a non-profit effectively, marketing must be built into the total design."

REFERENCES

1. Garland, Susan, "On the Road with Your Favorite Museum", *BusinessWeek*, (January 17, 2005), pp. 84–85;   Venice, Deborah, "The Art of the Craft", *Marketing News*, (June 15, 2005); pp 19–20.

2. McKenna, Regis, *Relationship Marketing*, Reading MA: Addison-Wesley, (1991).

3. Schonberger, R., *Building a Chain of Customers: Linking Business Functions to Create the World Class Company*, New York: McMillan Inc., (1990).

4. Levitt, Theodore, "Marketing Myopia", *Harvard Business Review*, (July–August 1960); pp. 45–66.

3

APPROACHING THE MARKET

To succeed in our over communicated society, a company must create a position in the prospect's mind, a position that takes into consideration not only a company's own strengths and weaknesses, but those of its competitors as well.

—Al Reis and Jack Trout

Low graduation rates have plagued the student athlete for decades. Not only do athletes graduate at a much lower rate than the general student population, but there are also concerns about the rigor of their majors and related courses. Critics employ these statistics to either diminish the over-inflated value of sports on many campuses, or to raise the playing field so that athletes must meet the same standards as nonathletes.

To combat this dire situation, the National Collegiate Athletic Association (NCAA) has created its own set of measures assessing graduation rates. For example, in January of 2006, they reported that more than three in four Division I athletes are graduating within six years, compared to just 62 percent reported by the U.S. Department of Education, during that same period (1995 to 1996 and 1998 to 1999).

The NCAA produced its statistics with a new formula known as the Graduation Success Rate, which the association plans to use to hold colleges more accountable for the academic performance of their athletes. Unlike the federal rates, the NCAA rates account for incoming transfer students and do not penalize institutions for athletes who transfer to other colleges, as long as those students leave in good academic standing. (Twenty-five percent of the 91,000 athletes that the NCAA tracked had transferred at least once.)

Two groups have been vocal critics of this new measure—the Knight Foundation Commission on Intercollegiate Athletes and the Drake Group—positing that the NCAA's formula obscures greater problems in the college game. Too many athletes are loading up on easy courses, barely passing their courses, and failing to meet the more rigorous academic standards the NCAA recently established.

Colleges and universities take these numbers very seriously. The University of Texas at Austin had a Graduation Success Rate of 40 percent, and a 31 percent federal rate. In an attempt to improve those numbers, the university has spent $18 million upgrading its academic-support center for athletes, having more tutors, and buying laptops for many of its players. Some critics question the real intent of these expenditures. R. Gerald Turner, president of Southern Methodist University and a vice-chair of the Knight Commission, expresses the opinion of many skeptics: "Far too many schools are reaping financial rewards for postseason play, while they're failing to graduate the athletes who have enabled their success on the field."[1]

INTRODUCTION

The student athlete and nonathlete together represent the entire market for colleges and universities. Yet, the very fact that a small percentage of that market is comprised of scholarship athletes has a tremendous impact on the marketing effort. This chapter discusses the concept of market; how it can be viewed and how it can be approached. Specifically, this chapter presents three topics: defining the nature of markets; identifying the types of markets; and a discussion of product differentiation, market segmentation, and positioning.

DEFINING THE MARKET

The market can be viewed from many different perspectives, and consequently, is impossible to define precisely. In order to provide some clarity, we provide a basic definition of a market: *a group of potential buyers with needs and wants and the purchasing power to satisfy them*. Rather than attempting to cut through the many specialized uses of the term, it is more meaningful to describe several broad characteristics and use this somewhat ambiguous framework as the foundation for a general definition.

The Market Is People

Since exchange involves two or more people, it is natural to think of the market as people, individuals, or groups. Clearly, without the existence of people to buy and consume goods, services, and ideas, there would be little reason for marketing. Yet this perspective must be refined further if it is to be useful.

People constitute markets only if they have overt or latent wants and needs. That is, individuals must currently recognize their needs or desires for an existing or future product, or have a *potential* need or desire for an existing or future product. While the former condition is quite straightforward, the latter situation is a bit more confusing, in that it forces the marketer to develop new products that satisfy unmet needs. Potential future customers must be identified and understood.

When speaking of markets as people, we are not concerned exclusively with individual ultimate consumers. Although individuals and members of households do constitute the most important and largest category of markets, business establishments and other organized behavior systems also represent valid markets. People (individually or in groups), businesses, and institutions create markets.

However, people or organizations must meet certain basic criteria in order to present a valid market:

- There must be a true need and/or want for the product, service, or idea; this need may be recognized, unrecognized, or latent.
- The person/organization must have the ability to pay for the product via means acceptable to the marketer.
- The person/organization must be willing to buy the product.
- The person/organization must have the authority to buy the product.
- The total number of people/organizations meeting the previous criteria must be large enough to be profitable for the marketer.

The Market Is a Place

Thinking of the market as a place, "the marketplace," is a common practice of the general public. Such locations do exist as geographical areas within which trading occurs. In this context, we can think of world markets, international markets, American markets, regions, states, cities, and parts of cities. A shopping center, a block, a portion of a block, and even the site of a single retail store can be called a market.

While not as pervasive as the "people" component of the market, the "place" description of a market is important too. Since goods must be delivered to, and customers attracted toward, particular places where transactions are made, this identification of markets is useful for marketing decision-making purposes. Factors such as product features, price, location of facilities, routing salespeople, and promotional design are all affected by the geographic market.

Even in the case of immeasurable fields, such as religion, a marketplace might be Yankee Stadium, where Billy Graham is holding a revival. Finally, a market may be somewhere other than a geographical region, such as a catalog or ad that allows the customer to place an order without the assistance of a marketing intermediary or an 800 number.

The Market Is an Economic Entity

In most cases, a market is characterized by a dynamic system of economic forces. The four most salient economic forces are supply, demand, competition, and government intervention. The terms *buyer's market* and *seller's market* describe different conditions of bargaining strength. We also use terms such as *monopoly, oligopoly*, and *pure competition* to reflect the competitive situation in a particular market. Finally, the extent of personal freedom and government control produces free market systems, socialistic systems, and other systems of trade and commerce.

Again, placing these labels on markets allows the marketer to design strategies that match a particular economic situation. We know, for instance, that in a buyer's market, there is an abundance of product, prices are usually low, and customers dictate the terms of sale. U.S. firms find that they must make tremendous strategy adjustments when they sell their products in Third World markets. The interaction of these economic factors is what creates a market.

There is always the pressure of competition as new firms enter and old ones exit. Advertising and selling pressure, price and counterprice, claim and counterclaim, service and extra service are all weapons of competitive pressure that marketers use to achieve and protect market positions. Market composition is constantly changing.

TYPES OF MARKETS

Now that we have defined markets in a general sense, it is useful to discuss the characteristics of the primary types of markets: 1. consumer markets, 2. industrial markets, 3. institutional markets, and 4. reseller markets. It should be noted that these categories are not always clear-cut. In some industries, a business may be in a different category altogether or may even encompass multiple categories. It is also possible that a product may be sold in all four markets. Consequently, it is important to know as much as possible about how these markets differ so that appropriate marketing activities can be developed.

Consumer Markets

When we talk about *consumer markets*, we are including those individuals and households who buy and consume goods and services for their own personal use. They are not interested in reselling the product or setting themselves up as a manufacturer. Considering the thousands of new products, services, and ideas being introduced each day and the increased capability of consumers to afford these products, the size, complexity, and future growth potential of the consumer market is staggering.

Industrial Markets (Business)

The *industrial market* consists of organizations and the people who work for them, those who buy products or services for use in their own businesses or to make other products. For example, a steel mill might purchase computer software, pencils, and flooring as part of the operation and maintenance of their business. Likewise, a refrigerator manufacturer might purchase sheets of steel, wiring, shelving, and so forth, as part of its final product. These purchases occur in the industrial market. There is substantial evidence that industrial markets function differently than do consumer markets.

Institutional Markets

Another important market sector is made up of various types of for-profit and nonprofit institutions, such as hospitals, schools, churches, and government agencies. *Institutional markets* differ from typical businesses in that they are not motivated primarily by profits or market share.

Rather, institutions tend to satisfy somewhat exoteric, often intangible, needs. Also, whatever profits exist after all expenses are paid are normally put back into the institution. Because institutions operate under different restrictions and employ different goals, marketers must use different strategies to be successful. For the most part, this is the market served by nonprofit institutions.

Reseller Markets

All intermediaries that buy finished or semifinished products and resell them for profit are part of the *reseller market*. This market includes approximately 383,000 wholesalers and 1,300,000 retailers that operate in the United States. With the exception of products obtained directly from the producer, all products are sold through resellers. Since resellers operate under unique business characteristics, they must be approached carefully. Producers are always cognizant of the fact that successful marketing to resellers is just as important as successful marketing to consumers.

APPROACHING THE MARKET

All the parties in an exchange usually have the ability to select their exchange partner(s). For the customer, whether consumer, industrial buyer, institution, or reseller, product choices are made daily. *For a product provider, the person(s) or organization(s) selected as potential customers are referred to as the target market.*

Still, the way we approach the market dictates how we do marketing, regardless of the target market(s) selected. The various approaches are shown in Exhibit 3.1. Each path will suggest a unique strategy and set of tactics. These concepts are explained in the following sections.

The Undifferentiated Market (Market Aggregation)

The undifferentiated (aggregated) approach occurs when the marketer ignores the apparent differences that exist within the market and uses a marketing strategy that is intended to appeal to as many people as possible. In essence, the market is viewed as a homogeneous aggregate. Admittedly, this assumption is risky, and there is always the chance that it will appeal to no one, or that the amount of waste in resources will be greater than the total gain in sales.

For certain types of widely consumed items (e.g., gasoline, soft drinks, white bread), the undifferentiated market approach makes the most sense. One example was the campaign in which Dr. Pepper employed a catchy general-appeal slogan, "Be a Pepper!," that really said nothing specific about the product, yet spoke to a wide range of consumers. Often, this type of

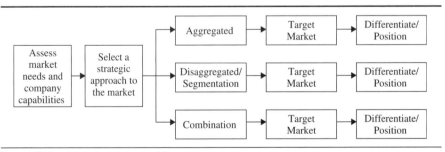

EXHIBIT 3.1   APPROACHES TO THE MARKET

general appeal is supported by positive, emotional settings, and a great many reinforcers at the point-of-purchase. Walk through any supermarket and you will observe hundreds of food products that are perceived as nearly identical by the consumer and are treated as such by the producer—especially knock-off or generic items.

Identifying products that have a universal appeal is only one of many criteria to be met if an undifferentiated approach is to work. The number of consumers exhibiting a need for the identified product must be large enough to generate satisfactory profits. A product such as milk would probably have universal appeal and a large market; a set of dentures might not. In respect to the former product category, the "Got Milk?" advertising campaign was very successful, yet it made no attempt to differentiate people who have different uses for milk. They treated all milk users the same. However, adequate market size is not an absolute amount and must be evaluated for each product.

Two other considerations are important: the per-unit profit margin and the amount of competition. Bread has a very low profit margin and many competitors, thus requiring a very large customer base. A product such as men's jockey shorts delivers a high profit but has few competitors.

Success with an undifferentiated market approach is also contingent on the abilities of the marketer to correctly identify potential customers and design an effective and competitive strategy. Since the values, attitudes, and behaviors of people are constantly changing, it is crucial to monitor these changes. Introduce numerous cultural differences, and an extremely complex situation emerges. There is also the possibility that an appeal that is pleasing to a great diversity of people may not then be strong or clear enough to be truly effective with any of these people.

Finally, the competitive situation might not promote an undifferentiated strategy. All would agree that Campbell's dominates the canned soup industry, and that there is little reason for them to engage in much market differentiation. Clearly, for companies that have a very large share of the market, undifferentiated market coverage makes sense. For a company with small market share, it might be disastrous.

The Segmented Market (Disaggregation)

This premise of *segmenting* the market theorizes that people and organizations can be most effectively approached by recognizing their differences and adjusting accordingly. By emphasizing a segmentation approach, the exchange process should be enhanced, since a company can more precisely match the needs and wants of the customer. Even these soft drink manufacturers have moved away from the undifferentiated approach and have introduced diet, caffeine-free, and diet-caffeine-free versions of their basic products.

While it is relatively easy to identify segments of consumers, most firms do not have the capabilities or the need to effectively market their product to all of the segments that can be identified. Rather, one or more target markets (segments) must be selected. In reality, market segmentation is both a disaggregating and aggregating process. While the market is initially reduced to its smallest homogeneous components (perhaps a single individual), business in practice requires the marketer to find common dimensions that will allow him to view these individuals as larger, profitable segments. Thus, market segmentation is a two-fold process that includes: 1. identifying and classifying people into homogeneous groupings, called *segments*, and 2. determining which of these segments are viable target markets. In essence, the marketing objectives of segmentation analysis are:

- To reduce risk in deciding where, when, how, and to whom a product, service, or brand will be marketed
- To increase marketing efficiency by directing effort specifically toward the designated segment in a manner consistent with that segment's characteristics

Segmentation Strategies

There are two major segmentation strategies followed by marketing organizations: a concentration strategy and a multisegment strategy.

An organization that adopts a *concentration strategy* chooses to focus its marketing efforts on only one market segment. Only one marketing mix is developed. For example, the manufacturer of Rolex watches has chosen to concentrate on the luxury segment of the watch market. An organization that adopts a concentration strategy gains an advantage by being able to analyze the needs and wants of only one segment and then focusing all its efforts on that segment. This can provide a differential advantage over other organizations that market to this segment but do not concentrate all their efforts on it. The primary disadvantage of concentration is related to the demand of the segment. As long as demand is strong, the organization's financial position will be strong. But if demand declines, the organizations' financial position will also decline.

The other segmentation strategy is a *multisegment strategy*. When an organization adopts this strategy, it focuses its marketing efforts on two or more distinct market segments. The organization does so by developing a distinct marketing mix for each segment. They then develop marketing programs tailored for each of these segments. Organizations that follow a multisegment strategy usually realize an increase in total sales as more marketing programs are focused at more customers. However, the organization will most likely experience higher costs because of the need for more than one marketing program.

Base of Segmentation

There are many different ways by which a company can segment its market, and the chosen process varies from one product to another. Further, the segmentation process should be an ongoing activity. Since markets are very dynamic, and products change over time, the bases for segmentation must likewise change. (See Exhibit 3.2.)

In line with these basic differences, the following factors are used to segment ultimate consumers.

Segmenting Ultimate Consumers

Geographic Segments Geography probably represents the oldest basis for segmentation. Regional differences in consumer tastes for products as a whole are well-known. Markets according to location are easily identified and large amounts of data are usually available. Many companies simply do not have the resources to expand beyond local or regional levels; thus, they must focus on one geographic segment only. Domestic and foreign segments are the broadest type of geographical segment.

Closely associated with geographic location are inherent characteristics of the location: weather, topography, and physical factors such as rivers, mountains, or ocean proximity. Conditions of high humidity, excessive rain or drought, snow or cold all influence the purchase of a wide spectrum of products. While marketers no longer segment markets as being east or west of the Mississippi River, people living near the Mississippi may constitute a viable

Primary Dimensions	Bases
Characteristics of Person or Organization	Geography, Age, Sex, Race Income, Life Cycle, Personality, Lifestyle
Purchase Situation	Purpose, Benefits, Purchase Approach, Choice Criteria, Brand Loyalty, Importance

EXHIBIT 3.2 BASES FOR SEGMENTATION

segment for several products, such as flood insurance, fishing equipment, and dredging machinery.

Population density can also place people in unique market segments. High-density states such as California and New York and cities such as New York City, Hong Kong, and London create the need for products such as security systems, fast-food restaurants, and public transportation.

Geographic segmentation offers some important advantages. There is very little waste in the marketing effort, in that the product and supporting activities such as advertising, physical distribution, and repair can all be directed at the customer. Further, geography provides a convenient organizational framework. Products, salespeople, and distribution networks can all be organized around a central, specific location.

The drawbacks in using a geographic basis of segmentation are also notable. There is always the obvious possibility that consumer preferences may (unexpectedly) bear no relationship to location. Other factors, such as ethnic origin or income, may overshadow location. The stereotypical Texan, for example, is hard to find in Houston, where one-third of the population has immigrated from other states. Another problem is that most geographic areas are very large, regional locations. It is evident that the Eastern seaboard market contains many segments. Members of a geographic segment often tend to be too heterogeneous to qualify as a meaningful target for market action.

Demographic Segments Several demographic characteristics have proven to be particularly relevant when marketing to ultimate consumers. Segmenting the consumer market by age groups has been quite useful for several products. For example, the youth market (approximately aged 5 to 13) not only influences how their parents spend money, but also makes purchases of their own. Manufacturers of products such as toys, records, snack foods, and video games have designed promotional efforts directed at this group. More recently, the elderly market (ages 65 and over) has grown in importance for producers of products such as low-cost housing, cruises, hobbies, and healthcare. An example of how nonprofit organizations have employed age as a basis for segmenting markets is their appeal to Generation X, defined by demographers as those born in 1965 through 1981. Some charities have developed young professionals' boards for those 35 and under to get involved in decision-making roles about fund raising. An example is Project Sunshine, which helps sick children and has chapters throughout the United States. Their programs have focused largely on providing volunteer opportunities for people younger than 40, and supplementing those volunteer efforts with fund-raising efforts specifically geared toward that generation. Thus far, 40 percent of their volunteers and 45 percent of their donations have come from that segment.

Gender has also historically been a good basis for market segmentation. While there are some obvious products designed for men or women, many of these traditional boundaries are changing, and marketing must apprise themselves of these changes. The emergence of working women, for instance, has made determination of who performs certain activities in the family (e.g., shopping, car servicing), and how the family income is spent more difficult. New magazines such as *Men's Guide to Fashion, Modern Black Man, Sportswear International, NV,* and *Vibe* indicate how media is attempting to subsegment the male segment. Thus, the simple classification of male versus female may be useful only if several other demographic and behavioral characteristics are considered as well.

Another demographic trait closely associated with age and sex is the *family life cycle*. There is evidence that, based on family structure (i.e., number of adults and children), families go through very predictable behavioral patterns. For example, a young couple who have one young child will have far different purchasing needs than a couple in their late fifties whose children have moved out. In a similar way, the types of products purchased by a newly married couple will differ from those of a couple with older children.

Income is perhaps the most common demographic basis for segmenting a market. This may be partly because income often dictates who can or cannot afford a particular product. It is quite reasonable, for example to assume that individuals earning minimum wage could not easily purchase a $35,000 sports car. Income tends to be a better basis for segmenting markets as the price tag for a product increases. Income may not be quite as valuable for products such as bread, cigarettes, and motor oil. Income may also be helpful in examining certain types of buying behavior. For example, individuals in the lower-middle income group are prone to use coupons. *Playboy* recently announced the introduction of a special edition aimed at the subscribers with annual incomes over $100,000.

Several other demographic characteristics can influence various types of consumer activities. *Education*, for example, affects product performances as well as characteristics demanded for certain products. *Occupation* can also be important; individuals who work in hard physical labor occupations (e.g., coal mining) may demand an entirely different set of products than a person employed as a teacher or bank teller, even though their incomes are the same. *Geographic mobility* is somewhat related to occupation, in that certain occupations (e.g., military, corporate executives) require a high level of mobility. High geographic mobility necessitates that a person (or family) acquire new shopping habits, seek new sources of products and services, and possibly develop new brand preferences. Finally, *race and national origin* have been associated with product preferences and media preferences. Black Americans have exhibited preferences in respect to food, transportation, and entertainment, to name a few. Hispanics tend to prefer radio and television over newspapers and magazines as a means of learning about products.

Even *religion* is used as a basis for segmentation. Several interesting findings have arisen from the limited research in this area. Aside from the obvious higher demands for Christian-oriented magazines, books, music, entertainment, jewelry, educational institutions, and counseling services, differences in demand for secular products and services have been identified as well. For example, the Christian consumer attends movies less frequently than consumers in general and spends more time in volunteer, even non-church related, activities.

Notwithstanding its apparent advantages (i.e., low cost and ease of implementation), considerable uncertainty exists about demographic segmentations. The method is often misused. Take, for example, the use of a disability as a basis for segmenting markets. While it is appropriate to base the initial segmentation on a physical impairment (i.e., sight, hearing, movement), the problems of having a disability tend to be multifaceted. Often, a disabled person has several deficiencies, some related to the primary problem, others secondary. Also, all disabilities have levels of severity. Research indicates that the attitudes of the person toward their handicap and the resulting quality of life all play an important role in assessing how a disabled person should be categorized. Therefore, the creation of a Braille keyboard for the blind is just a starting point if that person is to be totally satisfied. This warning is particularly relevant for nonprofits that wish to employ a segmentation strategy based on demographics, yet deal with complex problems.

Usage Segments In 1964, Dik W. Twedt, first president of Division of Consumer Psychology, made one of the earliest departures from demographic segmentation when he suggested that the heavy user, or frequent consumer, was an important basis for segmentation. He proposed that consumption should be measured directly, and that promotion should be aimed directly at the heavy users. This approach has become very popular, particularly in the beverage industry (e.g., beer, soft drinks, and spirits). Considerable research has been conducted with this particular group, and the results suggest that finding other characteristics that correlate with usage rate often greatly enhances marketing efforts.

Four other bases for market segmentation have evolved from the usage-level criteria. The first is *purchase occasion*. Determining the reason for an airline passenger's trip, for instance, may be the most relevant criteria for segmenting airline consumers. The same may be true for products such as long-distance calling or the purchase of snack foods.

The second basis is *user status*. It seems apparent that communication strategies must differ if they are directed at different use patterns, such as nonuser versus ex-users, or one-time users versus regular users. New car producers have become very sensitive to the need to provide new car buyers with a great deal of supportive information after the sale in order to minimize unhappiness after the purchase. However, determining how long this information is necessary or effective is still anybody's guess.

The third basis is *loyalty*. This approach laces consumers into loyalty categories based on their purchase patterns of particular brands. A key category is the brand-loyal consumer. Companies have assumed that if they can identify individuals who are brand loyal to their brands, and then delineate other characteristics these people have in common, they will locate the ideal target market. There is still a great deal of uncertainty as to how to correctly measure brand loyalty.

The final characteristic is *stage of readiness*. It is proposed that potential customers can be segmented as follows: unaware, aware, informed, interested, desirous, and intend to buy. Thus if a marketing manager is aware of where the specific segment of potential customers is, he or she can design the appropriate marketing strategy to move them through the various stages of readiness. Again, these stages of readiness are rather vague and difficult to accurately measure.

Psychological Segments Research shows that the concept of segmentation should recognize psychological as well as demographic influences. Evidence suggests that attitudes of prospective buyers towards certain products influence their subsequent purchase or non-purchase of them. If persons with similar attitudes can be isolated, they represent an important psychological segment. *Attitudes* can be defined as predispositions to behave in certain ways in response to given stimulus.

Personality is defined as the long-lasting characteristics and behaviors of a person that allow them to cope and respond to their environment. Very early on, marketers were examining personality traits as a means for segmenting consumers. None of these early studies suggest that measurable personality traits offer much prospect of market segmentation. However, an almost inescapable logic seems to dictate that consumption of particular products or brands must be meaningfully related to consumer personality. It is frequently noted that the elderly drive big cars, that the new rich spend disappropriately more on housing and other visible symbols of success, and that extroverts dress conspicuously.

Motives are closely related to attitudes. A motive is a reason for behavior. A buying motive triggers purchase activity. The latter is general, the former more specific. In theory, this is what market segmentation is all about. Measurements of demographic, personality, and attitudinal variables are really convenient measurements of less conspicuous motivational factors. People with similar physical and psychological characteristics are presumed to be similarly motivated. Motives can be positive (convenience), or negative (fear of pain). The question logically arises: why not observe motivation directly and classify market segments accordingly?

Lifestyle refers to the orientation that an individual or a group has toward consumption, work, and play and can be defined as a pattern of attitudes, interests, and opinions held by a person. Lifestyle segmentation has become very popular with marketers, because of the availability of measurement devices and instruments, and the intuitive categories that result from this process. As a result, producers are targeting versions of their products and their promotions to various lifestyle segments. Thus, companies like All State Insurance are designing special programs for the good driver, who has been extensively characterized through a lifestyle segmentation approach.

Lifestyle analysis begins by asking questions about the consumers' activities, interests, and opinions. If a man earns $60,000 to $80,000 per year as an executive, with a wife and four children, what does he think of his role as provider versus father? How does he spend his spare time? To what clubs and groups does he belong? Does he hunt? What are his attitudes toward advertising? What does he read?

AIO (activities, interests, opinions) inventories, as they are called, reveal vast amounts of information concerning attitudes toward product categories, brands within product categories, and user and nonuser characteristics. Lifestyle studies tend to focus upon how people spend their money; their patterns of work and leisure; their major interests; and their opinions of social and political issues, institutions, and themselves.

Single-Base and Multi-Base Segmentation

So far, we have talked about the use of individual bases for market segmentation. The use of a *single-base segmentation strategy* is a simple way to segment markets, and is often very effective. Clearly, the use of bases such as gender (cosmetics), or age (healthcare products, music), or income (auto-mobiles), provides valuable insights into who uses what products. But the use of a single base may not be precise enough in identifying a segment for which a marketing program can be designed. Therefore, many organizations employ *multi-base segmentation strategies*, using several bases to segment a total market. For example, the housing market might be segmented by family size, income, and age.

American Log Home, for example, offers a wide variety of packages and options to its customers based on their needs, incomes, skills, family size, and usage. Packages range from one-room shelters designed primarily for hunters to a 4,000 square-foot unit complete with hot tub, chandeliers, and three decks. Customers can select to finish part of the interior, part of the exterior, or to have the entire structure finished by American Log Home.

The resulting huge array of products is a disadvantage of multi-base seg-mentation as a strategy. When using several bases that vary in importance, considering all to be equal could produce misdirected efforts.

Qualifying Customers in Market Segments

Clearly it is important to employ appropriate factors to identify market seg-ments. Equally important is qualifying the customers who make up those segments. Qualifications involve judgment. Marketers must be able to dif-ferentiate between real prospects and individuals or firms who have some similar characteristics but cannot be converted to purchasers.

It should be clear that not all market segments present desirable marketing opportunities. Traditionally, five criteria have been employed to gauge the relative worth of a market segment:

1. *Clarity of identification*: The degree to which we can identify who is in and who is outside the segment. Part of this process also involves the delineation of demographic and social characteristics that make it easier to measure and track the identified segment. Unfortunately, obtaining segment data is not always easy, especially when the segment is defined in terms of behavioral or benefits characteristics. Sex is a clear basis for segmenting a product such as brassieres.

2. *Actual or potential need:* Needs that reflect overt demands for existing goods and services, or needs that can be transformed into perceived wants through education or persuasion, constitute a segment. It is fur-ther assumed that this need exists in a large enough quantity to justify a separate segmentation strategy. This criterion requires the ability to

measure both the intensity of the need and the strength of the purchasing power supporting it. A 40-story building has a clear need for elevators.

3. *Effective demand:* It is not enough for an actual or potential need to exist; purchasing power must also exist. Needs plus purchasing power create effective demand. The ability to buy stems from income, savings, and credit. Purchasing power derived from one or more of these three sources must belong to the members of a market segment in order for it to represent a meaningful marketing opportunity. The possession of a valid Visa or other credit card meets these criteria for most products.

4. *Economic accessibility:* The individuals in a market segment must be reachable and profitable. For example, segments could be concentrated geographically, shop at the same stores, or read the same magazines. Regrettably, many important segments—those based on motivational characteristics, for instance—cannot be reached economically. The elderly rich represent such a segment.

5. *Positive response:* A segment must react uniquely to marketing efforts. There must be a reason for using different marketing approaches in the various segments. Different segments, unless they respond in unique ways to particular marketing inputs, hardly justify the use of separate marketing programs.

The Strategy of Market Segmentation

During the last two decades, a more complete and concise understanding of market segmentation has emerged. This is not to say that there are not still unsettled issues, measurement problems, and other issues to consider. If meaningful segmentations depend on finding patterns in your customers' actual buying behavior, then to construct one properly, you need to gather the relevant data. Depending on the question your exercise is ultimately aimed at answering, you would want information about, say, which benefits and features matter to your customers. Or which customers are willing to pay higher prices or demand lower ones. Or the relative advantages and disadvantages customers identify in your existing offerings. You'll also need data on emerging social, economic, and technological trends that may alter purchasing and usage patterns.

Armed with such data, you can then fashion segments that are both revealing and applicable. Such segments will:

*   Reflect the company's strategy;

- Indicate where sources of revenue or profit may lie;
- Identify consumers' values, attitudes, and beliefs as they relate specifically to product or service offerings;
- Focus on actual customer behavior;
- Make sense to top management;
- Accommodate or anticipate changes in markets or consumer behavior.

The segmented approach will be described throughout this book in greater detail. At this point, it is sufficient to know that the segmentation strategy is the primary marketing approach used by a majority of producers. Combined with product differentiation, it is the essence of a contemporary marketing strategy.

Combination

It is often the case that an organization will employ both an aggregated and disaggregated approach to the market. For example, a company such as Nestle employs an aggregated strategy in selling their powdered and canned baby formula worldwide, but segments on their many other products. Therefore, a combination approach is dictated by the situation faced by the organization, relative to their product offerings and the market characteristics. It is typical for a company that has a global presence to segment in more developed markets such as the United States and Europe, and aggregate in Third World countries. When combining market strategies the guidelines outlined for both approaches must be applied.

TARGET MARKET SELECTION

Once a company has opted into one of the three approaches toward the market, the next step is to select one or more target markets. None of the rest of marketing is likely to succeed unless the target market selection process is done correctly. To quote marketing expert Philip Kotler: "To get it right the first time, the most time, the most important steps are targeting and positioning. If you nail these two components of strategy, everything else follows."[2]

Yet we find that targeting—and market segmentation generally—is one of the least well-developed skills in marketing today. Some markets don't even seem to realize they need to specify a target market. This is particularly true with many of the new Internet companies and Web site developers who obsess over maximizing the number of "eyeballs" at their site. Yet, not all eyeballs are created equal and a firm should make every effort to assess which eyeballs would be most profitable to attract.

Even marketers that do have a targeting strategy often identify targets that are dreamlike, rather than based on facts. Here is an example of a target that is intuitively appealing, but in actuality, provides very little real information:

"Female heads of households who are time-pressured and yet, at the same time, want to meet their families' expectations of them as a wife, mother, keeper of the home." Does this not describe virtually all female heads of households?

Fortunately, there are companies that do conduct major research projects designed to develop, with serious quantitative data, a segmentation of the marketplace with the aim of finding one or more highly profitable targets to pursue. This process is costly and time consuming, but necessary if the optimum target markets are to be selected.

The following criteria should be considered, regardless of whether it is part of an undifferentiated market or one of several possible market segments.

- Decision making power
- Strong sales potential
- Strong growth potential
- High lifetime value
- High retention
- Common motivations
- Common problems
- Responsive to marketing efforts
- Use similar media
- Ease of access

Naturally, all these criteria will be further developed for each company. Here is an example of how one company operationalized their target market statement:

- It is sufficient in size to merit disproportionate attention (i.e., 10 to 30 percent).
- It is growing rather than shrinking over time.
- It is different attitudinally/behaviorally and therefore differentially reachable with media, through direct mail, promotions, public relations, sales force, and so forth.
- It has "problems/needs/wants" distinctly different from other segments.
- It represents potential profitability considerably greater than its size (i.e., 50 to 75 percent).

PRODUCT DIFFERENTIATION

Both undifferentiated and segmented markets contain a high level of competition. How does a company compete when all product offerings are basically the same and many companies are in fierce competition? The answer is to engage in a strategy referred to as *product differentiation*. It is an attempt to tangibly or intangibly distinguish a product from that of all competitors in the eyes of customers. Examples of tangible differences might be product features, performance, endurance, location, or support services, to name but a few. Chrysler once differentiated their product by offering a 7-year/70,000-mile warranty on new models. Pepsi has convinced many consumers to try their product because they assert that it really does taste better than Coke. Offering products at a lower price or at several different prices can be an important distinguishing characteristic, as demonstrated by Timex watches.

Some products are in fact the same, and attempts to differentiate through tangible features would be either futile or easily copied. In such cases, an *image* of difference is created through intangible means that may have little to do with the product directly. Soft drink companies show you how much fun you can have by drinking their product. Beer companies suggest status, enjoyment, and masculinity. Snapple may not taste the best or have the fewest calories, but may have the funniest, most memorable commercials. There tends to be a heavy emphasis on the use of mass appeal means of promotion, such as advertising when differentiating through intangibles. Microsoft has successfully differentiated itself through an image of innovation and exceptional customer service. This challenge of differentiating a product through intangible benefits or features is the fate of most nonprofit organizations. How does the local Baptist church differentiate itself? What are its products? These issues will be addressed in chapter 6 when we discuss the strategic adjustment needed when marketing service products, which include nonprofits.

There are certain risks in using product differentiations. First, a marketer who uses product differentiation must be careful not to eliminate mention of core appeals or features that the consumer expects from the product. For example, differentiating a brand of bread through its unique vitamin and mineral content is valid as long as you retain the core freshness feature in your ad. Second, highlighting features that are too different from the norm may prove ineffective. Finally, a product may be differentiated on a basis that is unimportant to the customer or difficult to understand. The automobile industry has learned to avoid technical copy in ads since most customers don't understand it or don't care.

POSITIONING

Regardless of whether an organization follows an aggregated (undifferentiated) or disaggregated (segmentation) approach to the market, a position will emerge. The customer may create the position or you may create your own position. The latter is preferred. A *positioning* must be one, two, or three words, phrases or sentences about your organization (brand) that you want to imprint in the heads of key stakeholders. Close your eyes and what are the first words that come to your mind when I say Volvo? Sears? Microsoft? Iraq? The American Heart Association? If these organizations have done their job correctly, these words will be positive and reflect the mission of the organization. This image, this *reason* you're giving consumers to buy your product comes about through the positioning strategy. A *positioning strategy* includes product differentiation factors plus how these factors will be combined, how they will be communicated, and who will communicate them. The following table shows examples of past and present great positions.

GREAT POSITIONS, PAST AND PRESENT

Archer Daniels Midland	Supermarket to the world
BMW	The ultimate driving machine
Burger King	Have it your way
Google	Most powerful search engine
IBM	Fast, flexible solutions
jetBlue	Cheap flights with style
SAS	Gives you the power to know
Volvo	Personal safety

Given this context, the word "positioning" includes several of the common meanings of a position: A place (what place does the product occupy in its market?), a rank (how does the product fare against its competitors in various evaluative dimensions?), a mental attitude (what are consumers' attitudes?), and a strategic process (what activities must be attempted in order to create the operational product position?). Thus, positioning is both a concept and a process. The positioning process produces a position for the product, just as the segmentation process produces alternative market segments. Positioning can be applied to any type of product at any stage of the life cycle. Approaches to positioning range from gathering sophisticated market research information on consumers' preferences and perceptions of brands to the intuition of the product manager or a member of her staff.

There are several bases for creating a position. The following are the most prevalent:

- product features (e.g., quality, strength, size, speed)
- product benefits (e.g., convenient, fast, safe)
- usage occasions (e.g., vacation, entertainment, party)
- user category (e.g., one-time users, moderate users, heavy users)
- competitors (e.g., direct comparison, similar comparison, number 1)
- reputation (e.g., history, awards, J.D. Powers)
- promotional elements (e.g., inexpensive, events, sponsorship)

These bases can be employed to a more general positioning strategy. The three most popular are:

1. **Consumer positioning**—position a product to appeal to a specific market segment (target) or group of segments. The bases that have proven most effective in consumer positioning include: product claims, imagery, usage, and user categories.
2. **Competitive positioning**—position a product against one or more of its competitors. Several considerations are made when positioning against competitors: to name or not to name the competition; to take the dominant or underdog position; to try to reposition competition via unknown facts.
3. **Social accountability positioning**—position a product as superior in respect to social support issues such as green marketing and cause marketing.

Products and brands are constantly being repositioned as a result of changes in competitive and market situations. *Repositioning* involves changing the market's perceptions of a brand or product so that it can compete more effectively in its present market or in other market segments. Changing market perceptions may require changes in the tangible product, its selling price, or how it is better than a competitor. Often, however, the new differentiation is accomplished through a change in the basic marketing message. To evaluate the position and to generate diagnostic information about the future positioning strategies, it is necessary to monitor the position over time. A product position, like a celebrity, may change readily; keeping track and making necessary adjustments is very important. It may be just as determinate that a company has no position, or one created by the consumer or a competitor, as a position that is not correct.

Ultimately, the positioning strategy is a five-step process:

Step 1. Access where you are positioned now. In doing this, a marketer would examine the evaluative criteria used by consumers, with a focus on product attitudes and stereotypes related to these attributes. As an example, from the consumer's perspective Wal-Mart is viewed as "good value" while K-mart is viewed as "cheap."

Step 2. Access the position of all current and potential competitors. The key here is to correctly identify the primary attributes consumers use to compare competitors in marketing choices. It is often the case that competitors compare well on the top two or three attributes, such as price and quality, and it is not until you get to "convenience" that consumers distinguish competitors.

Step 3. Determine your capabilities of establishing and keeping a position. While every university would like the same position as Stanford or Yale, it is highly unlikely they can do this profitably or permanently. Conversely, a retailer who is cursed with an inconvenient location may be able to reposition themselves by employing Internet technology as a substitute. This is an instance when an outside consultant should be called in to conduct this assessment

Step 4. Analyze which of the marketing communication tools would be most effective in delivering this position to the target audience. Personal selling, advertising, sales promotion, and public relations, which are the primary communication devices, each have their strengths and weaknesses in creating accurate positions. For example, the more complex the position, the more likely you would be to use personal selling and the less likely you would be to use advertising. Experts in marketing communication must make an objective evaluation of all these elements.

Step 5. Determine the legality of your position. A good lawyer familiar with communication, claims, and counterclaims should be hired to examine your proposed position in order to consider improper claims, possible deception, and a host of other legal problems that can become part of a positioning strategy.

In the end the best axiom to follow is to base your positioning on "real customer problems." Otherwise you take the risk of creating a position that is based on perspective of top management rather than customers. In addition, the consumers must find your position to be distinctive, superior, and believable. Achievement of all four of these requirements ensures the nonprofit marketer that they are on the road to success.

All nonprofit organizations must have a basic understanding of the market(s) in which they operate. Prior to that, however, they must determine how they are going to approach the market. The initial decision is whether to assume the market is homogeneous, where everyone is essentially the same, or heterogeneous, where important differences are noted. Each has important strategic implications for all the marketing efforts that follow. Thus it would be a serious mistake to gloss over the discussion of how to approach your market.

REFERENCES

1. Adapted from: Brad Wolverton, "Under New Formula, Graduation Rates Rise", *The Chronicle of Higher Education*, January 6, 2006, p. A49.

2. Drucker, Peter F., *Managing the Non-Profit Organization*, New York: Collins Business (1990); p. 74.

4

MARKETING RESEARCH: THE FOUNDATION FOR PLANNING

The use of marketing research has been identified as a source of a firm's marketing orientation that allows it to obtain a sustainable competitive advantage.

—Albert Kohli

Sharon Silva, Director of Research & Analysis for the American Red Cross (ARC), faced a tough challenge following the events of 9/11. Before that date, polls indicated that the "trust" the public had in the Red Cross was 82 percent (high level of trust). After 9/11, this number dropped to 73 percent with no apparent explanation. Initial research suggests that since 9/11 there has been greater donor awareness, but with it has come a greater interest in accountability and adherence to best practices. Also, it was determined that donors did not really understand what the Disaster Relief Fund was and how it operated. In February and March 2002, 12 focus groups comprised of long-time ARC donors as well as 9/11 donors were conducted by Wirthlen Worldwide. They also took a poll of a random sample of 2,000 U.S. citizens. The findings indicated the following:

- People value and support the "first on the scene" role of the Red Cross.
- They see the Red Cross as playing a key role in providing basic necessities to disaster victims.
- They have a very limited understanding of how Disaster Relief funding works, but they would like to learn more.

- When the fund is explained, donors are enthusiastic; it shows that the American Red Cross is efficient and effective in delivering disaster services.
- Donors expect the Red Cross to use funds appropriately.
- No fundraising message was 100 percent clear.

The results of this marketing research served as the basis for the new Donor DIRECT program in May 2002.

DONOR + INTERNET + RECOGNITION + CONFIRMATION = TRUST

This program serves as the marketing platform even today. It is an example of how good marketing research can lead to good marketing strategy.

INTRODUCTION

Marketing research addresses the need for quicker yet more accurate decision making by the marketer. The impetus for this situation is the complex relationship between the business firm and the ever-changing external environment. In particular, most marketers are far removed from their customers; yet must know who their customers are, what they want, and what competitors are doing. Often the marketer relies on salespeople and dealers for information, but more and more, the best source of information is marketing research.

It should be noted that most marketing decisions are still made without the use of formal marketing research. In many cases, the time required to do marketing research is not available. In other cases, the cost of obtaining the data is prohibitive or the desired data cannot be obtained in reliable form. Ultimately, successful marketing executives make decisions on the basis of a blend of facts and intuition.

In this chapter, we provide an overview of the marketing research process. We start the discussion with a look at business information. As noted in Exhibit 4.1, marketing research is applicable throughout the marketing planning process. More importantly, it is just as important in nonprofit organizations as it is in for-profit organizations.

THE NATURE AND IMPORTANCE OF MARKETING RESEARCH

Informal and, by today's standards, crude attempts to analyze the market date back to the earliest days of the marketing revolution. Only in recent years,

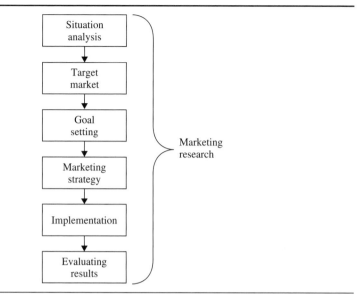

EXHIBIT 4.1 THE MARKETING PLANNING PROCESS AND THE ROLE OF MARKETING RESEARCH

however, has the role of research as it relates to management been clearly recognized.

Reflecting this change in orientation, the following definition of marketing research is offered: *marketing research* is the scientific and controlled gathering of nonroutine marketing information undertaken to help management solve marketing problems. There is often hearty disagreement over the answer to the questions of whether marketing research is a science. One's answer depends on the employed definition of "science." To be specific, a research activity should use the scientific method. In this method, hypotheses (tentative statements of relationships or of solutions to problems) are drawn from informal observations. These hypotheses are then tested. Ultimately, the hypothesis is accepted, rejected, or modified according to the results of the test. In a true science experiment, reproducible, verified hypotheses are turned into "laws." In marketing research, verified hypotheses become the generalizations upon which management develops its marketing programs. (To simplify our discussion, we will use "questions" as synonym for "hypothesis.")

The mechanics of marketing research must be controlled so that the right facts are obtained in the answer to the correct problem. The control of fact-finding is the responsibility of the research director, who must correctly design the research and carefully supervise its execution to ensure that it goes according to plan. Maintaining control in marketing research is often diffi-cult because of the distance that separates the researcher and the market and because the services of outsiders are often required to complete a research project.

WHAT NEEDS RESEARCHING IN MARKETING?

An easy and truthful answer to this question is "everything." There is no aspect of marketing to which research cannot be applied. Every concept pre-sented in this marketing text and every element involved in the marketing management process can be subjected to a great deal of careful market-ing research. One convenient way to focus attention on those matters that especially need researching is to consider the elements involved in market-ing management. Many important questions relating to the consumer can be raised. Some are:

- Who is/are the customer(s)?
- What does he/she desire in the way of satisfaction?
- Where does he/she choose to purchase?
- Why does he/she buy, or not buy?
- When does he/she purchase?
- How does he/she go about seeking satisfaction in the market?

Another area where research is critical is *profits*. Two elements are invol-ved. First, there is the need to forecast sales and related costs—resulting in profits. Second, there is the necessity of planning a competitive mar-keting program that will produce the desired level of sales at an appropri-ate cost. Sales forecasting is the principal tool used in implementing the profit-direction element in the marketing management concept. Of course, the analysis of past sales and interpretation of cost information are important tools in the evaluation of performance and provide useful facts for future planning.

A great deal of marketing research is directed toward rather specialized areas of management. These activities are broken down into five major areas of marketing research. Briefly, these activities are:

1. *Research on markets*—market trends, market share, market potentials, market characteristics, completion, and other market intelligence.
2. *Research on sales*—sales analysis, sales forecasting, quota-setting, sales territory design, sales performance measurement, trade channels, distribution costs, and inventories.

3. *Research on products* — new product research, product features, brand image, concept tests, product tests, and market tests.

4. *Research on advertising and promotion* — promotion concepts, copy research, media research, merchandising, packaging, advertising effectiveness measurement.

5. *Research on corporate growth and development* — economic and technological forecasting, corporate planning inputs, corporate image, profitability measurement, merger and acquisition studies, and facilities location.

PROCEDURES AND TECHNIQUES IN MARKETING RESEARCH

Considering the relatively short span of time in which marketing research has developed since the 1930s, it is quite remarkable that so sophisticated and thorough a collection of procedures and techniques should have been devised. In many respects, marketing research has advanced faster than any other specialized area in marketing management. In view of the highly specialized nature of marketing research, it is not possible in this discussion to present more than an outline of the basic procedures and techniques.

It is important for a marketing manager to be familiar with the basic procedures and techniques of marketing research. It is true that many businesspeople will never have occasion to engage personally in marketing research. However, it is quite likely that they will be faced with a need either to supervise an internal marketing research activity or to work with an outside marketing research firm. The manager who understands the research function is in a position to judge intelligently the proposals made by research specialists and to evaluate their findings and recommendations. Occasionally, the manager herself will have to seek solutions to marketing problems as it may not be possible to obtain the service of marketing research specialists. The manager who is familiar with the basic procedures of fact-finding in marketing should be able to supervise a reasonably satisfactory search for the information required.

There is no single set of steps in a market research procedure that is accepted by all. Indeed, each marketing research problem requires, to some degree, its own particular procedure. However, there is general agreement that four specific activities should be performed in any thorough marketing research project. These are: 1. making a preliminary investigation; 2. creating the research design; 3. conducting the investigation; and 4. processing the data/reporting results (see Exhibit 4.2).

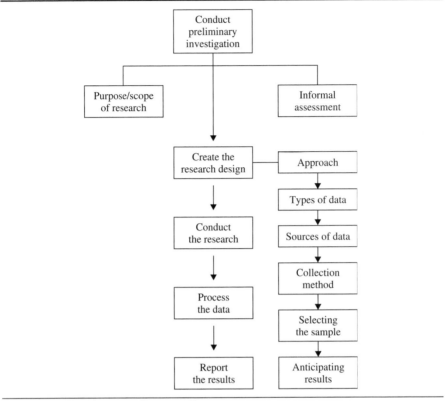

Exhibit 4.2   The Marketing Research Process

Making a Preliminary Investigation

There are two phases of activity in the preliminary investigation. The first of these involves the determination of the purpose and scope of the research. The second, called the informal assessment, involves an investigation into the marketing environment.

Determining the Purpose and Scope of the Research

The basic and critical problem in marketing research is seldom the problem that appears on the surface. It is therefore necessary to explore beneath the surface to ascertain the true nature and size of the problem. This is the vital first step and must be done correctly, since every subsequent phase of the project is directed at solving the basic problem. For the research to be worthwhile (indeed, for it not to be a waste of resources), the problem must be stated clearly and correctly. Failure to do so is one of the most serious and common mistakes in any project.

Correctly defining the research problem should lead to the establishment of the research parameters. A research study could be restricted by function (advertising); customer group (heavy users); market (Far East); and time frame (2005 to 2006). Because research is so costly, it is imperative that parameters are established and maintained.

The Informal Assessment

The second important phase of the preliminary investigation is called the informal assessment. This is an unstructured search of the marketing environment. It enables the researcher to become familiar with the problem setting. This is particularly important for the outside consultant who needs to become acquainted with the company, its customers, its products, and all of the marketing conditions surrounding the problem(s). But it is also wise for the researcher within the company to refresh his or her knowledge of the internal factors bearing on the problem and also to discover the external elements involved.

The informal investigation goes beyond merely "getting acquainted" with the problem and its marketing setting, however. The final result of the preliminary investigation is the creation of a set of research questions. In marketing research, these questions can be stated as a tentative explanation of the problem that the research is designed to solve. For example, if a marketing manager is trying to figure out why he has lost a large market share in a particular area of the country, an informal investigation might reveal three possible reasons for the decline in market position. These reasons, until verified by thorough study, can best be stated as research statements:

1. The decline in market share is the result of increased competitive advertising in the area.
2. The decline in market share is the result of the test marketing of a new product by a major competitor.
3. The decline in market share is the result of "stock outs" at the retail level caused by a trucking strike in the area.

In attempting to verify one or more of these hypothetical statements, the researcher must examine company records to uncover new sources of information or to discover relationships in old data that have bearing on the current problem. Interviews with company executives and operating personnel are often conducted. Interviews should also be conducted with various people outside the company whose opinions might have some relevance to the problem. The preliminary search is always limited to obtaining insight into the problem and into possible solutions for it.

In the final phase of the preliminary investigation, the researcher should analyze the results he has obtained thus far and restate them in the form of research questions to be tested in subsequent research steps.

Creating the Research Design

The design of a marketing research project is the plan proposed for testing the research questions as well as collecting and processing information. The administration of the project according to the design insures that the fact-finding process will be adequately controlled. "Design" means more than simply using good market research procedures. Every research project should be individually designed to produce the kinds of information needed to solve a particular problem. For this reason, no two market research projects are ever exactly alike.

Six steps are involved in creating a research design: choosing the approach, determining types of data needed, locating data sources, choosing a method of collecting data, selecting the sample, and anticipating/collecting the results.

Step 1. Choosing the Approach

Three alternative approaches are possible in creating a research design. They are not mutually exclusive, but in most cases, the design of a research plan is limited to the use of one of the three.

The first approach is the *experimental approach*. This approach requires that certain procedural rules must be followed. Essentially, the variable of interest—e.g., price level, message type—must be manipulated and every consumer participating in the experiment must have a "known and equal chance" of being selected to receive one version of the price or message.

In a market experiment, information relating to the basic problem is obtained through the use of a small-scale simulated program designed to test a specific research hypothesis. Suppose, for example, that we wish to test the question that families of similar size and economic characteristics living in three different cities purchase different amounts of a particular formula of a soft drink, such as Dr. Pepper. The first step would be to establish the research question: "For Time Period X, were the average fluid ounces of a Formula A, B, or C purchase in each city the same?" Next, a sample of the families in each city would be selected and randomly assigned to taste either formula A, B, or C. Next, a survey would be taken to determine the number of ounces subsequently purchased by each family. Once this was done, a statistical test would be used to test the research question. If statistically significant differences in purchases of Formula A, B, or C of Dr. Pepper were noted, it could be concluded that taste does influence the amount of this soft drink purchased by families who were randomly selected and assigned taste alternatives.

Of course, other hypotheses about soft drink purchasing could also be tested using a slightly different method. For example, the effect of television advertising on the purchase of Dr. Pepper might be studied by inspecting purchases in two or more cities that are in the same general area of the country (such as the Southwest) but in which different levels of television advertising have been used. This second method is the *historical approach*. In this approach, reliance is placed on past experiences in seeking solutions to marketing problems. Historical marketing facts are relevant only to the degree that they can be projected into the future. Fortunately, in many areas of marketing, this can be done with a good deal of confidence. Certain types of changes, such as populations and income distribution, come about rather slowly. The day-to-day effect of these changes on marketing is almost imperceptible. Projections of future population, gross national product, and consumer purchasing power are quite reliable. Historical analyses of such factors as consumer behavior, competitive selling tactics, and distributors' buying practices tend also to be fairly reliable indicators of future behavior by these same marketing components. Often it is possible to track the experiences of organizations similar to your own and assess how they dealt with similar problems. There are literally hundreds of case studies on companies such as Microsoft that are useful to many business functions. Learning from the mistakes of others makes good business sense.

The third approach that can be used in designing a marketing research plan is the *survey approach*. In the survey approach, marketing information is collected either from observation or by questionnaire or interview. In contrast to the experimental and historical methods, in which the data are more or less directly related to the problem, the survey approach necessarily involves far more subjectivity and intuition on the part of the researcher. Watching a customer purchase a new TV reveals something about his motives; simply asking him why he is buying that particular brand of television yields a much more accurate result. Drawing conclusions from either observations of behavior or from the opinions offered by a respondent creates important insights. The survey method is flexible. It can be adapted to almost any type of research design. For this reason, and because of the difficulties in creating marketing experiments and in collecting pertinent historical data, the survey approach is the one most often used in marketing research.

Step 2. Determining the Types of Data Needed

Three types of data are used when conducting marketing research: facts, opinions, and motivational information. The types of data required are partly identified by the nature of the problem to be solved. For instance, if the problem relates to production and inventory scheduling, the facts that are needed relate to market and sales potential. On the other hand, if the problem revolves around the choice between two new products, the opinions of potential customers are important considerations. Finally, if a problem involves the choice of an appropriate selling appeal, buyers' motivations are probably most important. Facts are quantitative or descriptive information that can be verified. Opinions are ideas relating to a problem that are expressed by people involved in the solution. Motivations are basic reasons, recognized or unrecognized, that explain action. They are extremely difficult to discover.

Step 3. Locating the Sources of Data

There are two general sources of data, primary sources and secondary sources. *Secondary source* information has been previously published and can be either internal or external. Company records and previously prepared marketing research reports are typical of internal secondary source material. External secondary sources are widely available and can be found outside the organization. Excellent bibliographies of secondary data sources are available, especially online. There are eight primary sources of secondary market information:

Public libraries.
Universities—library facilities and bureaus of business and economic research.
Government agencies—especially departments of commerce, agriculture, and labor.
Professional and trade associations.
Commercial publishers—especially trade publications.
Research and nonprofit organizations.
Conferences and personal contact.
Computer-provided search systems.

Undoubtedly, the Internet offers the cheapest and most efficient mechanism for gathering secondary data. The following are available to nonprofits:

Search Tools

- Search engines
    - general/subject specific
    - use to identify sources, not answers
    - use more than one
    - learn to use advanced/special features
- Directories
    - a.k.a. portals/gateways/indexes
    - hand-selected links
    - general/subject specific
    - browse subjects/search
- Government resources
    - use for statistics
    - use for demographics
    - use SEC filings for ownership information, corporate giving, executive biographies/salaries
- Online databases
    - fee-based (expensive)
    - subscription or pay-as-you-go (e.g., America Online)
    - library databases, which are usually free (e.g., Lexus-Nexus)
    - directories, news, journals (e.g., CanPo)

There are tremendous advantages in using data from secondary sources. First, the expense of gathering information from secondary sources is a fraction of the cost of collecting primary data. The time required to collect data is also less. Frequently, the information required to solve a management problem must be obtained quickly. Thanks to computer technology, it is now possible to gather, merge, and recalculate many secondary sources of data. This capability has made secondary data even more attractive.

The inherent limitations of using secondary sources data are twofold. First, the information is frequently dated. Second, seldom are secondary data collected for precisely the same reasons that the information is sought to solve the current marketing problem. In spite of these limitations, the advantages of secondary research are so great that it is a common procedure not to proceed with the collection of primary data until after a thorough search of secondary information sources has been completed.

Primary information is obtained directly from its source. It involves data that are not available in published form or in company records. It is gathered specifically to answer your research question. The sources of primary information, however, cannot be as easily identified as can the sources of secondary market data. Having identified the information required to help management solve a problem, it is usually possible to identify the person or persons possessing the information desired. In some cases, the information can be obtained from one of several sources. In other situations, the information can be obtained only by contacting specific sources. For example, a manufacturer of vitamins for children discovered that it was necessary to obtain information from the users (children), purchasers (parents), sellers (for the most part, pharmacists), and purchase influencers (pediatricians). Similarly, a manufacturer of feed for dairy cattle found it desirable to seek market information from farmers, feed dealers, and dairy specialists. Obviously, it is expensive to collect marketing information from multiple sources, and often it is rather time-consuming. These two disadvantages are offset by the fact that the information obtained is tailored to the specific problem at hand. Ultimately, the question as to which source of market information to use depends on the value of the information in relationship to the time and cost required to gather it.

Step 4. Choosing the Method of Collecting Data

There are various methods of collecting data, both secondary and primary. Secondary sources of information, listed earlier, can be gathered through a number of means. A company may establish a data-gathering/storage system as part of their computer system. Sales, expenses, inventory, returns, and customer complaints are then gathered automatically. Or, a company may subscribe to one or more public research companies that gather relevant information. Finally, a company can obtain information on a problem-by-problem basis.

There are three common methods used to collect primary information: observation, questionnaire, and self-report. *Observational data* collection may be the oldest method. Since the beginning of commerce, merchants have been watching their customers and noncustomers engage in a variety of behaviors. Examples include shopping, purchase, return, complaint behavior, and so forth. A local fast food manager might simply observe the expression on customers' faces as they eat a new sandwich. More formal observation techniques are also employed. Video cameras or audio systems can be targeted at customers, although this must be done with complete knowledge and permission. Researchers can also be hired to do license plate surveys in parking lots or simply record observations in a prescribed manner. There are even observational techniques that are quite intrusive. For instance, in the case of a pantry (cabinet) audit, the researcher comes to the consumer's home and actually takes an inventory of products found. Ethnography requires that the researcher practically move in with the consumer and observe various relevant behaviors. The observation technique can provide important research insights, especially if consistent patterns are noted. The less invasive forms of observational data are relatively inexpensive to collect and can be implemented and completed quickly. Unfortunately, interpreting an observation is still very subjective and mistakes are made.

Gathering information through a *questionnaire* format reflects the most popular research technique. There are two interrelated issues: the design of the questionnaire and the administration of the questionnaire. There are several rules of thumb that should be followed when designing a questionnaire. For example, a good questionnaire should be like a well-written story; it should be logical, relevant, easy to follow, and interesting to the reader/respondent. There are also a host of techniques and related guidelines. For example, Exhibit 4.3 illustrates the forms questions can take. A yes/no question is considered a closed-ended dichotomous question (i.e., the respondent must check one of two possible answers). Questions 4 and 5 in Exhibit 4.3 are two types of scaled questions. Questions 6 through 8 are open-ended, in that respondents can provide any answer desired. Closed-ended questions are best used when the researcher desires a particular set of answers or feels the respondent is unlikely to come up with an original answer. Open-ended questions allow the respondent to come up with personal answers. Of course, there is always a risk that the respondent will have no answer.

Other considerations are whether to place the easier questions at the beginning of the questionnaire, group similar questions, or place demographic questions at the end of the questionnaire. Again, the goal is to enable the respondent to answer the questionnaire easily and accurately.

The design of a questionnaire is a function of how the questionnaire is administered, and vice versa. Four techniques for administering a questionnaire are currently used: mail, telephone, personal interview, and online. In the mail technique, the questionnaire is distributed and returned through the mail. A typical packet might contain a cover letter explaining the purpose of the research, a copy of the questionnaire, a stamped self-addressed return envelope, and an incentive for compliance (cash, merchandise, contribution to charity, or copy of report). Mail questionnaires allow the researcher to ask a large number of questions over a broad range of topics. They also allow the respondent to answer the questionnaire at their leisure. Finally, the standardized format does not allow for subjective bias. Unfortunately, these advantages can become limitations. The longer the questionnaire, the less likely the individual will respond. In fact, without an incentive, a response rate of 10 to 20 percent is common. Also, control is lost through the mail process. Did the targeted person receive the questionnaire? Did the respondent understand the questions? Did she/he complete the questionnaire? Was the questionnaire returned on time? The loss of control also means that the interviewer cannot probe further into an interesting or controversial answer.

A more convenient and faster way of gathering marketing information is to conduct a telephone survey. Names and related telephone numbers can be obtained directly from a telephone directory or from an internally or externally generated database. Telephone surveys are limited in several important ways, such as the difficulty of reaching the correct respondent, the problem of completing the interview if the respondent decides to hang up, and the inability to eliminate the bias introduced by not interviewing those without phones or individuals with unlisted numbers. Also, 10 to 15 questions are likely to be the maximum number that the respondent will allow to be asked. Therefore, only a limited number of topics can be addressed. In spite of these limitations, the telephone survey method has grown in popularity. The costs are relatively low, research companies can provide well-trained and technically supported interviewers, and the technique works if the research questions are limited and require a quick answer. Still, keep in mind that most potential respondents feel it would be better if you didn't call them while they were eating dinner. In other words, people are busy, and gaining their trust and cooperation over the telephone can be difficult.

Although often very costly and time-consuming, personal interviews may constitute the best way of collecting survey information (see Exhibit 4.3). Once compliance is gained, the well-trained interviewer can make sure the right person is answering; ask as many questions as necessary to address new issues, and encourage the respondent to complete the questionnaire. Note however, that with freedom comes bias. It is sometimes difficult for an interviewer to maintain objectivity. Asking questions with a certain intonation, changing the wording, or changing the ordering of questions can all modify responses.

There are several online information-gathering techniques that allow the respondent more freedom in providing answers. As one would expect, there has been a recent rapid technological evolution in this area. Online questionnaires can help Web site sponsors to gauge customer satisfaction, profile visitors, and provide a way to measure traffic for advertisers beyond banner click-throughs. By using research tools such as exit surveys, e-tailers can find out why people are leaving their sites—and why they might not come back.

A. DIRECT QUESTIONS/CLOSED-ENDED

1. HAVE YOU PURCHASED A NEW AUTOMOBILE SINCE JANUARY 1 OF THIS YEAR:

      YES   NO

2. IF YOU HAVE PURCHASED A NEW AUTOMOBILE, WHAT MAKE AND MODEL DID YOU BUY

    MAKE:_____ MODEL:_____

3. IF YOU HAVE NOT PURCHASE A CAR SINCE JANUARY 1, DO YOU NOW PLAN TO BUY A NEW AUTOMOBILE BEFORE DECEMBER 31 OF THIS YEAR?

      YES   NO

4. IF YOU HAVE NOT DECIDED WHETHER OR NOT YOU WIL BUY A NEW AUTOMOBILE, DO YOU NOW THINK THAT IT IS

—EXTREMELY LIKELY
—QUITE LIKELY
—UNLIKELY
—EXTREMELY UNLIKELY

THAT YOU WILL BUY A NEW AUTOMOBILE BETWEEN NOW AND DECEMBER 31?

5. I TEND TO RELY HEAVILY ON THE REPUTATION OF A CAR BRAND

      DISAGREE   AGREE
        1   2   3   4   5

B. DEPTH QUESTION/OPEN-ENDED

6. IF YOU HAVE NOT PURCHASED A NEW AUTOMOBILE, WHAT IS THE MOST IMPORTANT REASON FOR YOUR DECISION NOT TO BUY A NEW CAR?

7. THAT IS VERY INTERESTING. TELL ME MORE ABOUT THAT.

8. ANY OTHER REASONS?

EXHIBIT 4.3 EXAMPLES OF QUESTIONS USED IN MARKETING RESEARCH

There are four popular types of online research. Pop-up surveys occur when visitors are intercepted as they leave certain pages of the Web site. A questionnaire then appears in a box at the top of their main browser screens asking for responses. With e-mail/Web surveys, a company sends an e-mail message asking the recipient to complete a survey. Sometimes the survey is embedded in the e-mail itself. Other times the e-mail lists either a password-protected location to visit or a unique location that only the addressee can access to fill out the survey. Online groups are much like traditional focus groups, but are conducted in a Web-based chat room where select individuals are invited by the company or its research firm. Finally, in the case of moderated e-mail groups, discussions take place over a period of time with a group communicating via e-mail. A moderator compiles the answers and sends the summary back to the group for comments and follow-up.

The third technique used to gather research information is *self-reporting*. This technique allows the respondent to deliver the information in a somewhat unstructured format. One very popular version of this technique is the focus group. A *focus group* takes place in a room where approximately 8 to 10 individuals and a trained moderator gather to discuss a particular business problem or set of problems. Often, the room contains a two-way mirror, which the sponsors of the research sit behind in order to observe the process. The proceedings are audiotaped and/or videotaped. Focus groups have been an extremely popular type of data collection technique for a long time. A great deal of diverse information can be gathered quickly (assuming there is a well-trained moderator). However, there are serious limitations. It's still a subjective process and interpretation is necessary. It is also expensive; often several thousand dollars per focus group. Finally, it is difficult to control the behavior of the participants. Some dominate and some say nothing. And some become the equivalent of professional focus group members and therefore are no longer are able to provide the hoped-for spontaneity.

According to a psychologically proven premise, by making the questions impersonal, it is possible to obtain information from a respondent that he or she would not, or could not, otherwise provide. This method involves the use of the *projective technique*, and represents a second type of self-report technique. The intent of the projective technique is to give respondents an opportunity to answer questions without the embarrassment or confusion created by direct involvement. Several projective techniques are employed:

- *Word association tests*. In the word association test, the respondent is asked to say the first word that comes into mind upon the presentation of another word stimulus. The most obvious applications of this test are in research on brand recognition, company image, and advertising appeals.
- *Sentence completion tests*. In a sentence completion test, the respondent is asked to complete a number of sentences with the first words that come to mind. A series of sentence completion questions used by a supermarket chain were: a. I like to shop in an AG supermarket because...; b. I think that food prices are...; c. The thing that bothers me most about food shopping in an AG store is....

The sentence completion test is relatively simple to administer and easy to interpret. It is usually difficult, however, to reduce the findings from a sentence completion test to statistical form.

- *Psychodrama*. In the psychodramatic type of question, the respondent is asked to project himself into an artificial marketing situation. The obvious artificiality of the situation makes the psychodrama a role-playing experiment in which the respondent provides information based on his personal attitudes through his explanation of the artificial situation.

Perhaps the greatest deficiency of projective techniques is the difficulty of presenting the findings. The identification of attitudes, motives, opinions, and so forth is not difficult; however, it is extremely hard to measure the importance of these factors.

Step 5. Selecting the Sample

In most marketing research, it is seldom necessary to conduct a complete census (to talk to 100 percent of the target segment). To do so is time-consuming, expensive, and often impossible. For this reason, most marketing surveys make use of samples. A *sample* is a group of elements (persons, stores, financial reports) chosen from among a "total population" or "universe." The value of a research project is directly affected by how well the sample has been conceived and constructed.

The selection of the sample to be investigated requires a master list, or a framework, from which respondents may be selected. The sampling frame is the "population" or statistical "universe" from which the sample units will be selected. The frame for a survey of attitudes of credit customers of a department store would be the company's list of customers who make purchases from their store via charge accounts. Databases can be purchased according to specified characteristics and are generally affordable to nonprofits.

Although there are many kinds of sample designs, all of them can be classified as either *probability samples* or *nonprobability samples*. In a probability sample, each unit has a known chance of being selected for inclusion in the sample. Its simplest version is the random sample, in which each unit in the sample frame has exactly the same chance of selection. Examples of this include flipping a fair coin, whose sides have a 50 percent chance of turning up, and throwing an unloaded die, whose sides have a 16-2/3 percent chance of turning up. This same principle can be applied to the previous department store example. A sample of names could be selected from the company's list of charge customers according to a random process, such as using a table of random digits.

While in a probability sample the sampling units have a known chance of being selected, in a nonprobability sample the sampling units are selected arbitrarily. To return to our department store example, instead of using a table of random numbers to select a sample of charge customers, an arbitrary and more convenient method would be to take the first 50 names on the list.

Step 6. Anticipating the Results/Making the Report

The research plan should provide for: 1. procedures for processing the data, 2. procedures for interpretation and analysis of the findings, and 3. an outline of the final report. In reaching these decisions, it is usually helpful to work from the form and content of the final report. The report should present a summary of findings and recommendations for management action drawn up in the light of the reasons for the research. The kinds of facts to be presented and the manner of their presentation dictate the type of analysis to be undertaken. The kinds of analysis will, in turn, often suggest the method of data processing. *Data processing* in general refers to the procedures for sorting, assembling, and reporting data. It can be done manually using worksheets or by computer programming. The method of data processing has important bearing upon the manner in which the data are collected and reported. Thus, the design of the project is often expedited by a thorough consideration of the kinds of results that are expected and how they will be handled in the final report.

Anticipating the results of the project and preparing a dummy or draft final report has another advantage. It is often helpful to use the results of this step in the research design to demonstrate to management the kind of project that is going to be undertaken. Getting management to agree that the kinds of information anticipated will assist in the solving of a marketing problem is helpful in obtaining approval for the project and in restraining management expectations so that they align with the scope and purpose of the project.

CONDUCTING THE RESEARCH

The attention devoted in the previous paragraphs to the design of the research plan might leave the impression that once a marketing research project has been carefully designed, the job is almost done. Clearly, this is not the case. The implementation of a research plan is seldom an easy task. Often a research program requires extra effort from already-busy personnel in the company. In other cases, outsiders must be recruited, hired, and trained.

In either situation, carrying out a marketing research plan is difficult and requires very close supervision and control. To the extent that the plan has been well conceived, supervision and control are restricted to making sure that the research activities called for in the plan are carried out according to schedule and in the manner prescribed.

PROCESSING THE DATA

Processing the data obtained in a market survey involves transforming the information into a report to be used by management. Four steps are involved: 1. editing the data; 2. tabulating the data; 3. interpreting the data; and 4. presenting the report. If, in the anticipation of the results of the survey, the procedures for handling the data have been set forth and the form of the final report conceived, these final four steps in the research procedure may be quite mechanical. A good plan for the analysis and interpretation of the data is of immense assistance in bringing a project to a successful conclusion, but it should never limit the kinds of interpretations that eventually are made or restrict the content of the final report.

The final report of a marketing research study should ordinarily be written. Since vast amounts of data often are involved, the written report is the only appropriate method of presenting these findings. The written report also has the advantage of being permanent, thus permitting management to study the findings carefully and to refer to them in the future. Unfortunately, many marketing research projects are never translated into management action—sometimes because the research conclusions do not directly contribute to the solution of the problem, sometimes because the report is too technical and difficult to understand, and sometimes because the report writer has not offered specific suggestions as to how the report should be translated into management strategy.

THE VALUE OF MARKETING RESEARCH

It is important to point out that it is not always necessary to conduct research before attempting to solve a problem in marketing management. The manager may feel that he already knows enough to make a good decision. In a few instances, there may be no choice among alternatives and hence no decision to make. It is rather pointless to study a problem if there is only one possible solution. But in most business situations, the manager must make a choice among two or more courses of action. This is where fact-finding enters in to help make the choice.

But even if a manager would like more information in order to make a decision, it is not always wise for her to conduct the research that would be required. One reason is that the time involved may be too great. Another more compelling reason is that the cost of the research may exceed its contribution. In principle, it is easy to understand how such a cost test might be applied. If the cost of conducting the research is less than its contribution to the improvement of the decision, the research should be carried out. If its cost is greater, it should not be conducted. The application of this principle in actual practice is somewhat more complex. Finally, good research should help integrate marketing with the other areas of the business.

MARKETING RESEARCH FOR NEXT TO NOTHING

For most companies, money for marketing research is just part of the annual budget. Yet, for nonprofit organizations operating on already-slim budgets, spending a lot of money on research isn't a realistic option. It behooves nonprofits to identify sources of marketing research that are inexpensive or even free. Here are a few suggestions:

- Partner with a college or university. Professors are often looking for projects to assign to their marketing research classes and are inclined to conduct research for nonprofits.
- Tap current donors or board members to conduct research, especially prospect research. Often, individuals with business experience are familiar with the basics of marketing research and can perform adequately.
- Partner with noncompeting nonprofits. Typically, nonprofits that are not direct competitors collect similar data, especially if they are operating in the same geographic market. Be proactive in locating such research partners.

SUMMARY CASE

As noted throughout this chapter, conducting marketing research is a necessary but expensive activity. For many nonprofits it is somewhat impractical. Still, the research created and implemented by Philip Mangano[1], head of the federal government's Interagency Council on Homelessness, illustrates an effective and professional marketing research plan. It started with secondary data: on any given night, perhaps two million Americans are homeless, but only about 10 percent are chronically so (on the streets for a year or more).

The chronically homeless are overwhelmingly male, and almost all have some impairment—mental illness, disease, disability, drug or alcohol abuse. Also, life on the streets is not cheap. It costs the city of New York at least $40,000 for each chronically homeless person for jail time, shelter costs, emergency room visits, and hospital stays. In Dallas, researchers put the figure at $50,000; in San Diego, it is as much as $150,000.

Via cost-benefit analysis, Mangano estimates that it costs less to get people off the street than letting them stay there. His program has been adopted by over 200 U.S. cities. The first step is to establish a baseline of just how big the market is. This is typically done by a street count—going out at night and counting how many people are sleeping out of doors. Accountability comes about by setting benchmarks for improvement and rewarding those who meet the numbers.

The next step is to talk to the homeless themselves. The marketing research is done the usual way—asking what they want. The typical response is emphatic. They don't want a 12-step program or a bed in a shelter. What they want is a room of their own.

The results then contribute to a strategic plan, Housing First. The plan is simple: if you give people what they want (not what you think they should want), they might just accept it. It entails getting people a room or apartment, by either renting in the private sector or building permanent supported housing, and then bringing social services to the tenant.

In New York City, the success rate has been 88 percent, at a cost of about $22,000 a year per person. A similar program in Phoenix reports a rate of 92 percent, at a cost of $19,800. San Francisco has seen a 40 percent drop in homelessness.

For most nonprofit organizations, investing in marketing research is a tough decision. To do it right, marketing research requires a large investment in time, dollars, and expertise. Moreover, it tends to slow down the decision making process. There seems to be an acceptable adage in the nonprofit sector—as long as no other nonprofits engage in marketing research, you shouldn't have to either. Yet, the advantages of having your decisions guided by good marketing research are enormous. Thanks to the Internet, there is no longer an excuse not to do the basics, at the very least.

REFERENCE

1. "Weapons of Mass Displacement," *Street Sheet* (San Francisco: Thomas Jefferson Area Coalition for the Homeless, 2004), pp. 1–2.

5

EXTERNAL CONSIDERATIONS IN MARKETING INTRODUCTION

In Chapter 1 we introduced the impact of Hurricane Katrina on the nonprofit world. Most notably, events such as national disasters, while identifying a host of recipients needing aid from nonprofits, also may have positive or negative effects on other nonprofits. For example, a survey of small- and medium-sized nonprofits in late 2005 found that fundraising efforts for 71 percent of nonprofits that responded were negatively affected by donation campaigns for large disaster-relief missions. As a result, about 60 percent of nonprofits said they would eliminate programs or reduce budgets. More than 32 percent of donors said they had shifted all or a portion of their donations away from nonprofit groups they typically support and toward disaster-relief funds. These giving declines could particularly hamper human service organizations that typically see increased demand during the winter months.

These results highlight the importance of monitoring events and variables that are outside the control of the nonprofit organization. Such awareness is the first step of the marketing planning process. It is the front half of the situation analysis introduced in Chapter 2, and serves as input in identifying potential opportunities and threats.

INTRODUCTION

As shown in Exhibit 5.1, marketing managers are confronted with many environmental concerns, including technology, customer, competitor, ethical/legal, economic, demographic, and social trends. All organizations should continuously appraise their external situation and adjust their strategy to adapt to their environment.

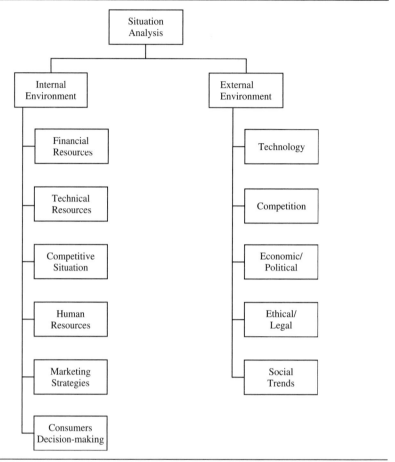

EXHIBIT 5.1   ENVIRONMENTAL FACTORS AFFECTING THE ORGANIZATION

One technique used by organizations to monitor the environment is known as *environmental scanning*, which refers to activities directed toward obtaining information about events and trends that occur outside the organization and that can influence the organization's decision making. In a sense, such data collection scanning acts as an early warning system for the organization. It allows marketers to understand the current state of the environment and to predict trends. A formal but simple strategic information scanning system can enhance the effectiveness of the organization's environmental scanning efforts.

A good strategic plan requires careful monitoring of the marketing organization's external environment. The external environment represents sources of opportunities and threats. If the marketing organization is to align its capabilities and resources with opportunities and threats, it must know what those threats are. It is important that marketing organizations have a strategy to uncover relevant strategic opportunities and threats early. As threats and opportunities appear, marketing organizations should develop strategies to deal with them.

Another problem is that at any one time, there may appear to be a great many opportunities and threats looming. Marketers must be able to prioritize these opportunities and threats according to such factors as their relevance to the organization, the cost effectiveness of strategies to deal with the threats and opportunities, and the urgency of the threat or opportunity. Organizations are inundated with information and must therefore have an effective mechanism for sorting out that information which is relevant to the organization.

Only after the marketing environment is thoroughly understood can an organization spot trends and determine whether they represent market opportunities or market threats.

EXTERNAL FACTORS THAT AFFECT PLANNING

There are many marketplace changes occurring that marketers cannot control but affect what marketers do. Faced with these environmental uncertainties, successful marketers will be those who recognize the changes that are occurring and who make effective adjustments.

There are a number of external factors that constitute the external environment. Our approach is not to attempt to present an all-encompassing view of the elements of the external environment. Rather, it is to briefly describe each of the components and show how external factors affect marketing strategy.

Competitors

As with other external forces, management must also prioritize the importance of the factors that affect competition. The relationships among these elements and competition must be understood if the organization is to be able to develop and sustain a competitive advantage.

Competitive analysis focuses on opportunities and threats that may occur because of actual or potential competitive changes in strategy. It starts with identifying current and potential competitors. Who are your competitors? Before answering that question you must put aside the traditional notion in the nonprofit community that "because you are all doing work that benefits society, competition doesn't exist." This perspective is both naive and harmful. In fact, all nonprofit organizations are your competitors in one way or another. Givers of money, time, and expertise have a limited amount of each to donate and they choose between your competitors and you. Although it may not be necessary to treat these competitors as enemies, you must be aware that they are out there.

Viewing competitors from the point-of-view of the customer also requires that your definition of competition is broad and complete. Exhibit 5.2 illustrates the breadth of competition. As indicated, the inner circle represents "direct" competitors who have similar titles and purposes. These are the nonprofit organizations that seek to cure physical diseases, such as cancer, muscular dystrophy, and heart disease.

Indirect competitors are all other nonprofit organizations, in that we assume that the concept of nonprofit per se appeals to certain kinds of customers. The *need-based* competitors describe the for-profit organizations that provide the customer a solution to a category of needs. For example, the YMCA and Boys Club satisfy the need for exercise and recreation. So do Bally's and a plethora of health clubs that seek profits. Ultimately, the nonprofit marketer must identify its competitors at all three levels.

In addition to identifying a competitor from the perspective of the customer, other criteria might be the geographic location of competitors, relative size, history, channels of distribution, and common tactics.

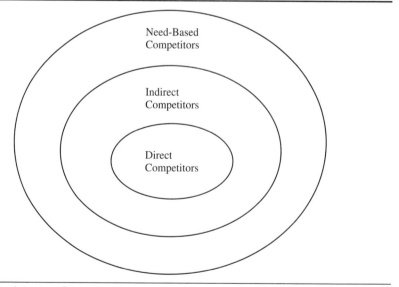

EXHIBIT 5.2 LEVELS OF COMPETITION

A second question to consider is the following: "What criteria do we need to use to make sure that our competitors are 'correctly' identified?" One way of answering this question is to track the customer's perceptions of product groupings and substitution. Do they change over time? Likewise, tracking expected competitors over time may prove insightful.

Once competitors are correctly identified, it is helpful to assess them relative to factors that drive competition: entry, bargaining power of buyers and suppliers, existing rivalries, and substitution possibilities. These factors relate to a firm's marketing mix decisions and may be used to create a barrier to entry, increase brand awareness, or intensify a fight for market share.

Barriers to entry represent business practices or conditions that make it difficult for new or existing firms to enter the market. Typically, barriers to entry can be in the form of capital requirements, advertising expenditures, product advantages, distribution access, or switching costs. Japan has been accused of having unofficial cultural-based barriers to the Japanese market.

In industries such as steel, automobiles, and computers, *the power of buyers and suppliers* can be very high. Powerful buyers exist when they are few in number, there are low switching costs, or the product represents a significant share of the buyer's total costs. This is common for large nonprofit organizations such as the National Red Cross and the Bill and Melinda Gates Foundation.

Existing competitors and possible substitutes also influence the dynamics of the competition. For example, in slow-growth markets, competition is more severe for any possible gains in market share. High fixed costs also create competitive pressures for firms to fill production capacity. For example, hospitals are increasing their advertising in a battle to fill beds, which represents a high fixed cost.

Legal/Ethical Factors

Every marketing organization's activities are influenced by ethical and legal factors that establish the rules of the game. These laws, agencies, policies, and behavioral norms are established to ensure that marketers compete legally and ethically in their efforts to provide want and need satisfying products and services. The various legal issues with which marketers must be knowledgeable include the following:

- *Monetary and fiscal policy*. Marketing decisions are affected by factors such as tax legislation, the money supply, and the level of government spending. The tendency of a Republican Congress to spend on defense and not on the environment is an example.

- *Federal legislation*. Federal legislation exists to ensure such things as fair competition, fair pricing practices, and honesty in marketing communications. Anti-tobacco legislation affects the tobacco and related industries.
- *Government/industry relationships*. Agriculture, railroads, shipbuilding, and other industries are subsidized by government. Tariffs and import quotas imposed by government affect certain industries (e.g., automobile). Other industries are regulated (or no longer regulated) by government (e.g., rail, trucking, and airlines). Deregulating the utilities industry had a tremendous negative effect on the California power industry in 2001.
- *Social legislation*. Marketers' activities are affected by broad social legislation such as the civil rights laws, programs to reduce unemployment, and legislation that affects the environment (e.g., water and air pollution), and most recently, the Patriot Act. The meat processing industry has spent billions of dollars trying to comply with water pollution legislation.
- *State laws*. State legislation affects marketers in different ways. For example, utilities in Oregon can spend only ½ percent of their net income on advertising. California has enacted legislation to reduce the energy consumption of refrigerators and air conditioners. In New Jersey, nine dairies have paid the state over $2 million dollars to settle a price-fixing lawsuit.
- *Regulatory agencies*. State regulatory agencies (e.g., the Attorney General's Office) actively pursue marketing violations of the law. But federal agencies including the Federal Trade Commission and the Consumer Product Safety Commission concern themselves with all facets of business.

Literally every facet of business is affected by one or more laws. It would be impossible to adequately cover them all in the space allotted. However, we will briefly discuss the three areas receiving the most notice in nonprofit marketing.

Product Liability

The courts are increasingly holding sellers responsible for the safety of their products. The courts generally hold that the producer of a product is liable for any product defect that causes injury in the course of normal use. Liability can even result if a court or a jury decides that a product's design, construction, or operating instructions and safety warnings make the product unreasonably dangerous to use.

Regulation

Deregulation means the relaxation or removal of government controls over industries that were thought to be either "natural monopolies," such as telephones, or essential public services like airlines and trucking. When regulated, industries got protection against renegade competition.

Industries such as the airlines, banking, railroads, communications, and trucking have long been subject to government regulation. A marketplace shockwave hit these industries as they were deregulated. Each of these industries saw the birth of many new competitors attempting to take advantage of market opportunities uncovered by deregulation. For example, US Airways, Midway, People Express, AirCal, Golden West, Muse Air, and Texas Air all started after the airline industry was deregulated. Not all of them survived. The result was that competition intensified, prices were lowered (sometimes below cost), and many once-stable organizations suffered huge financial losses.

As deregulation unfolded, new competition was permitted and rate regulation was loosened or abandoned—the vicious cycle began to reverse itself. For example, before deregulation AT&T had been slow to adopt fiber-optic cable. In 1985, there were only 136,000 miles of it in AT&T's system. Sprint and MCI had more. AT&T responded. By 1994, it had 1.3 million miles of fiber-optic cable (slightly more than MCI and Sprint). Airlines, freed of the Civil Aeronautics Board's (CAB) routine restrictions, organized "hub and spoke" systems—routing passengers via major transfer points—that provided more connections. In 1978, about 14 percent of all passengers had to change airlines to reach their destinations; by 1995, this number fell to about 1 percent.

Consumer Protection

Since the beginning of the twentieth century, there has been a concerted effort to protect the consumer. For example, the Food, Drug, and Cosmetic Act (1938) was aimed principally at preventing the adulteration or misbranding of the three categories of products. The various federal consumer protection laws include more than 30 amendments and separate laws relating to food, drugs, and cosmetics, such as the Infant Formula Act (1980) and the Nutritional Labeling and Education Act (1990). Perhaps the most significant period in consumer protection was the 1960s, with the emergence of *consumerism*. This was a grassroots movement intended to increase the influence, power, and rights of consumers in dealing with the institutions. The Consumer Product Safety Act (1972) established the Consumer Product Safety Commission.

Ethics is generally referred to as the set of moral principles or values that guide behavior. There is a general recognition that many, if not most, business decisions involve some ethical judgment. Consider the following dilemma. An athletic shoe company is considering whether to manufacture shoes in a country with a very poor record on human rights. The new facility will improve the company's competitive position, but the host government will also make a considerable profit, a profit that will be enjoyed by the ruling elite, not by the people of the country who will be employed at meager wages. Will the firm support a corrupt government in order to make higher profits?

Firms hope that a consideration of ethical issues during the decision-making process will be helpful in preventing or at least decreasing the frequency of unethical behavior. Having a corporate ethics policy also seems to facilitate the process of recovery after an ethical scandal—although firms may wish otherwise, unethical acts do occur and do not often go unnoticed. The lack of respect many people feel towards business today, the press's propensity for investigative reporting, and the willingness of many insiders to blow the whistle on unethical corporate behavior increase the likelihood that such behaviors will eventually be discovered (see Exhibit 5.3).

Ethical problems faced by marketing professionals stem from conflicts and disagreements. They tend to be relationship problems. Each party in a marketing transaction brings a set of expectations regarding how the business relationship will exist and how transactions should be conducted. For example, when you as a consumer wish to purchase something from a retailer, you bring the following expectations about the transaction: 1. you want to be treated fairly by the salesperson, 2. you want to pay a reasonable price, 3. you want the product to be available as advertising says it will and in the indicated condition, and 4. you want it to perform as promised. Unfortunately, your expectation might not be in agreement with those of the retailer. The retail salesperson may not have time for you, or the retailer's notion of a reasonable price may be higher than yours, or the advertising for the product may be misleading.

While ethics deal with the relationship between buyer and seller, there are also instances when the activities of marketing influence society as a whole. For example, when you purchase a new refrigerator, there is a need to discard your old refrigerator. Thrown in a trash dump, the old refrigerator may

Marketing professionals were asked to describe the most difficult ethical issue they face.

Issue	Percentage of Marketing Professionals Responding
Bribery: Gifts from outside vendors, payment of questionable commissions, "money under the table"	15%
Fairness: Unfairly placing company interests over family obligations, taking credit for the work of others, inducing customers to use services not needed, manipulation of others	14%
Honesty: Lying to customers to obtain orders, misrepresenting services and capabilities	12%
Price: Differential pricing, charging higher prices than firms with similar products while claiming superiority, meeting competitive prices	12%
Product: Product safety, product and brand infringement, exaggerated performance claims, products that do not benefit consumers	11%
Personnel: Firing, hiring, employee evaluation	10%
Confidentiality: Temptations to use or obtain classified, secret, or competitive information	5%
Advertising: Crossing the line between exaggeration and misrepresentation, misleading customers	4%
Manipulation of Data: Falsifying figures or misusing statistics or information, distortion	4%
Purchasing: Reciprocity in the selection of suppliers	3%

Source: Lawrence B. Chonko and Shelby D. Hunt, "Ethics and Marketing Management: An Empirical Examination," *Journal of Business Research*, Vol. 13, 1985, pp. 339-359.

EXHIBIT 5.3 ETHICAL ISSUES IN MARKETING

pose a safety risk, or contaminate the soil, and certainly will contaminate the aesthetics of the countryside, thus requiring society to bear part of the cost of your purchase. This example illustrates the issue of *social responsibility*, the idea that organizations are part of a larger society and are accountable to society for their actions. The well-being of society at large should also be recognized in an organization's marketing decisions. In fact, some marketing experts stress the *societal marketing concept*, the view that an organization should discover and satisfy the needs of its consumers in a way that also provides for society's well-being. A definition for social marketing is provided by Alan Andreasen:

> Social marketing is the adaptation of commercial marketing technologies to programs designed to influence the voluntary behavior of target audiences to improve their personal welfare and that of the society of which they are a part.

There is little doubt that the importance of social marketing is growing, and that for many marketers, it will become part of their competitive advantage.

Economic/Political Issues

Various economic forces influence an organization's ability to compete and consumer's willingness and ability to buy products and services. The state of the economy is always changing. Interest rates rise and fall. Inflation increases and decreases. Consumers' ability and willingness to buy changes. The economy goes through fluctuations. Two aspects of the economy are consumers' buying power and the business cycle.

Consumer Buying Power

A consumer's buying power represents his or her ability to make purchases. The economy affects buying power. For example, if prices decline, consumers have greater buying power. If the value of the dollar increases relative to foreign currency, consumers have greater buying power. When inflation occurs, consumers have less buying power. A list of several aspects of consumer buying power is presented next. Each can be measured relative to a marketer's external environment.

- *Buying power*: A consumer's ability to make purchases
- *Income*: The amount of money an individual receives from wages, rents, investments, pensions, and/or subsidies
- *Disposable income*: The income available for spending after taxes have been paid

- *Discretionary income*: Disposable income available for spending or saving after basic necessities (e.g., food, housing, clothing) have been purchased
- *Credit*: An individual's ability to buy something now and pay for it later
- *Wealth*: The accumulation of past income and other assets including savings accounts, jewelry, investments, real estate, and the like
- *Willingness to spend*: An individual's choice of how much disposable income to spend and what to spend it on
- *Consumer spending patterns*: Amount of money spent on certain kinds of products and services each year
- *Comprehensive spending patterns*: The amount of income individuals allocate to expenditures for classes of products and services
- *Product spending patterns*: The amount of income spent for specific products in a product class

The Business Cycle

Fluctuations in our economy follow a general pattern known as the *business cycle*. The fluctuations in economic conditions affect supply and demand, consumer buying power, consumer willingness to spend, and the intensity of competitive behavior. The four stages in the business cycle are prosperity, recession, depression, and recovery.

- *Prosperity* represents a period of time during which the economy is growing. Unemployment is low, consumers' buying power is high, and the demand for products is strong. During prosperity, consumer disposable incomes are high and they try to improve their quality of life by purchasing products and services that are high in quality and price. The U.S. economy was in a period of prosperity from 1991 to 2000. For marketers, opportunities were plentiful during prosperity, and they attempted to expand product lines to take advantage of consumers' increased willingness to buy.
- *Recession* is characterized by a decrease in the rate of growth of the economy. Unemployment rises and consumer buying power declines. Recession tends to occur after periods of prosperity and inflation. During a recession, consumers' spending power is low, as they are busy paying off debts incurred through credit purchases during more prosperous times. During recessions, marketing opportunities are reduced. Because of reduced buying power, consumers become more cautious, seeking products that are more basic and functional.

- *Depression* represents the most serious economic downturn. Unemployment increases, buying power decreases, and all other economic indicators move downward. Consequently, consumers are unable or reluctant to purchase products, particularly big-ticket items. Also, consumers tend to delay replacement purchases. Although many marketers fail during this period, insightful marketers can gain market share.
- *Recovery* is a complicated economic pattern, in that some economic indicators increase while others may stay low or even decrease. Much of what happens during a recovery may be a result of intangibles, such as consumer confidence or the perception of businesses that things will get better. Tentative marketers take serious risks. Premature marketers may face dire consequences.

For marketers, an important task is to attempt to determine how quickly the economy will move into a situation of prosperity. Improper forecasting can lead some firms to overextend themselves, as consumers may be slow to change purchase habits they have been accustomed to in the more difficult economic times.

The economy is cyclical in nature. We know that the cycles will occur. We just cannot predict exactly when, or how severe the cycles will be. Assumptions must be made about money, people, and resources. For example, many organizations become less aggressive when they believe the economy is not going to grow. If they are right, they may do well. But if they are wrong, those organizations that are more aggressive can perform very well—often at the expense of the conservative organizations. Assumptions must also be made about such economic factors as interest rates, inflation, the nature and size of the workforce, and the availability of resources such as energy and raw materials.

Experts posit that the U.S. economy is looking up in 2007. However, there are also serious concerns. The following summary points reflect both positives and negatives:

- Economic signals such as consumer confidence, housing, and employment statistics have weakened significantly following the worst hurricane season on record, during which Katrina and Rita helped drive up already steep energy and commodity prices. All these factors could imply that corporate profits could come under severe pressure.
- Higher energy costs are taking their toll on U.S. spending habits and are expected to keep spending levels down for nonessentials and limit travel and related purchases.

- Soaring energy costs are fueling higher operating costs throughout the manufacturing supply chain—including raw materials, factory overhead, and transportation—further affecting profit margins of consumer-product companies.
- Following a nearly perfect economy during the 1990s in which the economic volatility transferred to the capital markets, the U.S. economy hits a capital goods recession due to over-production and cutbacks in employee hours and wages.
- The self-correction of the capital markets over the past three or four years suggests that the economy is poised for an upward bounce, especially in the computer semiconductor and healthcare sectors.
- Saving more would help the trade deficit, but cut economic growth—the U.S. is imbalanced compared to the world when considering savings.
- There have been increasing military and humanitarian expenditures related to the war on terrorism.
- The shift of white-collar work to offshore locations has threatened jobs in the United States.
- There has been an increase in savings and money management as many workers approach retirement.

The Job Market

The U.S. job market remains soft, spending and wages are down. Hiring came to a near standstill in 2004, with recent increases below projections. More than a million jobs have been added back to the 2.6 million lost since President Bush took office, but they pay less and offer fewer benefits, such as health insurance. The new jobs are concentrated in health care, food services, and temporary employment firms, all lower paying jobs. Temp agencies alone account for about a fifth of all new jobs. In fact, three in five new jobs pay below the national median hourly wage, which is $13.53. On a weekly basis, the average wage of $525.84 is at the lowest level since October 2001.

Economists say wages should rise as companies boost hiring but the growing gap between the haves and have-nots will remain. Technology has eliminated many U.S. jobs, as has global competition and outsourcing, particularly from low-wage countries such as China and India.

Technology

Technology is the knowledge of how to accomplish tasks and goals. Technology affects marketers in several ways. First, aggressively advancing technology is spawning new products and processes at an accelerating rate that threatens almost every existing product. Second, competition continues to intensify from broad and new organizations, and many substitute technologies compete with established products. Third, product innovations that result in superior performance or cost advantages are the best means of protecting or building market position without sacrificing profit margins. This is especially true in today's world, when many markets are experiencing flat or slow growth and excess capacity is commonplace.

History provides many examples of companies that have lost their competitive advantage—and perhaps even their entire business—because a competitor came into the market with a product that had superior cost advantage or performance characteristics. These examples are not limited to small or weak companies; even industrial giants like IBM, General Electric, and AT&T have seen certain parts of their markets eroded by competition that surprised them with a distinctly superior product. IBM, despite its dominant position in the computer market, lost position in the late 1970s to several smaller companies that were first to develop powerful minicomputers to replace the larger mainframe computers that were the cornerstone of IBM's business.

All organizations must make assumptions about the future in technology and its impact on their business activities. The results of technology cannot be ignored. For example, the Japanese promote the use of electronic circuits and have used them almost exclusively in their controls. However, U.S.-based organizations have been slower to change and many have continued to use electromechanical controls in their products.

Everyone enjoys thinking about the future and the kinds of technology that will evolve. Let's fast-forward a few years to see what opportunities technology will open up for marketers: the speed of technological development during the last decade has been phenomenal. The following points represent the more important technological trends.

- Advances in cell phones, laptop, and email technology have made it feasible for people to carry their jobs around with them, with many people feeling they have no choice but to do so. Most knowledge workers are never quite off the job, even on vacation, adding to already high stress levels. Technology also makes identity theft easier; as such, people are increasingly concerned about providing personal data that might enable this form of theft.
- People are also turning to technology-based social networks, such as blog networks, and network software such as Orkut and Friendser.

- Ajax and other software tools make browser-based applications behave more like software running on a PC. This allows new data to trickle in, so for example, rather than creating a new Web page, updating the content of the page can take place on the fly.
- Deep Web search provides access to hidden corporate firewalls or in databases waiting to be indexed.
- Biogenerics allows a pharmaceutical company to clone a protein, with its complex molecular structure. This ability has the potential to capture 11 percent of the total biodrug market.
- Hybrid cell phones are Wi-Fi-enabled cell phones that bring together cellular and landline phone systems.
- Micro fuel cells are batteries for portable electronic devices that use a refillable external fuel supply, from hydrogen to natural gas, methane, ethanol, and sodium borohydride.
- Wi-Max is like Wi-Fi on steroids, with a theoretical range of 30 miles.
- The next revolution in information technology is a combination of commoditized technologies, wired employees, cheap storage and processing powers—all married to ubiquitous radio frequency identification (RFID) sensors; all will allow companies to monitor where their products are made, distributed, and sold—all in real time.
- Electrical therapy is approaching an historic transition. Using advances in pacemaker technology, researchers and doctors are finding that rapid-fire bursts of low-voltage electricity can alleviate symptoms in an astonishing number of illnesses in many other parts of the human body, (e.g., depression, post-stroke paralysis, migraines, angina, obesity, Alzheimer's disease, Tourette's syndrome), and other brain ailments.
- Post-9/11 snooping technologies are evolving faster than laws to control them. Surveillance devices aimed at humans are proliferating at an unprecedented rate, from basics that can monitor members of a crowd for abnormal vital signs, to biometric scanners that pick out individual travelers at a distance and link them to vast commercial and government databases containing their detailed personal information.
- A powerful scanning technology known as functional magnetic resonance imaging (fMRI) is making its way out of the labs and into marketers' toolkits for studying consumers' emotions and motivations. The fMRI detects the ebb and flow of blood to the brain's centers of pleasure, thought, or memory.
- Advances in biotechnology, cosmetic surgery, and cancer drugs are being made every day.

All these miracles are possible in the amazing world of tomorrow. These are not technologies in a lab, but working prototypes, many just about to hit the market. The potential for marketers in just five years makes today's Web offerings look like a warm-up act. While these services will rely on the Internet to communicate between newfangled gadgets and more intelligent servers, most of the services won't be based on HTML, for practical reasons. For example, you can't effectively run a Web browser on a cell phone screen, and you don't want one inside your shirt.

The pitfalls for marketers are also obvious. While today's Web is open, each of these new technologies has a potential gatekeeper—cell phone operators, cable companies, appliance makers.

Social Trends

The social environment includes all factors and trends related to groups of people, including their number, characteristics, behavior, and growth projections. Since consumer markets have specific needs and problems, changes in the social environment can affect markets differently. Trends in the social environment might increase the size of some markets, decrease the size of others, or even help to create new markets. We discuss here two important components of the social environment: the demographic environment and the cultural environment.

Demographics

The term demographics is shorthand for "population characteristics." Demographics include age, income, gender, race, mobility (in terms of travel time to work or number of vehicles available), educational attainment, home ownership, employment status, and even location. The term demographics is often used erroneously for demography, the study of human population and its structure and change. Whereas demography is a descriptive and predictive science, demographics are an applied art and science. In both cases, however, the objects of study are the characteristics of human populations. Demographics is interested in any population characteristic that might be useful in understanding what people think, what they are willing to buy, and how many fit this profile.

Demographic Trends

Many demographic trends are quite easy to determine. This is due to the predictability of many demographic relationships. If, for example, the birth rate increases during certain years (as indeed happened during the Baby Boom years), we can determine that there will be an increase in the demand for baby furniture, diapers, and education. After two decades there will be an increased demand for university services, compact automobiles, rental apartments, wedding photographs, and vacations. Thus, the old saying, "demographics explain about two-thirds of everything."

Next, we examine nine demographic changes:

1. **Households are growing more slowly and getting older.** About half of all households are age 50 and older and growing at an annual rate of 1 percent compared with nearly 2 percent in the 1980s.

2. **The traditional family continues to go the way of the dinosaur.** Married couples are a slight majority of U.S. households. Only one-third of households have children under 18, and nearly one-fourth of households are people who live alone.

3. **The increase in education continues.** Most adults in the United States still have not completed college (approximately 67 percent), but that number continues to decline.

4. **Nonphysical jobs keep growing.** Jobs that don't require physical strength keep growing in number. Virtually all job growth during the next ten years will take place in service providers, especially in health-care and social services.

5. **The population is growing faster than expected.** Over 300 million people live in the United States. This is an increase of 29 million since 1990, and most of the growth has resulted from an unforeseen boom in birth and immigration.

6. **The growth of minority citizens continues.** Although white non-Hispanics have been the biggest contributors to the U.S. population growth in the 1990s, Hispanics have been a close second. The number of Hispanics in the United States increased from 22 million in 1990 to 41 million in 2004. Twenty-five years ago, Hispanics were only about 5 percent of the U.S. population. They're now 14 percent—twice the growth rate of African-Americans and Asians. By 2050 minorities will comprise 49 percent of the U.S. population.

7. **Baby Boomers have become middle-aged.** The oldest Baby Boomers are now aged 59. The largest ten-year age group, people aged 45 to 55, has been growing as it absorbs the younger half of the Baby Boom generation.

8. **People are moving south.** More than half of U.S. population growth (54 percent) between 1990 and 1999 occurred in ten southern states.

However, the fastest growth since 1995 has been in the eight southern states led by Texas, Florida, and North Carolina.

9. The middle-class gets hammered. According to the U.S. Census Bureau, the share of aggregate household income earned by the middle 60 percent of the households has shrunk from 52 percent in 1973 to 45 percent 30 years later.

Age

Dr. Kenneth Dychtwald (1989) describes the "Aging of America" and convincingly argues that the changing age distribution of the American population is "the most important trend in our time." He considers the consequences of demographic facts like: the over-50 age group owns 77 percent of all financial assets in America, accounts for more than 50 percent of all new car sales, spends more on travel and recreation than any other age group, and so forth. He asks what will happen to healthcare systems and social security entitlements (pension benefits) when the graying of America places additional demands upon the system.

Another way to look at age is as generational cohorts. A "generational cohort" has been defined as "the aggregation of individuals who experience the same events within the same time interval." The most definitive recent work on this concept was done by Schuman and Scott (1989) in 1985 in which a broad sample of adults of all ages were asked, "What world events over the past 50 years were especially important to you?" They found that 33 events were mentioned with great frequency. When the ages of the correspondents were correlated with the expressed importance rankings, seven distinct cohorts became evident.

Today we use the following descriptors for these cohorts:

- Depression cohort (born from 1912 to 1921)—strive for financial security, risk aversive, waste not want not attitude, strive for comfort.
- WWII cohort (born from 1922 to 1927)—value the novelty of sacrifices for the common good, patriotism, and being a team player.
- Post-war cohort (born from 1928 to 1945)—look for conformity, conservation, and traditional family values.
- Baby Boomer cohort #1 (born from 1946 to 1954)— seek to be experimental, individualistic, free spirited, and social cause oriented.
- Baby Boomer cohort #2 (born from 1955 to 1964)—are less optimistic, distrust the government, and exhibit cynicism.

- Generation X cohort (born from 1965 to 1976)—have a quest for emotional security, are independent, informal, and entrepreneurial.
- N Generation cohort also called Generation Y (born from 1983 to 2005)—quest for physical security and safety, patriotism, heightened fears, acceptance.

Population

To create projections about populations, demographers analyze birth rates, death rates, and immigration, and project forward three different numbers—one that indicates the highest possible number, one that indicates the lowest possible number, and one that is in between, a number known as "the middle series."

By 2025, the U.S. population is expected to exceed 350 million people—an increase of about 70 million and a boost of 25 percent. This puts the nation on a growth trajectory that's similar to the one experienced just after World War II. Expect record-breaking growth to continue, as Americans live longer, birth rates hold steady, and immigration continues at its current pace.

As the population increases, niche markets may become unwieldy for businesses to target with a single market strategy. For example, many companies have one marketing strategy to reach Hispanic consumers. But by 2025, the Hispanic market will double to 70 million consumers. As a result, the niche market of today will become a mass market in its own right, segmented not only by nationality (i.e., Mexican, Guatemalan) but also by spending behavior and other psychographic characteristics. Marketers will have to understand a vast array of rituals, customs, and languages to build trust and patronage.

The American Household

As the population age profile has changed, so has the structure of the American household. In 1960, 75 percent of all households consisted of married couples. Today, that type of household is just 50 percent of the population. Just 25 percent of households are married couples with children, and only 10 percent are households with working fathers and stay-at-home moms. Some of the fastest growing types of households are those with a single person, those with a single parent, and those with unmarried partners. The majority of divorced people (21.6 million) eventually remarry, which has given rise to the *blended family*.

Gender

One of the most underappreciated forces affecting life in the United States is the gender ratio. Generally defined as the number of males per 100 females, it has a profound bearing on several issues, not least of which is the status of women. Women's advantageous gender ratio (104:100), together with greater protections than ever before and their growing superiority in educational attainment, could lead, arguably, to the unprecedented situation in which they become the dominant sex.

This dominance is clearly played out in their purchasing power. In the United States, women handle 75 percent of the family finances and control $14 trillion in consumer spending each year. Their income has increased 63 percent over the last three decades when adjusted for inflation, while men's has grown just 0.6 percent. Today, women make or influence 80 percent of consumer purchases, buying 51 percent of electronics, 75 percent of over-the-counter drugs, and 65 percent of new cars.

Another relevant trend is the prevalence of women in the workforce, especially older women. According to the projections from the Bureau of Labor Statistics, the number of women aged 55 and older in the workforce will increase by a whopping 52 percent between 2000 and 2010, to 10.1 million from 6.4 million. Today, more than half of women ages 55 to 64 (51 percent), and more than three-quarters of women ages 45 to 54 (77 percent), work full or part time. Only a small percentage of women aged 65 to 74 (16 percent) continue to work.

But between 2010 and 2020, the full force of the Baby Boom will hit the 65 to 74 age cohort, resulting in at least a 50 percent jump in the number of women in that group.

Ethnicity

Twenty-five years ago, Hispanics were only about 5 percent of the U.S. population—they're now 13 percent—and were not considered a large enough group to warrant any special considerations. Census 2000 counted 35.5 million Hispanics versus 34.7 million African Americans. The Black and Hispanic markets are now roughly the same size. However, the Hispanic population's rapid growth indicates that it's soon likely to become the nation's largest minority group.

The new generation wants to become American but they don't want to deny their Hispanic roots. The implication is that America is much more of a salad bowl than a melting pot. In the nineteenth and early twentieth centuries, it was very common for children to be chastised for speaking a language other than English at school. Now the opposite is often the case, where people are often encouraged to retain their native language.

The other trend that is in question is whether the pressures of politics or economics will result in an increase or decrease in the rate of immigration from Asian countries. Various Asian economies are developing very rapidly, so it appears unlikely that there's going to be a huge increase in immigration from a country like China.

Income and Spending

In 2003, the Census Bureau reported that the number of Americans in poverty and without health insurance each rose by more than 1 million. The median household income was virtually unchanged ($43,318), but women lost ground against men for the first time since 1999.

The Census report also showed:

- Income fell among Hispanics and whites and the gender gap widened. The median full-time female worker made 75.5 cents for every dollar earned by a man.
- Poverty increased among whites and Asians, and at the fastest pace in a decade among children. It did not change significantly for Hispanics and Blacks. The poverty level for a family of four is considered to be an annual income of $18,660 or less.

There are also patterns across the three consumer income categories. *Gross income* is the total amount of money made in one year by a person, household, or family unit. The typical U.S. household earned about $43,318 in 2003. When gross income is adjusted for inflation, however, the income of that typical U.S. household was relatively stable from 1970 to 2002. The second income component, *disposable income*, is the money the consumer has left after paying taxes to use for food, shelter, clothing, and transportation. In recent years, consumers' allocation of income has shifted to new categories of "necessities" such as vitamins and supplements, antibacterial body washes, lotions and deodorants, and the like. The third component of income is *discretionary income*, the money that remains after paying for taxes and necessities. Discretionary income is used for luxury items such as entertainment, electronics, and recreation.

Perhaps most relevant is the fact that Hispanic households brought in about $9000 less in income than the average U.S. household in 2001, and the largest share of Hispanic households, 36.4 percent, earned less than $25,000.

Cultures and Subcultures

All of us are part of a cultural fabric that affects our behavior, including our behavior as consumers. *Culture* is the sum of learned beliefs, values, and customs that regulate the behavior of members of a particular society. Through our culture, we are taught how to adjust to the environmental, biological, psychological, and historical parts of our environment.

Beliefs and values are guides of behavior, and customs are acceptable ways of behaving. A *belief* is an opinion that reflects a person's particular knowledge and assessment of ("I believe that ....").

Values are general statements that guide behavior and influence beliefs and attitudes ("Honesty is the best policy."). A value system helps people choose between alternatives in everyday life.

Customs are overt modes of behavior that constitute culturally approved ways of behaving in specific situations. Customs vary among countries, regions, and even families. In Arab societies, for instance, usury (payment of interest) is prohibited, so special Islamic banks exist that provide three types of accounts: nonprofit accounts, profit sharing deposit accounts, and social services funds. A U.S. custom is to eat turkey on Thanksgiving Day. However, the exact Thanksgiving Day menu may depend on family customs.

Dominant cultural values are referred to as *core values*; they tend to affect and reflect the core character of a particular society. For example, if a culture does not value efficiency but does value a sense of belonging and neighborliness, few people in the culture will want to use automatic teller machines. What do Americans value? Clearly, a catchall phrase such as the "Protestant work ethic" no longer captures the whole value system.

Core values are slow and difficult to change. Consequently, marketing communication strategies must accurately portray and reflect these values.

Secondary values also exist in any culture. Secondary values are less permanent values that can sometimes by influenced by marketing communications. In addition, secondary values are often shared by some people but not others. These values serve as a basis for subcultures.

A natural evolution that occurs in any culture is the emergence of subcultures. Core values are held by virtually an entire culture, whereas secondary values are not.

A *subculture* is a group of people who share a set of secondary values. Examples include Generation X and environmentally concerned people. Many factors can place an individual in one or several subcultures. Five of the most important factors that create subcultures are:

- *Material culture*. People with similar income may create a subculture. The poor, the affluent, and the white-collar middle class are examples of material subcultures.

- *Social institutions*. Those who participate in a social institution may form a subculture. Examples include participation in marriage, parenthood, a retirement community, the army, and so on.
- *Belief systems*. People with shared beliefs may create a subculture, such as shared beliefs in religion or politics. For example, traditional Amish do not use several types of products, including electricity and automobiles. A whole set of factors has also been correlated with whether a person is a Democrat, Republican, Independent, Libertarian, or Socialist.
- *Aesthetics*. Artistic people often form a subculture of their own associated with their common interests, including art, music, dance, drama, and folklore.
- *Language*. People with similar dialects, accents, and vocabulary can form a subculture. Southerners and northerners are two traditional categories.

Understanding Other Cultures Around the World

Adjusting to cultural differences is perhaps the most difficult task facing marketing communicators who operate in other countries. Before entering a foreign market, a company must decide to what extent it is willing to customize its marketing efforts in order to accommodate each foreign market. Naturally, the more the company standardizes its effort, the less trouble it incurs and the greater the assumed profitability. But is some customization inevitable? More is said about this in Chapters 8–11.

6

TRANSITIONING TO SERVICES MARKETING

ENTREPRENEURS WANTED: Help to grow an enterprise from scratch in an industry that offers no barriers to entry, historically low margins, massive labor scarcity, no proprietary technology, few economies of scale, weak brand distinctions, and heavy regulatory oversight. Serious inquiries only.

—Roger Brown

A mass reverse exodus occurred in New Orleans during January 2006. Nearly five months after Katrina and Rita swept away many campuses, thousands of students, faculty, and administrators returned with the beginning of a new semester. Still, many important questions lingered. Could the now smaller, poorer colleges recover from multimillion-dollar damages? Could they recruit students and retain professors? Could they adapt to the new realities of New Orleans without sacrificing their missions? How can marketing facilitate this recovery? Indeed, there has been a drastic reduction of both products (programs/curriculum) and support staff. Southern University shut down 19 programs. Tulane University laid off more than 200 professors. And Dillard University and Xavier University of Louisiana cut their faculty and staff by more than a third. Dillard, a historically black institution, had particularly severe challenges. Nearly one-half of their original student body was temporarily housed in a high-rise Hilton, where they attended classes in 14 partitioned rooms created from the grand ballroom—hardly soundproof. The students were required to wear photo ID badges at all times. To buy textbooks, they had to hop on a shuttle bus that took them to the bookstore across town. Other buses ferried them to Tulane University, where the administration had agreed to let Dillard students use libraries and science labs.

By the time this book is published we will know whether Dillard's efforts will prove successful. After all, the university's insurance covered only a small part of the damage. And, federal aid dollars were going toward more important causes. We do know that a big part of their successful recovery will depend upon the soundness of their marketing plan and ensuing strategies. At least part of this planning process must accommodate the fact that nonprofit marketers sell service products, rather than goods products. The competitive advantage of a service product, such as a college, was implicitly expressed by Dillard senior, Christy Malbrew: "I love Dillard because there is such a sense of family. And we've become so much more unified now." Creating a profound brand loyalty such as this is not the same as the efforts of, say, tire giant Goodyear. The need for nonprofits to make adjustments within the context of services marketing will become evident as you read this chapter.

INTRODUCTION

It is the underlying assumption of this book that from this point forward in the marketing planning process, accommodations must be made for the inherent differences between for-profit and nonprofit organizations. Although we alluded to several of the structural differences in Chapter 1, there are additional differences that are inherent to the product exchange process, and thereby directly impact the marketing process. Nonprofit marketers must be made aware of a necessary transition from operating as a for-profit marketer, such as Federated Department Stores, to a traditional nonprofit, such as the Sailing Club of Puget Sound. Fortunately, there is a body of literature that facilitates this transition. *Services marketing* is a widely acknowledged sub-sector of marketing and offers a valid and reliable foundation for the study of nonprofit marketing.

The discussion that follows will employ the theories and principles related to services marketing. Virtually all nonprofit organizations sell service products. Therefore, offering this translation makes sense both intuitively and strategically. It offers a perspective that will greatly enhance the success of nonprofit marketing. When necessary, we will reexamine concepts already discussed with a service marketing approach.

DEFINING SERVICES AND SERVICE PRODUCTS

Although there are a number of definitions for *services*, it is easiest to think of them as *ideas, deeds, processes, and performance*. The term has been fur-ther extended into the concept of *service products*, as compared to *goods*

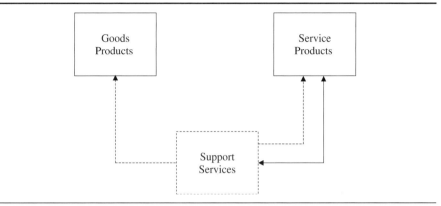

Exhibit 6.1   Service Products and Goods Products Are Different

products. Exhibit 6.1 illustrates the differences, as well as introducing the concept of *support services*. We can track these three concepts from a historical perspective. Initially, the exchange process included people making goods products (tangible things) and either bartering them or receiving payment from someone who needed that good. Often there was a direct transfer at a prescribed location. However, as our economy expanded, consumers purchased goods, such as furniture, tableware, and clothing, from more and more distant markets. This, in turn, required a mechanism for sorting, delivering, and collecting payments for this merchandise. Thus, warehouses, shipping lines, and accounting firms evolved as types of support services.

Support services provide support for a company's core products. They could include answering questions, taking orders, dealing with billing issues, handling complaints, and scheduling maintenance or repairs. To be specific, Dell offers repair and maintenance services for its equipment, consulting services for IT and commerce applications, training services, Web design and hosting, and other services. These services may include a final, tangible report; a Web site; or in the case of training, tangible instructional materials. But for the most part, the entire service is represented to the client through problem analysis activities, meetings with the clients, follow-up calls, and reporting—a series of deeds, processes, and performances.

Over time these support services became very successful and grew to become organizations needing their own cadre of support services. Thus, KLM Airlines has a long list of support services including food delivery, insurance, maintenance, and financial support. Similarly, a local brain injury organization needs support services such as Kinkos, Dial-a-Ride, and social service organizations.

With the growth of stand-alone service companies came the realization that the widely-accepted marketing strategies of the day did not work as well with service organizations. People who moved from packaged goods industries to marketing in health care, banking, and other service industries found their skills and experiences were not transferable. These people realized the need for new concepts and approaches for marketing and managing service businesses. Service marketers responded to these forces and began to work across disciplines and with academics and business practitioners from around the world to develop and document marketing practices for service industries. Beginning in the 1970s, services marketing emerged as a separate entity, worthy of study and application. Still, there are skeptics.

Suggesting that there are substantial differences between goods products and services products remains a source of great debate in marketing. Opponents of the division propose that "products are products," and just because there are some characteristics associated with service products and not goods products and vice-versa, does not mean that customized strategies are generally necessary for each. Advocates provide evidence that these differences are significant. It is the position in this book that in many relevant ways, service products are different than goods products, and that service products represent unique applications of marketing principles. Consequently nonprofit organizations that tend to offer service products should be enlightened about the necessary strategic adjustments. While all products share certain common traits, service products tend to differ from goods products in a number of ways. An important key to the success of any service organization is that the right strategies are chosen and that these strategies are implemented appropriately and well.

CHARACTERISTICS OF SERVICE PRODUCTS

Like goods products, service products are quite heterogeneous. Nevertheless, there are several characteristics that are specific to service products and distinguish them from goods products. Exhibit 6.2 identifies these various characteristics. Just as important, each of these characteristics are placed on a continuum, with "pure" goods products on the far left and "pure" service products on the far right. The notion of a continuum avoids the idea that products are a dichotomy. Rather, it suggests that many products have characteristics of both goods and services. In general, the further to the right your service product is characterized, the more likely your strategy is to move your product to the left.

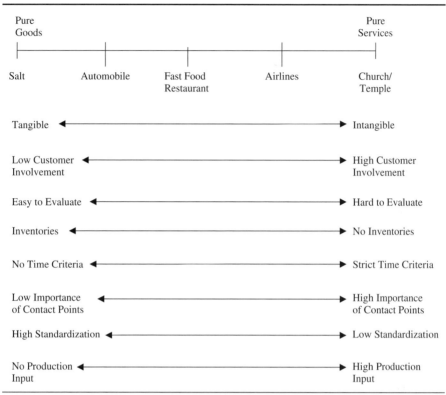

EXHIBIT 6.2   CHARACTERISTICS THAT DISTINGUISH GOODS FROM SERVICES

Intangible

With the purchase of a good you have something that can be seen, touched, tasted, worn, or displayed; this is not true with a service. Although you pay your money and consume the service, there is nothing tangible to assess or to show for it. For example, if you attend a professional football game, you spend $49.50 for a ticket and spend nearly three hours taking in the entertainment. Or if you donate $100 to the local Boys Club, you are left with a rather vague feeling of satisfaction. The challenge is how to tangibalize the intangible. The various blood banks have learned that giving 5-, 10-, and 20-gallon pins to donors does partially tangibalize the activity. Still, pure service products are intangible by their very nature, and the challenge facing nonprofit marketers is to make product characteristics as well as the benefits received from these products as real as possible. This may include physical elements or metaphors to demonstrate the competencies of the service firm and to illustrate the resulting benefits.

High Buyer Involvement/Inseparability

With many service products, the purchaser may provide a great deal of input into the final form of the product. For example, if you want to take a Caribbean cruise, a good travel agent will give you a large selection of brochures and pamphlets, describing the various cruise locations, and noting options provided in terms of cabin locations and size, islands visited, food, entertainment, prices, and whether the cruise line is set up for children. Although the task may be quite arduous, an individual can literally design every moment of the vacation. Similar alternatives may be available to potential volunteers at a nonprofit. In essence, volunteers are purchasing one of the products being offered by a nonprofit organization—feelings of contentment, use of spare time, and so forth. Defining the various tasks, scheduling alternatives, and offering possible rewards all allow the volunteer to design part of the service product received.

Hard to Evaluate

Because service products are mostly intangible, it is often impossible to evaluate the outcome. Was the sermon worth my time? Was a volunteer experience to Zambia worth the cost? The baselines we establish for such experiences are vague and may change from event to event or over time. Besides the attempt to provide tangible evidence mentioned earlier, it is helpful to educate the various stakeholders about the possible benefits they will receive. Blood donors not only get pins, they also get pamphlets explaining the technological advances in that sector of medicine, as well as concrete evidence as to how the various recipients will benefit.

No Inventories

We can store canned goods in our cabinets and use them at a later date. Service products have no such capabilities. (Exceptions include events that can be recorded.) If you miss a hair appointment or airline flight, you cannot store the product for a later date. If a nonprofit, such as National Public Radio (NPR), has an outdoor fundraising event and it rains, it is unlikely the event can be rescheduled. Consider how many colleges and other educational institutions located along the Gulf Coast lost sales because of Katrina. Many of these students moved to colleges in other states; temporarily or permanently. As noted earlier, for many a level of loyalty remained. In a less catastrophic example, Children's Hospital in Los Angeles lost several thousand dollars in donations because their Web site was down for 21 hours during the middle of a pledge drive. All these factors represent unique challenges for service marketers. Specifically, demand forecasting and creative planning for capacity utilization are challenging decision areas. The fact that services cannot typically be returned or reused also implies a need for strong recovery strategies when things go wrong.

Strict Time Criteria

Related to the inventory characteristics is the fact that many service organizations have specific and short windows of opportunity. Airlines have limited open dates, ski resorts have a season, churches are open on Sundays, surgeons operate on Tuesday and Thursday, and the Muscular Dystrophy Society (MDS) has a Labor Day telethon. If a service company cannot inform, educate, and persuade customers to take advantage of these windows, sales are lost. Nonprofit marketers must develop strategies to do all three. Or, they should research the use patterns of potential customers to learn when they are most amenable to taking prescribed action. For instance, service marketers should always consider how important the end of the tax year is for potential donors.

Importance of Contact Points

Any time the customer and service marketer interact it is considered a "contact." This can be a physical contact or a nonphysical contact. The former occurs when you meet face-to-face with a counselor, while the latter might be browsing Web sites looking for counselors. Because customers for service products do not have a physical entity to use as a reference point, each contact plays an important role in evaluation and decision making. Creating and managing these contact points is a challenge faced by nonprofit marketers.

Little Standardization

Because service products are so closely affected by available resources, ensuring service consistency from time to time is quite difficult. No two services will be exactly alike. Dentists have their bad days, not every baseball game is exciting, and the second vacation at Disney World may not be as wonderful as the first. Poor training, under-motivated staff and volunteers, and unclear guidelines that denote maximum or minimum performance are just a few factors that contribute to a lack of standardization. Ultimately, ensuring adequate service quality is the greatest challenge. Unfortunately, customers may not be able to articulate quality needs. Finally, parts of services may be delivered by third parties, further reducing standardization. From the customer's perspective, these subcontractors still represent the service organization. All must be managed.

Simultaneous Production and Consumption

Service products are characterized as being consumed at the same time they are being produced. The tourist attraction is producing entertainment or pleasure at the same time it is being consumed by the customer. In contrast, goods products are produced, stored, and then consumed. One result of this characteristic is that the provider of the service is often present when consumption takes place. Dentists, doctors, hair stylists, and ballet dancers are all present when the product is consumed. Likewise, a recipient of housing, food, and other provisions offered by a nonprofit, such as a homeless shelter, directly affects the creation of that package of benefits. This situation also means that frequently customers will interact with each other during the service production process and thus may affect each other's performance. Recall how the deplorable behavior of several survivors of Katrina impacted the quality of services offered at the New Orleans Superdome. In a similar fashion, survivors who could not clearly understand the various questions asked by volunteers often were denied benefits. Because services often are produced and consumed at the same time, mass production is difficult if not impossible. The quality of services and customer satisfaction will be highly dependent on what happens in real time, including actions of employees/volunteers and interactions between employees/volunteers and customers.

CLASSIFYING SERVICES

Placing concepts into appropriate classifications is helpful in order to better understand and manage that concept. In marketing, we start with the general classification of consumer and industrial goods. Most marketers will then move to classifications representing the core product delivered and/or the customer being served. Results include food, pharmaceuticals, steel, construction, telecommunications, patients, and Baby Boomers, to name but a few. Marketers are normally not interested in the manufacturing process. That is the responsibility of the operations people. However, the situation is different in service organizations, since the customer is often involved in the production of the service product. Consequently, a useful classification system for service products is to consider the nature of the process to which the

	Recipient	
Nature of Action	People	Objects
Tangible	People Processing – Target People's Bodies	Possession Processing – Target Physical Possessions
Intangible	Mental Processing – Target People's Minds	Information Processing - Target Intangible Assets

EXHIBIT 6.3 SERVICES CLASSIFIED BY PROCESSES

customer may be exposed. A *process* is a particular method of operation or a series of actions, typically involving multiple steps that often need to take place in a defined sequence. Processes can range from the very simple (e.g., mailing a letter), to the very complex (e.g., kidney replacement surgery and recovery). These processes can be illustrated via diagrams and flow charts.

When learning to understand a process, we begin with identifying the inputs and outputs. In the case of services two things get processed, people and objects. In understanding travel, the input tends to be people. In repairing a computer, the input tends to be an object. Exhibit 6.3 reflects a four-way classification of service products based primarily on an operational perspective. Each suggests fundamentally different processes that have vital implications for operations, human resources, and marketing.

People Processing

We all require certain inputs in order to maintain our physical being (food, medicine, shelter, beauty aids). To receive these benefits, the customer most often enters the service system. Thus, as an integral part of the process, we must be prepared to spend time and energy interacting and cooperating with the service producer—we must make an appointment and then go to the salon at the appointed time to get a haircut, for example. An individual experiencing blurred vision and living in the jungle of Brazil must commit to several stages of effort before being diagnosed, having surgery, and recovering.

Nonprofit marketers must analyze the process and possible outputs if they are to create an optimal sequence and ensure that the recipient will receive the benefits desired. Also, reflecting on the service process itself helps to identify some of the nonfinancial costs, such as time and mental and physical effort that customers incur in obtaining these benefits.

Possession Processing

For a variety of reasons, the United States has become a nation of pampered pets. In many sectors of society people spend more money on the health of their dog or cat than they do on their own health. As a result, veterinarians, pet spas, and even pet psychiatrists have grown in importance. Regardless of the level of attachment, pet care is a service performed on an owner's object, along with the repair of a computer, automobile, plumbing, and roof. In most cases, the customer's level of involvement with objects is much less than with people processing. Even Fluffy is delivered to the vet's office, picked up at a later time, and payment is made. Fed Ex and UPS have made their mark by making this process more convenient. In all instances, the service marketer must understand how the customer perceives the process, with an emphasis on the relative importance of the task and the willingness of the customer to assume responsibility for some of the process, and assess the expected output. Each customer has his or her own perception of importance and willingness to assume some responsibility. Imagine the response of an avid football fan who discovers that, two days before the Super Bowl, his high-definition TV is on the blink. In this instance, he is willing to pay double the usual rate to have it repaired on Saturday; and he must stay home from noon to 4 p.m. to wait for the repair person. Further imagine his reaction when, on Sunday morning, he learns that the set is still not working. Similar scenarios play out for nonprofits worldwide.

Mind Processing

Services that interact with people's minds include education, entertainment, consulting, psychotherapy, coaching, and news and information, to name but a few. These mind-shaping services can be profound and because there is potential for manipulation, strong ethical standards and constant monitoring are required. Unlike people processing, recipients do not need to be physically present. They simply have to be mentally in communication with the service product being provided. Long-distance learning provides an example where physical presence is necessary only a small percentage of the time, yet there are still requirements to prove that the recipient is participating at the expected level. All-day seminars offered by topic experts can be delivered live to an audience of 1,500 and via satellite to another 100,000. All pay the same $3,200 fee. Clearly, the audience attending electronically is not receiving the exact same benefits as the live group. Therefore, marketers of mind services must be extremely careful to analyze the needs and wants being met by the product, the ability of the recipient to receive this product satisfactorily, and the legal and ethical criteria to abide by.

Information Processing

Receiving information may be the most intangible service product. There are many service organizations responsible for collecting, processing, and distributing information. Examples include financial and professional services such as banks, investment consultants, accountants, law firms, marketing research organizations, management consultants, and medical testing labs. The face-to-face interaction between providers and recipients is often unnecessary in these exchanges, since technology can complete the transaction. However, based on tradition, trust, and the need for understanding, many customers prefer to engage in this process in person. The same rationale may be true for the provider who feels they learn more about their customer's needs, capabilities, and personality by meeting one-on-one. However, there is little evidence that building a personal relationship through this interaction is any more effective than one that can be created and maintained entirely via telephone, Web sites, or e-mail contact. As technology improves and people continue to become more comfortable with videophones or the Internet, we can expect to see a continuing shift to arm's-length transactions. Still, it is important to both honor and provide this old-fashioned delivery network if required. It is also critical that the needed information is provided in a comprehensible and timely manner.

BUILDING RELATIONSHIPS

Experts contend that finding new customers is eight times more expensive than keeping an existing customer. While building relationships with customers is the object of all marketing, it is particularly salient with service marketers. Primarily this is due to the prominent role played by people in the marketing exchange. People sell and deliver most service products to other people. And, because service products are intangible, these people become product surrogates and tangible representations. Some have argued that developing relationships has become the key focal point for marketing attention, replacing an earlier preoccupation with support services, and before that with product development.

It has been well-documented that the cost of establishing contact with a potential customer and making the first sale is quite high, often greater than the profit. It is only when a relationship is formed between the service provider and service customer that the exchange becomes profitable for both. Focusing on discrete, one-time, transactions is counter to one of the core principle of marketing—that marketing should revolve around systems where people or groups are interrelated.

Customers increasingly judge service providers on the basis of superior service relationships and reach a shared goal via relationships. The key problem is determining how to establish these relationships in a service exchange context.

In establishing and maintaining customer relationships for service exchanges, both the seller and customer offer a set of promises. Service providers promise to offer a service product that best meets the needs of the customer at a given price. They also promise to make sure the product is safe, the features are represented accurately, and the product will be available for a predictable period of time. In turn, the customer promises to honor his commitment as long as these benefits remain evident.

In some instances this relationship is between two parties, such as a patient and her physician or dentist. Here the relationship is based on a fundamental degree of trust. The customer assigns responsibility to a physician to monitor her health, provide solutions, and may even expect the doctor to warn her when maintenance is needed.

Today, the trend has gone away from one-on-one relationship building, so that health care trust has been transferred to groups and institutions such as clinics and HMOs. Consider the trust you assign to airlines, even though you have no relationship with the flight crew or ground maintenance. Airlines invent a relationship through frequent flyer programs, special prices, and a host of other privileges. However, there are usually restrictions in service relationships. Passengers cannot fly whenever they want, they must check baggage of certain sizes, they must be seated during certain periods of the flight, they cannot carry a weapon on board the plane, and so forth.

We are all aware of the fact that relationships have a kind of lifecycle, beginning with initial awareness and ending with dissolution. This natural progression should be followed if service marketers are to establish strong relationships with customers. The following strategies are offered to facilitate relationship building for nonprofit marketers:

- Create Awareness—In forming any relationship, the first step is to make sure the parties know each other exist. There is also a need to assess whether there is a mutual desire to enter into a relationship or transaction. The nonprofit marketer has a variety of cost-effective tools to create awareness. Direct mail, e-mail, and targeted advertising can all provide basic information. Simultaneously, the customer can provide feedback by sending back an information card, calling a 1-800 number, or purchasing the product, which also indicates a desire to form a relationship. Conversely, no response suggests that no relationship is desired. Because service products are intangible, it is important that this initial contact be made through elements having tangible characteristics, for example, a spokesperson or relevant imagery tend to be successful.

- Making Promises—Once contact is made, the next step in establishing a relationship is to establish the benefits shared. These early promises are based on the assumption that the marketer understands the expectations of the customer. This requires that the nonprofit marketer do the necessary research in order to identify these promises. It also means the marketer must have the capability to create and deliver these promises in a manner that is both consistent and profitable. In turn, the nonprofit marketer must identify the promises expected from the customer. While lifelong loyalty may be the ultimate goal, it is hardly ever realistic. A better baseline is to estimate how many purchases are necessary before the relationship becomes profitable. Finally, it is likely that different stakeholders are seeking different promises. Can the nonprofit profitably deliver on various promise packages?

- Maintenance—Many of us have maintained relationships for decades. Periodically, we renegotiate the promises so that an occasional e-mail or Christmas letter is all that is required. There is an understanding that the efficacy of the relationship could be reignited on a moment's notice. This scenario is not usually possible in a relationship between a service provider and a customer. Promises must be monitored and modified as deemed necessary. Often, additional rewards are offered. These incentives can be financial, such as money-off vouchers, continuity programs, or other credits. Companies can also add value to a relationship by offering nonfinancial incentives. For example, loyalty to the organization may be rewarded by specific privileges, such as first choice, better seating, or higher quality services.

- Dissolution—All relationships must end. For human friendships it may be one party dying or moving away, an argument, or simply boredom. The same is true with marketer-customer relationships. As we will discuss in chapter 12 on giving behavior, often people who donate to one charity switch to another because they are bored. Yet, it is likely that that relationship may be rekindled at a later time.

The service marketer would be wise to constantly monitor relationships in order to assess their mutual benefits. Anticipating where the relationship is headed allows the marketer to modify it if necessary or dissolve it if it is no longer beneficial to either party. There are three situations where the service marketer may wish to dissolve a relationship. First, the company may have targeted the wrong segment and can no longer meet the needs of specific customers: why would a legal services organization target clients who have problems that don't match their expertise? Second, organizations would not want to have long-term relationships with customers who are unprofitable. While it may be true that the company can provide for the needs of the customer, the segment may be too small or too costly to service. This is the burden many nonprofits face, yet some due diligence must be exercised. Finally, there are customers that are simply too much trouble. There are dysfunctional recipients, volunteers, donors, and board members in most every nonprofit. Research suggests that exposure to dysfunctional customer behavior can have psychological, emotional, behavioral, and physical effects on employees and other customers, and may even be detrimental to the success of the organization.

It is important not to burn any bridges. Anger at a former customer is just as deleterious as ignoring the requests of a current customer who is no longer wanted. Nonprofit marketers cannot afford to have enemies in the marketplace who may deliver negative word-of-mouth.

While relationships may endure as a result of one or both parties having no choice but to remain within the relationship, trust serves as a much better adhesive. Trust is a crucial element; it allows promises to be fulfilled and tensions to be worked out amicably. Today, consumers have more knowledge and confidence to venture outside a long-term relationship with a service provider. Keeping a customer means establishing trusting, mutually beneficial relationships. It is true that these alliances are more difficult to make, but they are critical for nonprofit marketers.

THE IMPORTANCE OF PEOPLE

Because people often become the service product and serve as the partner in customer relationships, they must be given special attention. Unlike goods products, the people engaged in producing service products are often not paid for their efforts. As a result, often they are not under strict control by management. From the customer's perspective, the encounter with service personnel is probably the most important element of the service product.

From the firm's perspective, the service levels and the way service is delivered by the front line can be an important source of differentiation as well as a competitive advantage. In addition, the strength of the customer/front line staff relationship is often an important driver of customer loyalty and can serve as the basis for optimal positioning.

Personnel Management

Given the essential role service personnel play in the success of the nonprofit firm, it is critical that they be effectively managed. Specifically, let us examine how a nonprofit should hire and motivate service personnel.

Hiring the Right People

There are specific guidelines that will facilitate the challenge of hiring the right people.

1. Become the preferred employer. Attracting the most talented people from a competitive job market is contingent on the value proposition offered by the nonprofit organization. This value proposition rests upon the image of the employer in the community, along with the reputation of the firm for delivering high-quality service products that make employees feel proud to be part of the team. Furthermore, despite the reputation of nonprofits for paying low salaries, the compensation package cannot be below average.

2. Identify the best candidates. There's no such thing as the perfect employee. For service organizations, there tends to be on-stage personnel (people who engage customers directly) and backstage personnel (people who do not work with customers). Regarding the former, it is often true that they possess qualities that cannot be taught. These qualities include neat appearance, effervescent personality, charm, empathy, and energy. Although innate, these characteristics can indeed be enhanced with on-the-job training or incentives. On-stage personnel often thrive on pleasant interaction and positive reinforcement from recipients. Conversely, the backstage personnel will do the work without immediate acknowledgement from the recipients. They may lack the qualities of the front line employee/volunteer, but are capable of performing the basic task at a high level. They require training, retraining, and appropriate incentives.

    In both groups, observing behavior may prove more effective than administering a battery of tasks. Behavior can be observed directly or indirectly by using behavioral stimulations or assessment center tests that use standardized situations in which applicants can be observed. Finally, it is advantageous to give applicants a realistic preview of the job. This gives candidates a chance to try on the job to see if it fits. At the same time, recruiters can observe how the candidate responds to the jobs realities and can manage the new employee's expectations.

3. Engage in active training. There must be a strong commitment of words, dollars, and actions toward training. This is true for paid employees as well as volunteers. At a minimum this training should include: a. an understanding of the organizational culture, purpose, and strategy, b. interpersonal and technical skills, and c. product knowledge. Of course, training must result in tangible changes in behavior. If staff members do not apply what they have learned, the investment is wasted.

4. Empower employees and volunteers. If a nonprofit does a good job on the first three suggestions, empowering employees is an effective next step. Virtually all successful service firms have legendary stories of employees who have walked the extra mile to make a customer's day or to avoid some kind of disaster for that client. For many service businesses, providing employees/volunteers with greater direction can enable them to provide superior service on the spot and establish important, long-lasting relationships.

Motivate Employees and Volunteers

Once a firm has hired the right people, trained them well, and empowered them into becoming an effective service delivery team, how can it ensure that they will deliver service excellence? Staff performance is a function of ability and motivation. Careful hiring, training, and empowerment give you able people; reward systems are the key to motivation. Many firms, including nonprofits, assume that money is the only proven motivator. The facts suggest that receiving a fair salary is an assumed element rather than a motivating factor. Paying more than what is seen as fair has only short-term motivating effects and wears off quickly. However, bonuses, which are contingent on performance, have to be earned again and again and therefore tend to be more lasting in their effectiveness. Other more lasting rewards are the job itself, recognition, feedback, and goal accomplishments.

The job itself can be a motivator if it offers a variety of activities, requires the completion of a "whole" and identifiable piece of work, seems significant in the sense that it has an impact on the lives of others, comes with autonomy, and has a source of direct and clear feedback about performance. This mandates that a job description be written for each job or job category. This can get very complicated or watered down in the case of nonprofits, where an individual may do multiple jobs.

Because humans need recognition and feedback, there must be a mechanism for employees to receive constant and fair feedback from customers, colleagues, and bosses. If employees and volunteers feel that they are being recognized and thanked for their excellent performance, they will desire to deliver it.

By nature, when we have stated goals we are more focused. Goals for people should be specific, challenging but attainable, and accepted by the staff as a high motivator leading to high performance. Goal-creation can be different for nonprofits where intangible customers are common and employee goals are often personal and not well defined.

EXPECTATIONS

Earlier we discussed the various attributes that distinguish goods products from service products. In most instances, intangibility and inseparability appear to have the most influence on the exchange process. Experts in services marketing have identified a key concept that is manifest because of intangibility and inseparability—expectations. This concept tends to occur prior to starting the decision-making process. That is, it is a concern to consumers simply because they are dealing with service products.

Consumer expectations are pretrial beliefs a consumer has about the performance of a service that are used as the standard or reference against which service performance is judged. We can think of expectations as shown in Exhibit 6.4. The top box indicates the "expected" service level desired by the consumer. Thus, if a patron visits a botanical garden she will have a baseline of expectations. The factors that contribute to this baseline include internal factors, external factors, and firm-produced factors. Examples of internal

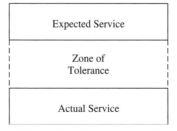

EXHIBIT 6.4   EXPECTED VERSUS ACTUAL SERVICE

factors include individual needs, level of involvement, past experience, and service philosophy. A person visits a botanical garden to satisfy what Maslow would call a need for social-belongingness. That particular individual likes to be part of a social sector that understands and appreciates plants. Similarly, if the person seeks a higher level of involvement, she may become a member, and/or donate time and money. If she had a very satisfactory experience with a similar organization in another city, she will use that as a reference point. Finally, we all have a service philosophy based on our hereditary model and past experience. Your mother loved plants and as a child she took you to beautiful gardens throughout the region. Consequently, your service philosophy or expected service is quite high.

There are also a number of external factors that impact expectations. In every buying opportunity there are competitive options. In the case of the consumer considering a visit to a botanical garden, there are likely to be several other educational and enjoyable alternatives competing for attention. Even a leisurely walk through a local park might suffice. However, in the case of a small or isolated city, the botanical garden may be the only option. Another factor is the desired social context. If the consumer is looking for a quiet and peaceful location where other consumers are like-minded, a botanical garden might make a great deal of sense. The type of word-of-mouth related to the service alternatives is a final external consideration. Positive word-of-mouth about the quality of the plants, educational information available, and friendliness of the staff will all contribute to a decision to visit.

Situational factors are temporary changes in the normal state of things. For example, imagine the state of mind of a family that has just been informed that their 11-year-old son has been diagnosed with muscular dystrophy. They want and need current information from a local hospital and/or the MDS. Their need is immediate and all-consuming. Consumer mood will definitely impact expectations. Individuals in a good mood tend to have lower expectations. Even weather can be a factor. This would certainly be the case with the botanical garden, where half the exhibits are outside—if rain is predicted, attendance will be lower. Similarly, time constraints usually mean that a consumer who has 90 minutes of free time will not visit an exhibit that takes 4 hours to see.

There are factors the service organization offers that may influence expectations. These factors are represented by the marketing mix discussed earlier. Marketing communications, in the form of advertising, sales promotion, public relations, and selling can influence more customers to purchase. Clearly, the free publicity the American Red Cross received after Katrina was a major factor in people donating. Even pricing can play a role. The Minneapolis Zoo has a free senior's day once a month; this generates thousands of additional customers who buy food and souvenirs. Even distribution has an impact on service expectations. The world-famous Brooklyn Botanical Garden is in a neighborhood that would be inconvenient and a security risk for some customers. Likewise, service personnel who are well trained, knowledgeable, and friendly are much more likely to attract customers than those who are not. Tangible cues are under the control of the nonprofit marketer and can have a direct bearing on expectations. Tangible cues consist of such things as the appearance of the interior and exterior of the facility, the furniture, the equipment used in the service, interior decor, cleanliness, signage, and the appearance of the firm's personnel. Tangible cues can sometimes be beyond the control of the nonprofit marketer. Other customers can be too loud, too rowdy, or simply too numerous.

All these factors contribute to the other two boxes (i.e., zone of tolerance and actual service) shown in Figure 6.4. The "actual service" is somewhat obvious. It is the real experience the customer receives. While Sam Smith expected the executive MBA program to be highly motivational and filled with interesting classmates and inspirational professors, this proved not to be the case. The "zone of tolerance" represents that difference. The gap may be quite small; suggesting that the consumer believes the actual product should come very close to expectations. Or, the gap may be wide, suggesting a very high tolerance. The former may be predicated on the fact that the consumer has had positive experiences with similar products and knows that the baseline is reasonable. The latter may be a function of few competitors and the very low price being charged. The zone of tolerance may also be very wide or very narrow, depending on the number of factors being considered. A consumer who visits a free blood pressure screening may only be concerned about the wait time.

It is critical that we as nonprofit marketers accurately measure these three concepts. It begins with identifying the criteria the customer employs in judging the product. Next, we must determine the relative level of these criteria. This is followed with an assessment of their importance. The last two measures create the zone of tolerance. Once the customer has experienced the nonprofit product, we can determine how well we deliver on each of these criteria. It is also possible that new criteria may have been added to (or deleted from) the equation. In turn, these changes may change the zone of tolerance as well.

Taking these measures is an ongoing process and serves as vital input to the rest of the marketing planning process. Unlike the marketing of tangible goods, the variables relevant to service products are different. As suggested in the next section, they also play a role in consumer decision making.

MARKETING MIX FOR SERVICES

As shown in Exhibit 6.5, services marketing has the ability to employ the traditional marketing mix (i.e., product, price, distribution, and communication), as well as extensions in the form of people, physical evidence, and process. The marketing mix contributes the elements the organization mostly controls and implements in order to achieve marketing objectives. The traditional mix, (also known as the four P's: price, place, product, promotion) are core decision variables and they should be totally interrelated (commonly known as integrated marketing). It is assumed that there is an optimal mix at any given point in time. These traditional mix elements were defined in Chapter 2 and will be elaborated upon further in future chapters. However, the differences introduced in Exhibit 6.2 suggest that additional mix elements are warranted.

People. The *people* element includes all the humans that play a role in the exchange of the service product. This includes employees, volunteers, customers, other customers, and influencers. Everything about these people, including their physical appearance, behavior, voice, attitudes, and perceived competencies may all impact the quality of the exchange process, as well as the resulting relationship. In fact, for some service products, such as consulting, counseling, education, and religion, people are the product. In other cases, the people may play a somewhat minor role or even a transitional role, such as the receptionist who schedules appointments at a clinic. The customer may never talk to this person again, yet they played a critical role early in the exchange. Referring back to Figure 6.2, with products in the middle of the continuum, people, such as a check-in clerk or bank teller, provide the service component while the retail store provides the tangible

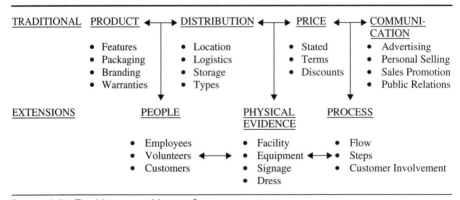

EXHIBIT 6.5   THE MARKETING MIX FOR SERVICES

element. Understanding the role people play in a service product exchange and managing them effectively is both a tool and challenge faced by non-profit marketers. It is also why continuous training is so important for the marketing success of nonprofits.

Physical Evidence. The tangible elements created to support the service product are all considered physical evidence. This includes, but is not restricted to, the building, the parking area, decorations, dress of employees, letterhead, business cards, Web site, signage, report forms, and equipment. All physical evidence should reflect the mission of the organization and be consistent as to paint an identifiable and clear picture of what the organization represents to its customers, donors, volunteers, and the world. It is important to know to what extent different target markets rely on different physical evidence. For example, many potential donors will consider a charity's Web site as a primary piece of physical evidence, followed by the receipt document, thank-you card, and information packet that follows. For others, the building or dress of employees is very relevant. In general, the less evidence available to judge the inherent quality of the service product, the more important surrogate physical evidence becomes.

Process The actual delivery steps the customer experiences, or the operational flow of the service, also give customers evidence on which to judge service products. When services are very complex it is often because the process is complex. It is wise to detail the process and identify potential redundancies or bottlenecks. There may be steps that the customer can perform, but may be unwilling to perform. Likewise, customers may be ill-equipped to perform various steps. Consider an animal shelter such as the Dumb Friends League. The donor goes through a somewhat simple process, beginning with a phone call or visit to a Web site, whereby the customer reads about the process and locates the facility. The donor brings their pet to the facility (no home pick-up), completes a lengthy questionnaire, and says goodbye to their pet. People who are adopting pets go through a reverse process. Imagine how the process would falter if donors had to have their pet examined first. The process characteristics are another form of evidence to gauge the acceptability of the service product exchange, service quality, and whether a relationship is likely.

UNDERSTANDING SERVICE QUALITY

Customers want to receive the highest level of quality in their service product as possible. Yet, because of all the differences between goods products and service products, gauging service quality has emerged as the ultimate

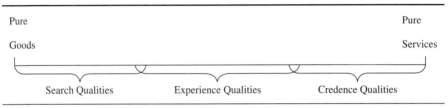

EXHIBIT 6.6   SERVICES PRODUCT QUALITIES

perceptual challenge faced by service marketers. One recipient contacts a local charity in the morning and judges the results to be extremely positive. Another recipient visits in the afternoon and emerges with exactly the opposite reaction.

Researchers in service marketing have concluded that the contract that best describes the criteria used by service customers is "quality." Quality has been further expanded into three types of qualities, as illustrated in Exhibit 6.6. Note that once again we are putting all products on a continuum, with pure goods products on the far left and pure services on the far right. As such, *search qualities* correspond with goods products, and represent attributes that can be judged prior to purchase via tangible characteristics. Search qualities include such characteristics as color, style, fit, smell, and price, to name but a few. *Experience qualities* are attributes that consumers can evaluate only during or after the recipient has experienced the service or event. Examples of products high in experience qualities are food catering services, entertainment, and cosmetic surgery. A face-lift is evaluated after the service has been completed and may take place several times for many months. *Credence qualities* are attributes that consumers have difficulty evaluating even after the consumption is complete. Examples include accounting services, education, religion, and consulting services. Few consumers have the expertise to accurately assess the results of these service products. Similarly, how does a nonprofit organization determine whether a $60,000 advertising campaign was successful? Clearly, evaluating service products high in credence qualities is difficult. They represent the ultimate *implied promise* of service products.

The primary challenges faced by service marketers in gauging service quality (both experience and credence) reflects back on the issues discussed earlier:

- Because of intangibility, service quality is difficult to assess
- Service quality is the consumers' perceptions of the expected and actual service delivered.

Ultimately, to customers who are evaluating the quality of a service product, it is their perceptions that count, not what the service provider thinks they are delivering. If the customer perceives he or she received a poor solution to the problem, then the decision about further patronage will be based on that perception.

Measuring Service Quality

The differences in consumers' perceptions makes it very difficult to standardize service quality. Thanks to the expansive research of marketing professors Parasuraman, Zethanel, and Berry (1981, 1985, 1988), we have the following definitions of some common terms in the services sphere[1].

- Tangibles—things that can be seen and touched including the service providers' physical facilities, their equipment, and the appearance of employees.
- Reliability—the ability of the service firm to perform the promised service dependably and accurately.
- Responsiveness—the willingness of the firm's staff to help customers and to provide them with prompt and accurate services.
- Assurance—refers to the knowledge and courtesy of the company's employees and their ability to inspire trust and confidence.
- Empathy—the caring, individualized attention the service firm provides each customer.

These same researchers developed an instrument called SERVQUAL to measure service quality. The instrument was based on the premise that service quality is the difference between customers' expectations and their evaluation of the service they received. This 22-question instrument is available for purchase and provides a baseline for assessing improvement in various parts of your marketing strategy. However, there are some problems with SERVQUAL. First, SERVQUAL may not transfer well to all service organizations. For example, seldom do patients see their physician at the appointed time, rendering this measure of reliability unrealistic. Second, expectations may change after the consumer experiences the service product, which could bias the results from time to time.

It might be simpler and less expensive for the service organization to create their own measure of service quality. Creating internal and customer performance measures may be derived by experience, recommendations, and observations. Keeping a record of customer complaints is a basic internal measure. Time of delivery or on-time rate may be two others. Collecting performance measures directly from customers is also beneficial. Creating a basic survey measuring attitudes and opinions (remember Chapter 4) would be a good start.

SPECIAL CHALLENGES OF SERVICE

In Chapter 1 we delineated the special challenges faced by marketers of non-profit organizations. Here we provide a list of challenges that supersede that earlier list, since nonprofit organizations are one type of service organization. Answers to questions such as these are still being addressed as the field evolves:

- How can the benefits and quality of service products be improved when essentially they are intangible?
- How can we communicate a consistent and relevant image when many aspects of the service product are created or influenced by the customer?
- How does the service organization deal with fluctuating and unpredictable demand when capacity is fixed and the service is perishable?
- How can we motivate employees, volunteers, and customers to deliver acceptable service products, when the product is intangible and these stakeholders are part of the product itself?
- How can we create a satisfactory value equation (price) when service products are mostly intangible and stakeholders are part of the product?
- How should the firm be organized so that good strategic and tactical decisions are made?

In the chapters that follow we will attempt to answer these questions. Next, we examine the strategic decisions that are part of marketing nonprofit products. We begin with product management.

REFERENCE

1. Parasuraman, A., Zeithmal, V., and L. Berry, "SERVQUAL: A Multiple Item Scale for Measuring Consumer Perceptions of Service Quality", *Journal of Retailing*, 64 (1988): 12–40; Zeithmal, V., Parasuraman, A., and L. Berry, *Delivering Quality Service* (New York: the Free Press, 1990); Zeithmal, V. and M.J. Bettner, *Services Marketing, Third Edition* (New York: McGraw-Hill), 2003.

7

DECISION MAKING BY TARGET MARKETS AND STAKEHOLDERS

When asked to give money or support, people ask themselves
whether it's really going to make a difference.

—Jack Calfee, resident scholar at the American Enterprise Institute

Farm Aid is a nonprofit organization dedicated to helping America's family farmers stay on their land. It was created in 1985 by Willie Nelson after he heard another musician, Bob Dylan, mention during his performance at that summer's Live Aid concert, a benefit for victims of African famine relief, that someone should mount such a show to help the American farmer. Since its inception, Farm Aid has harvested a total of $25 million from its concerts and other fund-raising efforts.

Recently, the Farm Aid organization has decided to broaden its mission. Even as it continued to ask for donations to help farmers in the Deep South whose livelihoods have been threatened by Hurricane Katrina, Farm Aid 2005 introduced its audiences to growers who have switched from conventional methods that use high concentrations of chemical fertilizers and hormones to techniques that are safe for consumers and the environment. Mr. Nelson, along with dozens of other entertainers, encouraged their audiences to support efforts to grow organic produce.

By enlarging its perspectives, Farm Aid is now in a better position to serve the 500,000 families nationwide who work the land for a living. Family farmers face challenges from large-scale growers, the low prices that farm produce commands in the marketplace, increasing poverty, and natural disasters that can sometimes force them off their homesteads.

To pay for much of its advocacy, emergency-aid, and other efforts on behalf of farmers—as well as the salaries of its nine-member staff—Farm Aid has expanded its fund raising beyond concerts. The organization has developed regular direct-mail campaigns, sold concert memorabilia on the online auction site eBay, sought out corporate sponsorships, stepped up Web solicitations, and redoubled its efforts with individual donors who have made larger gifts in the past. Moreover, Farm Aid has invested in a better understanding of how all these donors make their decisions to give or not give, to buy or not buy. This is the topic of this chapter.

INTRODUCTION

The potential buyers, in commercial situations, "vote" (with their dollars) for the market offering that they feel best meets their needs. An understanding of how they arrive at a decision allows the marketer to build an offering that will attract buyers.

Two of the key questions that a marketer needs to answer relative to buyer behavior are:

1. How do potential buyers go about making purchase decisions?
2. What factors influence their decision process and in what way?

The answers to these two questions form the basis for target market selection, and, ultimately, the design of a market offering. A clear understanding of how all possible stakeholders (decision makers) make decisions is critical if you are to create an effective marketing plan.

When we use the term "buyer," we are referring to an individual, group, or organization that engages in market exchange. In fact, there are differences in the characteristics of these three entities and how they behave in an exchange. The exchange process allows the parties to assess the relative trade-offs they must make to satisfy their respective needs and wants. For the marketer, analysis of these trade-offs is guided by company policies and objectives. For example, a company may engage in exchanges only when the profit margin is 10 percent or greater. The buyer, the other member in the exchange, also has personal policies and objectives that guide their responses in an exchange. Unfortunately, buyers seldom write down their personal policies and objectives. Even more likely, they often don't understand what prompts them to behave in a particular manner. This is the mystery or the "black box" of buyer behavior that makes the exchange process so unpredictable and difficult for marketers to understand.

Buyers are essential partners in the exchange process. Without them, exchanges would stop. They are the focus of successful marketing; their needs and wants are the reason for marketing. Without an understanding of buyer behavior, the market offering cannot possibly be tailored to the demands of potential buyers. When potential buyers are not satisfied, exchange falters and the goals of the marketer cannot be met. As long as buyers have free choice and competitive offerings from which to choose, they are ultimately in control of the marketplace.

Therefore, individuals and groups are traditionally placed in the *consumer* category, while *organization* is the second category. Let us now turn to consumer decision making.

BUYER BEHAVIOR AS PROBLEM SOLVING

Consumer behavior refers to buyers who are purchasing for personal, family, or group use. Consumer behavior can be thought of as the combination of efforts and results related to the consumer's need to solve problems. Consumer problem solving is triggered by the identification of some unmet need. For example, a family consumes all of the milk in the house or the tires on the car wear out or the bowling team is planning an end-of-the-season picnic. This presents the person with a problem that must be solved. Problems can be viewed in terms of two types of needs; physical (such as a need for food) or psychological (for example, the need to be accepted by others or rid oneself of guilt by donating).

Although the difference is a subtle one, there is some benefit in distinguishing between needs and wants. A *need* is a basic deficiency given a particular essential item. You need food, water, air, security, and so forth. A *want* is placing certain personal criteria as to how that need must be fulfilled. Therefore, when we are hungry, we often have a specific food item in mind. Consequently, a teenager will lament to a frustrated parent that there is nothing to eat, standing in front of a full refrigerator. Most of marketing is in the want-fulfilling business, not the need-fulfilling business. Timex doesn't want you to buy just any watch; they want you to want a Timex brand watch. Likewise, Ralph Lauren wants you to want Polo when you shop for clothes. On the other hand, the American Cancer Association would like you to feel the need for a check-up and doesn't care which doctor you go to. In the end, however, marketing is mostly interested in creating and satisfying wants.

Factors of Consumer Behavior

While the decision-making process appears quite standardized, no two people make a decision in exactly the same way. As individuals, we have inherited and learned a great many behavioral tendencies: some controllable, some beyond our control. Further, the ways in which all these factors interact with one another ensures uniqueness. Although it is impossible for a marketer to react to the particular profile of a single consumer, it is possible to identify factors that tend to influence most consumers in predictable ways.

The factors that influence the consumer problem-solving process are numerous and complex. For example, the needs of men and women are different with respect to cosmetics; the extent of information search for a low-income person would be much greater when considering a new automobile as opposed to a loaf of bread; a consumer with extensive past purchasing experience in a product category might well approach the problem differently from one with no experience. Such influences must be understood in order to draw realistic conclusions about consumer behavior.

For purposes of discussion, it may be helpful to group these various influences into related sets (Exhibit 7.1). Situational, external, and internal

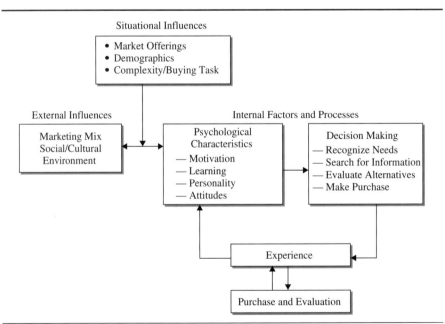

Exhibit 7.1 Elements That Influence the Consumer's Decision to Purchase and Evaluate Products and Services

influences are shown as having an impact on the consumer problem solving process. *Situation influences* include the consumer's immediate buying task, the market offerings that are available to the consumer, and demographic traits. *Internal influences* relate to the consumer's learning and socialization, motivation, personality, and lifestyle. *External influences* deal with factors outside the individual that have a strong bearing on personal behaviors. Current purchase behavior is shown as influencing future behavior through the internal influence of learning. Let us now turn to the nature and potential impact of each of these sets of influences on consumer problem solving.

Situational Influences

Buying Task. The nature of the buying task has considerable impact on a customer's approach to solving a particular problem. When a decision involves a low-cost item that is frequently purchased, such as bread, the buying process is typically quick and routinized.

A decision concerning a new car is quite different. The extent to which a decision is considered complex or simple depends on 1. whether the decision is novel or routine, and on 2. the extent of the customers' involvement with the decision. A great deal of discussion has revolved around this issue of involvement. *High-involvement* decisions are those that are important to the buyer. Such decisions are closely tied to the consumer's ego and self-image. They also involve some risk to the consumer; financial risk (highly priced items), social risk (products important to the peer group), or psychological risk (the wrong decision might cause the consumer some concern and anxiety). In making these decisions, it is worth the time and energy to consider solution alternatives carefully. A complex process of decision making is therefore more likely for high-involvement purchases. *Low-involvement* decisions are more straightforward, require little risk, are repetitive, and often lead to a habit; they are not very important to the consumer. Financial, social, and psychological risks are not nearly as great. In such cases, it may not be worth the consumer's time and effort to search for information about brands or to consider a wide range of alternatives. A low-involvement purchase therefore generally entails a limited process of decision making. The purchase of a new computer is an example of high involvement, while the purchase of a hamburger is a low-involvement decision. Similarly, the decision a person makes to volunteer two days each month at a charitable organization is likely a high-involvement decision. The decision to pledge $25 a month to one's synagogue is a low-involvement decision, requiring little complexity.

When a consumer has bought a similar product many times in the past, the decision making is likely to be simple, regardless of whether it is a high- or low-involvement decision. Suppose a consumer initially bought a product after much care and involvement, was satisfied, and continued to buy the product. The customer's careful consideration of the product and satisfaction has produced brand loyalty, which is the result of involvement with the product decision.

Once a customer is brand-loyal, a simple decision-making process is all that is required for subsequent purchases. The consumer now buys the product through *habit*, which means making a decision without the use of additional information or the evaluation of alternative choices.

Market Offerings. Another relevant set of situational influences on consumer problem solving is the available market offerings. The more extensive the product and brand choices available to the consumer, the more complex the purchase decision process is likely to be. For example, if you already have purchased or are considering purchasing a DVD, you know there are many brands to choose from—Sony, Samsung, Panasonic, Mitsubishi, Toshiba, and Sanyo, to name several. Each manufacturer sells several models that differ in terms of some of the following features—single or multiple event selection, remote control (wired or wireless), slow motion, stop action, variable-speed scan, tracking control, and so on. What criteria are important to you? Is purchasing a DVD an easy decision? If a consumer has a need that can be met by only one product or one outlet in the relevant market, the decision is relatively simple. Either purchase the product or let the need go unmet.

This is not ideal from the customer's perspective, but it can occur. For example, suppose you are a student on a campus in a small town many miles from another marketplace. Your town has only one bookstore. You need a textbook for class; only one specific book will do and only one outlet has the book for sale. The limitation on alternative market offerings can clearly influence your purchase behavior.

As you saw in the DVD example, when the extent of market offerings increases, the complexity of the problem-solving process and the consumers' need for information also increases. A wider selection of market offerings is better from the customer's point of view, because it allows them to tailor their purchases to their specific needs. However, it may confuse and frustrate the consumer so that less-than-optimal choices are made.

Demographic Influences. An important set of factors that should not be overlooked in attempting to understand and respond to consumers is demographics. Such variables as age, sex, income, education, marital status, and mobility can all have significant influence on consumer behavior. One study showed that age and education have strong relationships to store selection by female shoppers. This was particularly true for women's suits or dresses, linens and bedding, cosmetics, and women's sportswear.

People in different income brackets also tend to buy different types of products and different qualities. Thus various income groups often shop in very different ways. This means that income can be an important variable in defining the target group. Many designer clothing shops, for example, aim at higher-income shoppers, while a store like Target appeals to middle- and lower-income groups.

External Influences

External factors are another important set of influences on consumer behavior. Among the many societal elements that can affect consumer problem solving are culture, social class, reference groups, and family.

Culture. A person's culture is represented by a large group of people with a similar heritage. The American culture, which is a subset of the Western culture, is of primary interest here. Traditional American culture values include hard work, thrift, achievement, security, and the like. Marketing strategies targeted to those with such a culture heritage should show the product or service as reinforcing these traditional values. The three components of culture—beliefs, values, and customs—are each somewhat different. A *belief* is a proposition that reflects a person's particular knowledge and assessment of something (that is, "I believe that ..."). *Values* are general statements that guide behavior and influence beliefs. The function of a value system is to help a person choose between alternatives in everyday life. *Customs* are overt modes of behavior that constitute culturally approved ways of behaving in specific situations. For example, taking one's mother out for dinner and buying her presents for Mother's Day is an American custom that Hallmark and other card companies support enthusiastically.

The American culture with its social values can be divided into various subcultures. For example, African-Americans constitute a significant American subculture in most U.S. cities. A consumer's racial heritage can exert an influence on media usage and various other aspects of the purchase decision process.

Social Class. This is determined by such factors as occupation, wealth, income, education, power, and prestige, is another societal factor that can affect consumer behavior. The best-known classification system includes upper-upper, lower-upper, upper-middle, lower-middle, upper-lower and lower-lower class. Lower-middle and upper-lower classes comprise the mass market. The upper-upper class and lower-upper class consist of people from wealthy families who are locally prominent. They tend to live in large homes furnished with art and antiques. They are the primary market for rare jewelry and designer originals, as they tend to shop at exclusive retailers. The upper-middle class is made up of professionals, managers, and business owners. They are ambitious, future-oriented people who have succeeded economically and now seek to enhance their quality of life. Material goods often take on major symbolic meaning for this group. They also tend to be very civic-minded and are involved in many worthy causes. The lower-middle class consists of mid-level white-collar workers. These are office workers, teachers, small business people and the like who typically hold strong American values. They are family-oriented, hard-working individuals. The upper-lower class is made up of blue-collar workers such as production line workers and service people. Many have incomes that exceed those of the lower-middle class, but their values are often very different. They tend to adopt a short-run, live-for-the-present philosophy. They are less future-oriented than the middle classes. The lower-lower class consists of unskilled workers with low incomes. They are more concerned with necessities than with status or fulfillment.

People in the same social class tend to have similar attitudes, live in similar neighborhoods, dress alike, and shop at the same types of stores. If a marketer wishes to target efforts toward the upper classes, then the market offering must be designed to meet their expectations in terms of quality, service, and atmosphere. Golf, skiing, fine restaurants, and concerts are favored by members of the middle and upper classes. Fishing, bowling, pool, and fast food restaurants are more likely to involve members of the lower social classes.

Reference Groups. A *reference group* helps shape a person's attitudes and behaviors. Such groups can be either formal or informal. Churches, clubs, schools, notable individuals, and friends can all be reference groups for a particular consumer. Reference groups are characterized as having individuals who are opinion leaders for the group. *Opinion leaders* are people who influence others. They are not necessarily higher-income or better educated, but perhaps are seen as having greater expertise or knowledge related to some specific topic. For example, a local high school teacher may be an opinion leader for parents in selecting colleges for their children. These people set the trend and others conform to the expressed behavior. If a marketer can identify the opinion leaders for a group in the target market, then effort can be directed toward attracting these individuals. For example, if an ice cream parlor is attempting to attract the local high school trade, opinion leaders at the school may be very important to its success.

The reference group can influence an individual in three important ways.

1. Role expectations: The role assumed by a person is nothing more than a prescribed way of behaving based on the situation and the person's position in the situation. Your reference group determines much about how this role is to be performed. As a parent, you are expected to behave in a certain basic way under certain conditions.

2. Conformity: Conformity is related to our roles in that we modify our behavior in order to coincide with group norms. Norms are behavioral expectations that are considered appropriate regardless of the position we hold.

3. Group communications through opinion leaders: We, as consumers, are constantly seeking out the advice of knowledgeable friends or acquaintances who can provide information, give advice, or actually make the decision. For some product categories, there are professional opinion leaders who are quite easy to identify—auto mechanics, beauticians, stock brokers, and physicians are some examples.

Family. One of the most important reference groups for an individual is the family. A consumer's family has a major impact on attitude and behavior. The interaction between husband and wife and the number and ages of children in the family can have a significant effect on buying behavior.

One facet in understanding the typical nuclear family's impact on consumer behavior is identifying the decision maker for the purchase in question. In some cases, the husband is typically dominant, in others the wife or children, and still others, a joint decision is made. The store choice for food and household items is most often the wife's. With purchases that involve a larger sum of money, such as a refrigerator, a joint decision is usually made. The decision on clothing purchases for teenagers may be greatly influenced by the teenagers themselves. Thus, marketers need to identify the key family decision maker for the product or service in question.

Another aspect of understanding the impact of the family on buying behavior is the *family lifecycle*. Most families pass through an orderly sequence of stages. These stages can be defined by a combination of factors such as age, marital status, and parenthood. The typical stages are:

- The bachelor state: young, single people
- Newly married couples: young, no children
- The full nest I and II: young married couples with dependent children

- ○ Youngest child under six (Full nest I)
- ○ Youngest child over six (Full nest II)
- The full nest III; oldest married couples with dependent children
- The empty nest I and II; older married couples with no children living with them
  - ○ Adults in labor force (Empty nest I)
  - ○ Adults retired (Empty nest II)
- The solitary survivors: older single people
  - ○ In labor force
  - ○ Retired

Each of these stages is characterized by different buying behaviors. For example, a children's clothing manufacturer would target its efforts primarily at the full nest I families.

Thus, the family cycle can be helpful in defining the target customers. Consider where your primary donors would fall in the family lifecycle and how other responsibilities would affect their ability to donate.

Internal Influences

Each customer is to some degree a unique problem solving unit. Although they can be grouped into meaningful segments, in order to fully appreciate the totality of the buying process, a marketer needs to examine the internal forces that influence consumers. They are learning/socialization, motivation and personality, and lifestyle.

Learning and Socialization. As a factor influencing a person's perceptions, *learning* may be defined as changes in behavior resulting from previous experiences. However, learning does not include behavior changes attributable to instinctive responses, growth, or temporary states of the organism, such as hunger, fatigue, or sleep. It is clear that learning is an ongoing process that is dynamic, adaptive, and subject to change. Also, learning is an experience and practice that actually brings about changes in behavior. For example, in order to learn how to play tennis, you might participate in it in order to gain experience. However, your experience does not have to be an actual, physical one. It could be a conceptualization of a potential experience. In other words, you could learn to play tennis by reading about how to play without actually doing it. This is called *nonexperiential learning*.

Nonexperiential learning is particularly relevant in consumer behavior. For example, assume you are considering purchasing a bottle of Zinfandel wine. You ask the salesclerk what it tastes like, and he tells you it tastes like a strong ginger ale. Not liking the taste of ginger ale, you reject the purchase. Thus, you have learned that you do not like Zinfandel wine without having a direct taste experience. A great deal of our learning is of this type. This may be one reason why marketers try to identify opinion leaders who in turn tell others in the market about the benefits of the product.

Another characteristic of learning is the fact that there is no immediate evidence that learning has taken place is no reason to assume that learning has not occurred. We can store our learning until it is needed, and frequently do this in terms of making purchase decisions. For example, we are willing to learn about many product attributes even though we do not expect to buy that particular product in the near future.

As new information is processed and stored over time, consumer learning takes place. There are several theories of learning; one of the most useful to marketers is that of socialization. *Socialization* refers to the process by which people acquire the knowledge, skills, and dispositions that make them more or less able members of their society. The assumption made is that behavior is acquired and modified over the person's lifetime.

The social learning approach stresses sources of influence. "Socialization agents" (i.e., other people transmit cognitive and behavioral patterns to the learner). In the case of consumer socialization, this takes place in the course of the person's interaction with other individuals in various social settings. Socialization agents might include any person, organization, or information source that comes into contact with the consumer.

Consumers acquire this information from the other individuals through the processes of modeling, reinforcement, and social interaction. *Modeling* involves imitation of the agent's behavior. For example, a teenager may acquire a brand name preference for Izod from friends. Marketers can make use of this concept by employing spokespeople who have strong credibility with their target consumers to endorse their products and services. *Reinforcement* involves either a reward or a punishment mechanism used by the agent. A purchaser may be reinforced by good product performance, excellent postpurchase services, or some similar rewarding experience. The *social interaction* mechanism is less specific as to the type of learning involved; it may include a combination of modeling and reinforcement. The social setting within which learning takes place can be defined in terms of variables such as social class, gender, and family size.

These variables can influence learning through their impact on the relationship between the consumer and others. It should be noted that an individual who promotes learning can be anyone—a parent, friend, salesperson, or television spokesperson.

Motivation. Motivation is a concept that is difficult to define. In fact, the difficulty of defining motives and dealing with motivation in consumer research accounts for its limited application. A *motive* is the inner drive or pressure to take action to satisfy a need. To be motivated is to be a goal-oriented individual. Some goals are positive, some are negative, some individuals have a high level of goal orientation, some have a very low level. In all cases, the need must be aroused or stimulated to a high enough level so that it can serve as a motive.

It is possible (and usual) to have needs that are latent (unstimulated) and that therefore do not serve as the motive of behavior. The sources of this arousal may be internal (people get hungry), environmental (you see an ad for a Big Mac), or psychological (just thinking about food can cause hunger).

For motivation to be useful in marketing practice, a marketing manager must understand what motives and behaviors are influenced by the specific situation in which consumers engage in goal-directed, problem-solving behavior.

Motivation flows from an unmet need, as does all consumer problem solving. Perhaps the best known theory dealing with individual motivation is provided in the work of A.H. Maslow. One of the most important parts of Maslow's theory is his development of a model consisting of several different levels of needs that exist in a human being and relate to each other via a "need hierarchy". Maslow has differentiated between five levels of needs. The first of these concerns itself with physiological needs; that is, hunger, thirst, and other basic drives. All living beings, regardless of their level of maturity, possess physiological needs. Physiological needs are omnipresent and are of a recurrent nature.

Safety and security needs are second in Maslow's hierarchy. The difference between physiological needs and the need for safety and security is somewhat hazy. Safety and security imply a continued fulfillment of physiological needs. This is an extension of the more basic needs.

Third in Maslow's hierarchy of needs are the love needs. These are the needs for belonging and friendship. They involve a person's interaction with others.

The fourth level of needs in Maslow's hierarchy is the esteem needs. These are needs related to feeling good about oneself and having a positive self-image.

The fifth and highest level in Maslow's needs hierarchy is the need for self-actualization or self-fulfillment. This need can be defined as the need of a person to reach his full potential in terms of the application of his own abilities and interest in functioning in his environment.

It is important in discussing these levels of Maslow's hierarchy to point out two additional factors. First, Maslow has clearly indicated that these five levels of needs operate on an unconscious level. That is, the individual is probably not aware of concentration upon one particular need. One of the misunderstandings associated with Maslow's theory is that he believes the five needs to be mutually exclusive. That, in fact, is not Maslow's intent. To the contrary, several of these needs may occur simultaneously for any one individual; the relative importance of each need for any one individual determines the hierarchy involved.

Personality. Personality is used to summarize all the traits of a person that make him or her unique. No two people have exactly the same traits, but several attempts have been made to classify people with similar traits. Perhaps the best-known personality types are those proposed by Carl Jung, as a variation on the work of his teacher, Sigmund Freud. His personality categories are *introvert* and *extrovert*. The introvert is described as defensive, inner-directed, and withdrawn from others. The extrovert is outgoing, other-directed, and assertive. Several other more elaborate classifications have also been devised.

Various personality types, like people with various motives, are likely to respond in different ways to different market offerings. For example, an extrovert may enjoy the shopping experience and rely more on personal observation to secure information; thus, in-store promotion would become an important communication tool. Knowing the basic personality traits of target customers can be useful information for the manager in designing the marketing mix. Marketers have, however, found personality to be difficult to apply in developing marketing strategy. The primary reason for this is the lack of good ways to measure personality traits. Most available measures were developed to identify people with problems that needed medical attention. These have little value with consumers who are mentally healthy. As a result, most marketers have turned to lifestyle analysis.

Lifestyle. One of the new and increasingly important set of factors that is being used to understand consumer behavior is lifestyle. *Lifestyle* has been generally defined as the attitudes, interests, and opinions of the potential customer. Such variables as interest in hunting, attitude toward the role of women in society, and opinion on the importance of dressing well can be used to better understand the market and its behavior.

It is the multifaceted aspect of lifestyle research that makes it so useful in consumer analysis. A useful application of the lifestyle concept relates to consumer's shopping orientation. Different customers approach shopping in very different ways. They have different attitudes and opinions about shopping and different levels of interest in shopping. Once people know their alternatives, how do they evaluate and choose among them? In particular, how do people choose among brands of a product? Current description of this process emphasizes the role of attitudes.

Attitudes. An *attitude* is an opinion of a person, idea, place, or thing. Attitudes range based on a continuum from very negative to very positive. Traditionally, an attitude is broken down into three components: cognitive, affective, and behavioral. That is, an attitude is first what we know/believe, followed by what we feel, and ending with an action. Thus, we have learned that a particular company has been polluting a local river; we feel very strongly that business shouldn't do this and feel very angry; therefore, we boycott the product made by that company.

A great deal of marketing strategy is based on the idea that the cognitive, affective, and behavioral components of an attitude tend to be consistent. Thus, if it is possible to change what people believe about Yamaha CD players, for example, their feelings and their actions may eventually change as well. However, this relationship among the three components of an attitude seems to be situation- or even product-specific. For example, attitudes tend to predict behavior better in high-involvement decisions. Thus, if someone has a strong attitude about wearing stylish clothes, then it is possible to predict that the person will restrict purchases to a particular set of brands. Furthermore, we do not react to products in isolation. The situation, or our attitude toward the situation, plays an important role in how well attitudes predict behavior. For example, assume that a consumer likes pizza but doesn't like Ray's pizza. In a social setting where everyone wants to go to Ray's Pizza this person might eat this brand rather than not have pizza at all.

Despite limitations on the predictive power of attitudes, attitudes can help us understand how choices are made. However, we need to carefully assess the validity of the attitude–behavior relationships for each situation and product.

Given the hypothesis that attitudes influence buying behavior, how can a company bring its products and consumers' attitudes into a consistent state; that is, into a situation where consumers evaluate a given product or brand as satisfying their needs? Marketers have two choices; either they can change consumers' attitudes to be consistent with their product, or they can change the product to match attitudes. It is easier to change the product than to change consumers' attitudes. Nevertheless, attitudes can sometimes be modified.

Modifying attitudes might be the only reasonable choice, as when a firm is introducing a truly new product or an unusual new use for an existing one. Marketers should nevertheless face the fact that it is extremely difficult to change consumers' attitudes. If there is to be change, it is most likely to occur when people are open-minded in their beliefs or when an existing attitude is of weak intensity, that is, when there is little information to support the attitude or very little ego involvement on the individual's part. The stronger a person's loyalty to a certain brand, for example, the more difficult it is to change that attitude.

The Consumer Decision Process

Exhibit 7.1 also outlines the process a consumer goes through in making a purchase decision. Each step is illustrated in the following sections of this chapter. Once the process is started, a potential buyer can withdraw at any stage before making the actual purchase. The tendency for a person to go through all six stages is likely only in certain buying situations—a first-time purchase of a product, for instance, or when buying high priced, long-lasting, infrequently purchased articles.

For many products, the purchasing behavior is a routine affair in which the aroused need is satisfied in a habitual manner by repurchasing the same brand. That is, past reinforcement in learning experiences leads directly to buying, and thus the second and third stages are bypassed. However, if something changes appreciably (price, product, availability, services), the buyer may re-enter the full decision process and consider alternative brands. The first step is *need identification*.

Step 1. Need Identification

Whether we act to resolve a particular problem depends upon two factors;

1. the magnitude of the discrepancy between what we have and what we need, and
2. the importance of the problem. A consumer may desire a new Lexus and own a five-year-old Honda. The discrepancy may be fairly large, but relatively unimportant compared to the other problems he or she faces.

Conversely, an individual may own a car that is two years old and running very well. Yet, for various reasons, he or she may consider it extremely important to purchase a car this year. People must resolve these types of conflicts before they can proceed. Otherwise, the buying process for a given product stops at this point, probably in frustration.

Once the problem is recognized, it must be defined in such a way that the consumer can actually initiate the action that will bring about a relevant solution to the problem. Note that in many cases, problem recognition and problem definition occur simultaneously, such as a consumer running out of toothpaste. But consider the more complicated problem involved with status and image—how we want others to see us. For example, you may know that you are not satisfied with your appearance, but you may not be able to define it any more precisely than that. Consumers will not know where to begin solving their problem until the problem is adequately defined.

Marketers can become involved in the need recognition stage in three ways. First, they need to know what problems consumers are facing in order to develop a marketing mix to help solve these problems. This requires that they measure problem recognition. Second, on occasion, marketers want to activate problem recognition. This is prevalent with many nonprofits. A public service announcement espousing the dangers of cigarette smoking is an example. Weekend and night shop hours are retailers' response to the consumer problem of limited weekday shopping opportunities. This problem has become particularly important to families with two working adults. Finally, marketers can also shape the definition of the need or problem. If a consumer needs a new coat, does he define the problem as a need for inexpensive covering, a way to stay warm on the coldest days, a garment that will last several years, warm covering that will not attract odd looks from his peers, or an article of clothing that will express his personal sense of style? A salesperson or an ad may shape his answers.

Step 2. Information Search and Processing

Information Search. After a need is recognized, the prospective consumer may seek information to help identify and evaluate alternative products, services, and outlets that will meet that need. Such information can come from family, friends, personal observation, or other sources, such as Consumer Reports, salespeople, or the Internet. The promotional component of the marketers offering is aimed at providing information to assist the consumer in their problem-solving process. In some cases, the consumer already has the needed information based on past purchasing and consumption experience. Bad experiences and lack of satisfaction can destroy repeat purchases. The consumer with a need for tires may look for information in the local newspaper or ask friends for a recommendation. If he has bought tires before and was satisfied, he may go to the same dealer and buy the same brand.

Information search can also identify new needs. As a tire shopper looks for information, she may decide that the tires are not the real problem, her real need is a new car. At this point, the perceived need may change, triggering a new information search.

The information search involves mental as well as physical activities that consumers must perform in order to make decisions and accomplish desired goals in the marketplace. It takes time, energy, money, and can often involve foregoing more desirable activities. The benefits of the information search, however, can outweigh the costs. For example, engaging in a thorough information search may save money, improve quality of selection, or reduce risks. Undoubtedly the most important breakthrough in facilitating information search has been the development of search engines such as Google. In a matter of minutes, any connected consumer can gather information about hundreds of alternatives, make comparisons, and even request specific additional information. Clearly this has empowered today's consumer to be more demanding and to base their purchase decisions on more and better information.

Information Processing. Once the search actually occurs, what do people do with the information? How do they spot, understand, and recall information? In other words, how do they process information? This broad topic is important for understanding buyer behavior in general as well as effective communication with buyers in particular, and it has received a great deal of study. Assessing how a person processes information is not an easy task. Often observation has served as the basis. Yet there are many theories as to how the process takes place. One widely accepted theory proposes a five-step sequence, as follows:

Step 1. *Exposure*. Information processes starts with the *exposure* of consumers to some source of simulation such as watching television, going to the supermarket, or receiving direct mail advertisements at home. In order to start the process, marketers must attract consumers to the stimulus or put it squarely in the path of people in the target market.

Step 2. *Attention*. Exposure alone does little unless people pay attention to the stimulus. At any moment, people are bombarded by all sorts of stimuli, but they have a limited capacity to process this input. They must devote mental resources to stimuli in order to process them; in other words, they must pay *attention*. Marketers can increase the likelihood of attention by providing informational cues that are relevant to the buyer.

Step 3. *Perception*. *Perception* involves classifying the incoming signals into meaningful categories, forming patterns, and assigning names or images to them. Perception is the assignment of meaning to stimuli received through the senses.

Step 4. *Retention*. Storage of information for later reference, or *retention*, is the fourth step of the information-processing sequence. Actually, the role of retention or memory in the sequence is twofold. First, memory holds information while it is being processed throughout the sequence. Second, memory stores information for future, long-term use. Heavy repetition and putting a message to music are two things marketers do to enhance retention.

Step 5. *Retrieval and Application*. The process by which information is recovered from the memory storehouse is called retrieval. Application is putting that information into the right context. If the buyer can retrieve relevant information about a product, brand, or store, he or she will apply it to solve a problem or meet a need.

Variations in how each step is carried out in the information-processing sequence also occur. Especially influential is the degree of elaboration. *Elaborate processing*, also called *central processing* pays close attention to a message and thinks about it; he or she develops thoughts in support of or counter to the information received. In contrast, *nonelaborate*, or *peripheral processing*, involves passive manipulation of information. It is demonstrated by most airline passengers while a flight attendant reads preflight safety procedures.

Step 3. Identification and Evaluation of Alternatives

After information is secured and processed, alternative products, services, and outlets are identified as viable options. The consumer evaluates these alternatives, and, if financially and psychologically able, makes a choice. The criteria used in evaluation varies from consumer to consumer just as the needs and information sources vary. One consumer may consider price most important while another puts more weight upon quality or convenience.

The search for alternatives and the methods used in the search are influenced by such factors as: 1. time and money costs; 2. how much information the consumer already has; 3. the amount of the perceived risk if a wrong selection is made; and 4. the consumer's predisposition toward particular choices as influenced by the attitude of the individual toward choice behavior. That is, there are individuals who find the selection process to be difficult and disturbing. For these people there is a tendency to keep the number of alternatives to a minimum, even if they haven't gone through an extensive information search to find that their alternatives appear to be the very best. On the other hand, there are individuals who feel it necessary to collect a long list of alternatives. This tendency can appreciably slow down the decision-making function.

Step 4. Product/Service/Outlet Selection

The selection of an alternative in many cases will require additional evaluation. For example, a consumer may select a favorite brand and go to a convenient outlet to make a purchase. Upon arrival at the dealer, the consumer finds that the desired brand is out-of-stock. At this point, additional evaluation is needed to decide whether to wait until the product comes in, accept a substitute, or go to another outlet. The selection and evaluation phases of consumer problem solving are closely related and often run sequentially, with outlet selection influencing product evaluation, or product selection influencing outlet evaluation.

Step 5. The Purchase Decision

After much searching and evaluating, or perhaps very little, consumers at some point have to decide whether they are going to buy. Anything marketers can do to simplify purchasing will be attractive to buyers. In their advertising marketers could suggest the best size for a particular use, or the right wine to drink with a particular food. Sometimes several decision situations can be combined and marketed as one package. For example, travel agents often package travel tours.

To do a better marketing job at this stage of the buying process, a seller needs to know answers to many questions about consumers' shopping behavior. For instance, how much effort is the consumer willing to spend in shopping for the product? What factors influence when the consumer will actually purchase? Are there any conditions that would prohibit or delay purchase? Providing basic product, price, and location information through labels, advertising, personal selling, and public relations is an obvious starting point. Product sampling, coupons premiums, and rebates may also provide an extra incentive to buy.

Actually determining how a consumer goes through the decision-making process is a difficult research task. Refer back to Chapter 4 to recall the principles of marketing research.

Step 6. Postpurchase Behavior

All the behavior determinants and the steps of the buying process up to this point are operative before or during the time a purchase is made. However, a consumer's feelings and evaluations after the sale are also significant to a marketer because they can influence repeat sales and also influence what the customer tells others about the product or brand.

Keeping the customer happy is what marketing is all about. Nevertheless, consumers typically experience some postpurchase anxiety after all but the most routine and inexpensive purchases. This anxiety reflects a phenomenon called *cognitive dissonance*. According to this theory, people strive for consistency among their cognitions (knowledge, attitudes, beliefs, values). When there are inconsistencies, dissonance exists, which people will try to eliminate. In some cases, the consumer makes the decision to buy a particular brand already aware of dissonant elements. In other instances, dissonance is aroused by disturbing information that is received after the purchase. The marketer may take specific steps to reduce postpurchase dissonance. Advertising that stresses the many positive attributes or confirms the popularity of the product can be helpful. Providing personalized reinforcement has proven effective with big-ticket items such as automobiles and major appliances. Salespeople in these areas may send cards or may even make personal calls in order to reassure customers about their purchase.

DECISION MAKING BY NONPROFIT STAKEHOLDERS

Everything we have just discussed has applications to nonprofits. However, there are certain anomalies that exist in how individuals and groups make decisions in a nonprofit environment. These need to be noted and understood if the nonprofit marketer is to be successful. Because the process of understanding giving behavior (donating and awarding) is so critical to nonprofits, an entire chapter is dedicated to it (Chapter 12). Here, we simply provide an overall understanding of the variables and their linkages. We begin this discussion with an identification of the stakeholders impacting nonprofits.

Nonprofit Stakeholders

In Chapter 3 we discussed the notion of market and the selection of target markets from that market. We also indicated that there is an exchange between two primary parties, the marketer and the customer. While this remains the core element of marketing strategy (to facilitate exchange) there are other people and organizations that influence the decisions or are influenced by the decisions of the marketing organization. These are referred to as *stakeholders*, and must be acknowledged and accounted for throughout the life of the organization. As noted in Exhibit 7.2, for-profits and nonprofits share some stakeholders, while others are unique to each category.

Stakeholders

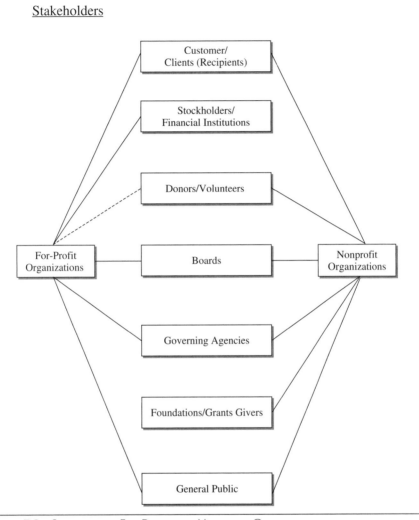

EXHIBIT 7.2   STAKEHOLDERS FOR PROFIT AND NONPROFIT ORGANIZATIONS

As indicated, both for-profits and nonprofits share a concern for customers/clients (recipients), boards, governing agencies, and the general public. For-profits also must pay great attention to stockholders and financial institutions, which are often their primary source of capital. Nonprofits, in contrast, must create marketing strategies for their primary sources of revenue—donors/volunteers and foundations/grant givers.

It is fairly safe to assume that foundations/grant givers share many of the same characteristics and decision-making traits discussed under individual decision making. That is, there is a prescribed process for applying to these organizations; there is a rational and sequential evaluation process; and, the decision tends to be made by a group of experts on the topic rather than an individual. Because these types of stakeholders are governed by such a rigid and unemotional process, nonprofits often hire or consult with individuals who have experience with working with this category of stakeholders and are somewhat analytical. Thus, understanding how these stakeholders make decisions is fairly clear and well documented. Typically, the decision to be made by the nonprofit marketer is whether he or she wants to engage in this exchange as it is so costly, competitive, time-consuming, and highly unpredictable.

The two remaining types of stakeholders are treated differently in the context of nonprofit. Both governing agencies and the general public interact differently with nonprofits as compared to for-profits. As noted in Chapter 5, both the laws governing nonprofits, as well as the ethical standards, are different for nonprofits. In general, virtually all the laws that apply to for-profits apply to nonprofits. In addition, there are laws that relate to a nonprofit's 501(c) (3) classification. Similarly, the very high legal standards applied to nonprofits spill over into ethical expectations. The public expects nonprofits to be honest, ethical, and transparent—always. Consequently, nonprofit organizations must constantly monitor their own legal and ethical behavior, and also monitor how the public and governing agencies are interpreting the law and ethical behavior. The recent resignations at the National Red Cross may play havoc with public opinion toward that organization for years to come. Monitoring both the legal community and the general public is the responsibility of the marketer. Making necessary changes is the marketer's charge as well.

Exhibit 7.3 shows a basic decision-making model relative to the two stakeholder groups most salient to the nonprofit marketer. This is a simplified version of the larger decision model presented and discussed in a later chapter.

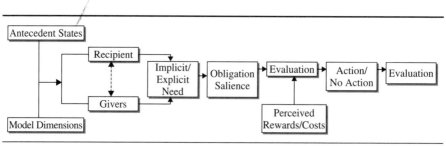

EXHIBIT 7.3　RECIPIENT AND GIVER DECISION MAKING

However, it does suggest that the process is different for nonprofits and quite complex. Yet, there are significant similarities with the concepts and processes discussed throughout this chapter.

Marketers directing nonprofit organizations must have an appreciation for the various stakeholders to which they are responsible. Likewise, they must understand how all these stakeholders view the nonprofit and the ensuing process they employ in order to engage in a transaction. Engaging in marketing research is a necessary prerequisite in order to gain these insights. It cannot be left to chance or the enlightened experience of nonprofit managers.

DECISION MAKING IN A SERVICE CONTEXT

We have already described the consumer decision-making process in Chapter 6. Although the process is similar when purchasing both goods and service products, there are some important differences.

Need Recognition

Recall that the Maslow Hierarchy included five levels: 1. physiological needs (food, water, shelter); 2. safety and security needs (shelter, protection, secure environment); 3. social needs (affection, friendship, acceptance); 4. ego needs (prestige, success, accomplishment, self-esteem), and 5. self-actualization (self-fulfillment, personal enrichment). While there are nonprofit organizations that provide for the first two levels, most focus on the bottom three. These needs are vague, transient, and easily dismissed; creating an awareness of these needs and tangibalizing them is the responsibility of the nonprofit marketer. Marketing education, self-improvement, and life-changing experiences is a tremendous challenge. It starts with a deep understanding of the core problems faced by the specific stakeholder. Often the customer cannot articulate his or her need clearly or completely. Feeling depressed is a symptom that comes from a host of needs. The rigor of the research required is high and may take expertise and dollars. In general, nonprofit organizations do not deal with obvious and superficial needs.

Information Search

Once they recognize the need, consumers obtain information about the service product that may satisfy that need. Finding information is a way of reducing risk and can be obtained through both personal and nonpersonal sources. For service products, personal sources are used most often. One benefit is that personal sources can directly relay information about the experience provided— they can rave about the vacation, religious service, or concert. Also, many nonprofits may not have the resources to provide nonpersonal information. Finally, since nonprofit products are complex and difficult to evaluate, relying on personal sources can provide important insights and reduce risk to the patron. Interestingly, the Internet has now become an important nonpersonal source of product information. It can provide visuals, photographs, virtual tours, online ratings, blogs, and even consumer complaint Web sites. Nonprofit marketers should identify and manage personal information sources, especially word-of-mouth. Yet, they should also create an awareness that basic information is available through nonpersonal sources as well—especially the Internet—and use those nonpersonal outlets to their full advantage.

Evaluation of Alternatives

The evoked set of alternatives—the group of products that a consumer considers acceptable options—tends to be smaller with service products than with goods products. Primarily, this is because nonprofit providers are not as numerous as for-profits. This is especially true once a nonprofit product category is selected. There is also the issue that nonprofit organizations are sometimes unable to provide adequate prepurchase information, thereby restricting fair comparisons. Faced with the task of collecting and evaluating experience qualities, consumers may simply select the first acceptable alternative rather than researching many alternatives. The Internet has the potential to widen the set of alternatives and already has done so in some industries. With regard to professional services, consumers must often choose between performing the service themselves or hiring someone to perform it. A case in point is a parent's decision to stay home to take care of the children or to engage a daycare center to provide child care. Thus, the customer's evoked set frequently includes self-provision of the service. Unless the nonprofit marketer can move its service into a customer's evoked set, purchase is unlikely. The challenge is to identify marketing strategies that will do just that.

Service Purchase

Following the evaluation of alternative solutions, consumers make a decision to purchase a service or do the task themselves. Since most service products are not fully produced at this point in time, the purchase decision is often based on an implied promise. This is when the benefit of being trusted becomes important. For many services, the purchase and production is almost simultaneous, as is the case with blood donation. At other times, consumers pay all or part of the purchase price up front for a service product they will not experience until it is produced for them later. A university education is an obvious example. Long-term donation commitments would also apply.

Because of the inherent risks in purchasing service products, some providers offer free (or deeply discounted) initial treats or extensive tours of facilities in order to reduce risk. It is also helpful to make the purchase process more concrete by spelling out all the details of the exchange in some sort of documentation. Donors receive a receipt, a "thank you" note, and an indication of how their donation will be used; all are attempts to tangibalize service products.

Ultimately, every phase of the purchase and use process must provide a high-level experience. It is how customers evaluate the experience, after all, that influences their decision to repurchase later. Therefore, it is advantageous for the marketer to view the purchase decision as a process, containing a sequence of steps, actions, and activities. It is this combination of steps, the flow of the activities, or the "experience" that is evaluated by the customer. Whether or not the provider acknowledges it or seeks to control this experience in a particular way, it is inevitable that the customer will have an experience—good, bad, or indifferent.

Postpurchase Evaluation

Recall that *dissonance* is a feeling or regret customers have after they make a purchase. It can occur immediately, or days, weeks, or months later. Hopefully, the customer does not experience dissonance and is pleased with the decision as evidenced by measures of satisfaction, exhibited loyalty, or positive word-of-mouth. Because service customers are strongly influenced by the personal opinions of others, understanding and controlling word-of-mouth communications becomes even more important for nonprofit companies. When a memorable and satisfying experience is provided, positive word-of-mouth is likely. When the experience is dissatisfactory, it is critical to have an effective response strategy. Because the customer may provide significant input into the production of the service product, it is possible that the customer may take partial responsibility for his or her dissatisfaction. Understanding this phenomenon is important if dissonance is to be handled effectively. Certainly, unfairly shifting the blame onto the customer is an unwise strategy.

Loyalty appears to be more prevalent with buyers of service products than with buyers of goods products. This difference is attributed to various factors that affect service loyalty: the cost of changing brands (switching costs), the availability of substitutes, social ties to the company, the perceived risk associated with the purchase, and the satisfaction experienced in the past. Because it may be more costly to change brands of services, because awareness of substitutes is limited, and because higher risks may accompany services, consumers are more likely to remain customers of service products longer. Loyalty, however, can quickly disappear if customer needs are not being met. Once again, constant customer monitoring is required.

Consumer behavior is the key element of the internal environment. Although other internal factors are important (e.g., financial condition, marketing strategy, human resources), they are topics beyond the scope of this book, and the reader is directed to one of the many references that illustrate an internal marketing audit. Understanding how the consumer (stakeholder) makes decisions and the variables that affect those decisions is the initial starting point for an effective marketing strategy.

8

CREATING AND MANAGING PRODUCTS

Blue Cross Blue Shield of Minnesota realizes it must adopt a more customer-centric approach and is personalizing the service experience.

—John Ounjian, CIO, Blue Cross Blue Shield of Minnesota

In two years, Habitat for Humanity International has more than doubled the amount it raises annually from companies that provide sponsorship fees, building supplies, and proceeds from the sale of products, and non-marketing promotions for the charity.

The key to expanding such donations to $41 million was not hiring more fund raisers to approach companies or designing new sponsorship opportunities. Instead, the critical factor for Habitat has been a single figure that fund raisers present to companies they are soliciting: $1.8 billion.

That's the value assigned to Habitat for Humanity by Interbrand, a New York consulting agency that analyzes how much corporate brands are worth.

Habitat asked the company to perform a similar evaluation of its "brand", but to adapt the corporate analysis to fit a charitable organization. The company based its evaluation on the amount that Habitat puts into building houses for the needy, after costs and overhead are deducted, forecasts for future income, and the loyalty of Habitat's donors. It also analyzed how the charity's work could be affected by events such as an economic downturn.

Such brand valuations, as they are called, "place a dollar amount on how much your good name is worth," says Jeff Parkhurst, managing director of valuation at Vivaldi Partners, another New York company that assesses corporate and charity brands.

If the estimates are accurate, charity brands are worth quite a bit. United Way of America's brand has a value of $34.7 billion. The Public Broadcasting

Service brand is worth $4.5 billion, enough to place it ahead of for-profit brands Kodak and KFC.

The interest in estimating the worth of a nonprofit brand marks a new phase in the growing sophistication of marketing efforts under way at the nation's charities. Since the late 1990s, many nonprofit groups have borrowed the techniques of corporate marketers and emphasized their brand in a number of ways, such as replacing public service announcements with paid advertising and trying to create consistent messages that aim to fulfill donor's wishes and expectations. The turbulent economy has also prompted many charities to seek ways to demonstrate their value to business leaders.

The importance of the brand was confirmed in a 2005 survey sponsored by the American Marketing Association Foundation. When respondents were asked to identify the three most important characteristics when deciding whether or not to give to a nonprofit charitable organization, the top answers were: "Trust in the Organization," "Personal Belief in the Organization's Goals," and the "Reputation of the Organization"—all brand attributes.[1]

INTRODUCTION

This chapter begins our discussion of the functional areas of marketing. Why do we begin our discussion with product rather than with promotion, distribution, or pricing? The answer is quite simple: none of those other functions serve any useful purpose without a company product that provides consumer satisfaction. Without a product, there is nothing to promote, nothing to distribute, nothing to price. This does not suggest that product is more important, rather, it is the impetus for the other marketing functions. Logically, we should start at the beginning, and the beginning of a marketplace is a set of correct decisions about the product offerings of the firm.

Recall from the previous chapter that service products are created and managed differently than goods products. Exhibit 6.2 depicted several characteristics that distinguish service products. The two most important differences are the fact that service products are mostly intangible, and service products are often inseparable from the customer. Keep these parameters in mind as you read this chapter.

DEFINING THE PRODUCT

In essence, the term "product" refers to anything offered by a firm to provide customer satisfaction, be it tangible or intangible. It can be a single product, a combination of products, a product-service combination, or several related products and services. It normally has at least a generic name (e.g., banana) and usually a brand name (e.g. Chiquita). Although a product is normally defined from the perspective of the manufacturer, it is also important to note two other points-of-view—those of the consumer and other relevant publics.

For a manufacturer like Kraft Foods, their macaroni-and-cheese dinner reflects a food product containing certain ingredients, packaged, distributed, priced and promoted in a unique manner, and requiring a certain return on their investment. For the consumer, the product is a somewhat nutritious food item that is quick and easy to prepare and is readily consumed by the family, especially the kids. For a particular public, such as the Food and Drug Administration, this product reflects a set of ingredients that must meet particular minimum standards, in terms of food quality, storage, and distribution.

Making this distinction is important in that all three perspectives must be understood and satisfied if any product will survive and succeed. Furthermore, this sensitivity to the perspectives of all three is the marketing concept in action. For example, a company might design a weight-reduction pill that not only is extremely profitable but also has a wide acceptance by the consumer. Unfortunately, it cannot meet the safety standards established by the federal government. Likewise, Bird's Eye Food might improve the overall quality of their frozen vegetables and yet not improve the consumers' tendency to buy that particular brand, simply because these improvements were not perceived as either important or noticeable by the consumer. Therefore, an appraisal of a company's product is always contingent upon the needs and wants of the marketer, the consumer, and the relevant publics. We define product as follows: *Anything, either tangible or intangible, offered by a firm; as a solution to the needs and wants of the consumer; is profitable or potentially profitable; and meets the requirements of the various publics governing or influencing society.*

There are four levels of product: core, tangible, augmented, and promised (see Exhibit 8.1). We begin with the notion of the *core product*, which identifies what the consumers feel they are *getting* when they purchase the product. The core benefits derived when an overweight 45-year old male purchases a $350 ten-speed bicycle is not transportation; it is the hope for better health and improved conditioning. In a similar vein, that same individual may install a $20,000 swimming pool in his backyard, not in order to obtain exercise, but to reflect the status he so desperately requires. Both are legitimate product core benefits. Because the core product is so individualized, and oftentimes vague, a full-time task of the marketer is to accurately identify the core product of a particular target market.

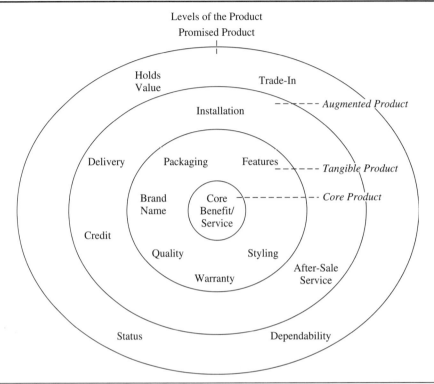

EXHIBIT 8.1 LEVELS OF THE PRODUCT

Once the core product has been indicated, the *tangible product* becomes important. This tangibility is reflected primarily in its quality level, features, brand name, styling, and packaging. Literally every product contains these components to a greater or lesser degree. Unless the product is one-of-a-kind (e.g., oil painting), the consumer will use at least some of these tangible characteristics to evaluate alternatives and make choices. In addition, the importance of each will vary across products, situations, and individuals. For example, for Mr. Smith at age 25, the selection of a particular brand of new automobile (core product = transportation) was based on tangible elements such as styling and brand name (choice = Corvette); at age 45, the core product remains the same, while the tangible components such as quality level and features become important (choice = Mercedes).

At the next level lies the *augmented product*. Every product is backed up by a host of supporting services. Often, the buyer expects these services and would reject the core-tangible product if they were not available. Examples would be restrooms and escalators/elevators in the case of a department store, and warranties and return policies in the case of a lawn mower. Dow Chemical has earned a reputation as a company that will bend over backwards in order to service an account. It means that a Dow sales representative will visit a troubled farmer after-hours in order to solve a serious problem. This extra service is an integral part of the augmented product and a key to their success. In a world with many strong competitors and few unique products, the role of the augmented product is clearly increasing.

The outer ring of the product is referred to as the *promised product*. Every product has an implied promise. An implied promise is a characteristic that is attached to the product over time. The car industry rates brands by their trade-in value. There is no definite promise that a Mercedes-Benz holds its value better than a BMW. There will always be exceptions. How many parents have installed a swimming pool based on the implied promise that their two teenagers will stay home more, or that they will entertain friends more often.

This four-ring perspective of a product changes when we consider a service product. Exhibit 8.2 illustrates the changes. Essentially, because of the intangibility of service products, we view product as three-circles, with the core need remaining in the centre, but the "promised" part of the product moving to the second circle position. "Tangible" and "augmented" merge into a third circle (differentiated), representing all the elements of the service product that can create tangibility and differentiation.

Let's take the example of a potential customer of a regional opera company. Mrs. Schmid is 74 years old and recently widowed, and has always enjoyed

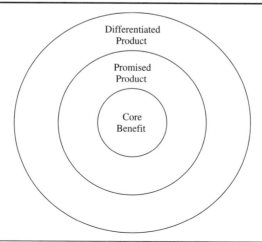

EXHIBIT 8.2   LEVELS OF THE SERVICE PRODUCT

opera, although her husband George refused to go. She received a direct mailer recently, outlining the opera's upcoming season and discounted prices for early subscribers. The core product she hopes to receive is entertainment via beautiful music. The promised product (implied) is a variety of intangibles, including companionship, avoiding loneliness, and spending time with other people who appreciate opera. Finally, there are a host of possible things that can supplement the core product and further differentiate it. Examples include marketing flyers and other communications that highlight the beautiful setting of the opera house, its historic building, the credentials of the direction and singers, the reputation of the opera company (brand), free parking/shuttle, and convenient restaurants. Further differentiation is possible at the opera event itself. Live Entertainment outside, well-trained ushers, and a champagne bar are all examples. Thinking about service products in this three-stage sequence will parallel the consumer's thought process and align the product management system accordingly.

PRODUCT PLANNING AND STRATEGY FORMULATION

The ultimate purpose of this chapter is to introduce the idea that products are planned, and that a whole series of decisions go into this planning process – from the moment the product idea is first conceptualized to the day it is finally deleted. The particular label placed on the company's plan for marketing its product is the *product strategy*. It is part of the marketing strategy and should harmonize with all the other decisions. Like the marketing strategy, it contains three important elements: 1. the determination of product objectives, 2. the development of product plans that will help reach product objectives, and 3. the development of strategies appropriate for the introduction and management of products.

The Determination of Product Objectives

Product objectives are derived from the marketing objectives that precede them. Virtually all the marketing objectives will have either an explicit or implicit impact on the product objectives. For example, the marketing objective: "increase market share in the 45- to 55-year-old market segment, by 8 percent, in the next year," might require the product's cost to be reduced by 20 percent (the product objective/implicit) or redesign the product (the product objective/explicit). Occasionally a marketing objective (e.g., introduce your product into Canada), will have little to do with product objectives, but have a major impact on manufacturing and distribution.

There are a great many objectives that relate to the product management effort. Rather than attempting to provide a complete list, a discussion of the most common product objectives will provide an adequate illustration.

It is safe to conclude that a universal objective is *growth in sales* as a result of the introduction of a new product or the improvement of an existing product. Certainly, there is little need to engage in either product activity unless this objective is present.

An objective related to growth in sales is *finding new uses for established products*. Since this process is generally easier than developing new products, the search for new uses of older products goes on endlessly. For example, Texas Instruments has found numerous uses for their basic product, the semiconductor.

Using excess capacity is another commonly stated product objective. This objective is prompted by the rapid turnover of products and the resulting changes in market share. Of course, such utilization is always a short-run consideration. In the long run, only those products that can generate a continuing level of profitability should be retained, regardless of the problem of excess capacity.

Maintaining or improving market share may also be an objective shared by many companies. In such cases, the emphasis of the firm is on the competitive position rather than attaining a target level of profits. Creating product differentiation is often the primary strategy employed to reach this objective.

Developing a full line of products is another typical objective. A company with a partial product line may well consider the objective of rounding out its product offerings. Often, the sales force provides the impetus for this objective in that they may need a more complete product line to offer their customers, or the resellers themselves may request a greater assortment.

Expanding a product's appeal to new market segments is a common objective. John Deere is attempting to increase its small share of the consumer power products market by aiming at suburbanites and women farmers. They have introduced a series of redesigned lawn and garden tractors, tillers, and snow blowers that are easier for women to operate.

Although this represents a limited selection of objectives, it does suggest that there must be a reason for all product-related activities. These reasons are best expressed in the form of specific objectives.

The Product Plan

Once a marketer has determined a set of product objectives, it is then possible to initiate the activities that constitute the product plan. Although there are a number of ways to look at this process, we have elected to explain this process through the product life cycle concept (PLC). It should be noted that the value of the PLC framework as a planning tool lies at the industry and/or product category level, not the brand level.

The Product Life Cycle

A company has to be good at both developing new products and managing them in the face of changing tastes, technologies, and competition. Evidence suggests that every product goes through a life cycle with predictable costs, sales and profits, as illustrated in Exhibit 8.3. As such, the manager must find new products to replace those that are in the declining stages of the *product life cycle* and learn how to manage products optimally as they move from one stage to the next.

The five stages of the PLC and their components can be defined as follows:

1. *Product development*: the period during which new product ideas are generated, operationalized, and tested prior to commercialization. Costs are high and there is no revenue.
2. *Introduction:* the period during which a new product is introduced. Initial distribution is obtained and promotion is obtained. Costs are very high and the revenue is usually low.
3. *Growth*: the period during which the product is accepted by consumers and the trade. Initial distribution is expanded, promotion is increased, repeat orders from initial buyers are obtained, and word-of-mouth advertising leads to more and more new users. Costs and revenue are approximately the same; with revenue a bit higher.

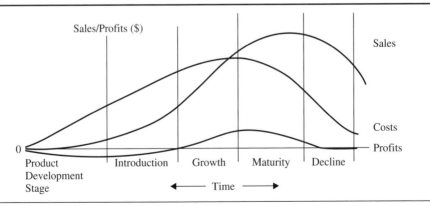

EXHIBIT 8.3 THE PRODUCT LIFE CYCLE

4. *Maturity*: the period during which competition becomes serious. Toward the end of this period, competitors' products cut deeply into the company's market position. Costs are low and revenue is high.
5. *Decline:* the period during which the product becomes obsolete and its competitive disadvantage results in a decline in sales, and eventually, deletion of that product. Costs are low and revenue is even lower.

It should be noted that the predictive capabilities of the product life cycle are dependent upon several factors, both controllable and uncontrollable, and that no two companies may follow the same exact pattern or produce the same results. For example, differences in the competitive situation during each of these stages may dictate different marketing approaches. Some argue that the competitive situation is the single most important factor influencing the duration or height of a product life cycle curve. A useful way of looking at this phenomenon is in the terms of *competitive distinctiveness*. Several years ago, it was suggested that a separation exists between products of *lasting* and *perishable* distinctiveness. Often, new products may, upon introduction, realistically expect a long period of lasting distinctiveness or market protection—through such factors as secrecy, patent protection, and the time and cash required to develop competitive products. However, almost all new products can expect fewer than 5, 10, or 15 years of market protection. In the consumer electronics sector, this may be months instead of years.

Of course, changes in other elements of the marketing mix may also affect the performance of the product during its life cycle. For example, a vigorous promotional program or a dramatic lowering of price may improve the sales picture in the decline period, at least temporarily. The black-and-white TV market illustrated this point. Usually the improvements brought about by nonproduct tactics are relatively short-lived and basic alterations to product offerings provide longer benefits.

Whether one accepts the S-shaped curve as a valid product-sales pattern or as a pattern that holds only for some products (but not of others), the product life cycle concept can still be very useful. It offers a framework for dealing systematically with product management issues and activities. Thus, the marketer must be cognizant of the generalizations that apply to a given product as it moves through the various stages. This process begins with product development and ends with the deletion (discontinuation) of the product.

Key Product Management Decisions

With every product, regardless of where it is in its life cycle, there are certain key decisions that must be made, perhaps repeatedly. These decisions include specifying product features, package design, branding decisions, establishing related services, and legal considerations. Although these decision areas are discussed separately, it should be noted that they all interact with one another, and are monitored and modified when necessary, throughout the life of the product.

Product Features

In a functional sense, the key question is, "Does the product do what the consumer wants it to do?" Does it get clothes clean? Does it quench your thirst? Does it save you money? Does it help me get a better job? Some of these questions can be answered only through product research, but consumer research provides more answers.

While the development of ultra-high-speed computer processing time was a research breakthrough, how the consumer perceives this benefit can be answered only by the consumer. It is possible that the product benefit is so great that it overwhelms the consumer or it is not believed by the consumer. Several new toothpaste manufacturers have recently come out with products that partially restore decayed tooth areas. They have intentionally kept this innovation very low-key, because they feared the consumer would not believe it. Conversely, teeth whitener strips are quite believable and have employed a great deal of marketing.

Product features include such factors as form, color, size, weight, odor, material, and tactile qualities. A new car can offer thousands of alternatives when one considers the exterior and interior options. The smell of fresh bakery products or a good Italian restaurant has clearly enticed many a customer. The product must also be aesthetically pleasing. When the entire product is put together, it must create an appealing, visually attractive and distinctive need satisfier. These same features can be used to tangibalize a service product.

Packaging

With the increased importance placed on self-service marketing, the role of packaging is becoming quite significant. For example, in a typical supermarket a shopper passes about 600 items per minute or one item every tenth of a second. Thus, the only way to get some consumers to notice the product is through displays, shelf-hangers, tear-off coupon blocks, other point-of-purchase devices, and, last but not least, effective packages. Common use of packaging includes protection, containment, communication, and utility/ease of use.

Clearly delineating the role of the product should lead to the actual design of the package: its color, size, texture, location of trademark, name, product information, and promotional materials. Although it many seem somewhat inconceivable, service products have packages as well. Whatever houses the core and promised aspects of the service product can be thought of as its package. A charitable organization is housed in a building along with adjoining parking lots, elevators, restrooms, the office itself, including furniture and artwork, and the appearance of the employees. All these elements represent the package for the organization, and may provide more information than a box of Duncan Hines cake mix. Essentially, the differentiated circle of the service product represents the nonprofit package.

Branding

Any brand name, symbol, design, or combination of these constitutes a branding strategy. The primary function of the *brand* is to identify the product and to distinguish it from those of its competitors. In addition, from the perspective of the buyer, it may simply represent consistent quality or satisfaction, enhance shopping efficiency, or call attention to new products. For the seller, selecting a brand name is one of the key new product decisions and reflects the overall position and marketing program desired by the firm. It is through a brand name that a product can: 1. be meaningfully advertised and distinguished from substitutes, 2. make it easier for the consumer to track down products, and 3. be given legal protection. Also, branding often provides an interesting carryover effect: satisfied customers will associate quality products with an established brand name.

Before going any further it is necessary to distinguish several terms:

- *Brand:* a name, term, sign, symbol, design, or a combination of these that is intended to identify the goods or services of one seller or group of sellers and to differentiate them from those of competitors.
- *Brand names:* that part of a brand that can be vocalized—the utterable.
- *Brand mark:* That part of a brand that can be recognized but is not utterable, such as a symbol, design, or distinctive coloring or lettering.
- *Trademark:* a brand or part of a brand that is given legal protection because it is capable of exclusive appropriation.

As was the case with product design and packaging decisions, branding requires a systematic effort at generating alternative brand names, screening them, and selecting the best alternative. However, before this process begins, a more basic decision must be made. What are the strongest benefits offered by my product? The brand name, logo, color, and music associated with the brand cannot proceed until you first answer this question. Nonprofits have a reputation for doing this backwards. A university will hire a brand consultant to create all the cool brand-related stuff and then determine whether the institution can deliver on the promises represented by the brand. This is a serious error in judgment. Once the first question has been answered, you can move onto the second. What is the basic branding approach to be employed? Three options are available.

First, a strict *manufacturer's branding policy* can be followed. This would mean that the producer refuses to manufacturer merchandise under brands other than his own, although he may sell seconds or irregulars on an unbranded basis. Everything Easter Seals produces has their brand on their products.

Second, an *exclusive distributor's brands policy* could be followed. In this case, the producer does not have a brand of his own but agrees to sell his products only to a particular distributor and carry his brand name (private brands). Many college bookstores sell a host of products, manufactured by someone else, but carrying their brand mark.

The final option is *mixed brand policy*, which includes elements of both extremes and leads to the production of manufacturer's as well as distributor's brands. For example, Firestone sells some tires under their own brand names, and some under private labels. For most companies, both brand names and trademarks are vital in the identification of products. The design process should be guided by research; often the advertising agency is brought in to help. Brand names are mandatory if the manufacturer or distributor intends to use mass advertising. Brand names also make word-of-mouth and advertising effective. Without them, repeat purchases of a particular product would be virtually impossible. Product identification through the brand name is a most important element in the product plan. Branding is critical for nonprofits.

Related Services

Behind every product is a series of supporting services, such as warranties and money-back guarantees. In fact, at times it is difficult to separate the associated services from the product features. This was discussed in reference to Exhibit 6.1. Consequently, companies must constantly monitor the support services offered by the company and its competitors. It is just as important to understand the perceived value of support services as it is to understand key product attributes.

Based on the results of data-gathering devices such as customer surveys, consumer complaints, and suggestion boxes, the product manager can determine the types of services to offer, the form the service will take, and the price charged. For example, consumers are very reluctant to purchase a computer that can be serviced only by sending it to the factory, and paying the postage and high service fee. Dell, however, has been very effective in selling their computers with service contracts and local repair. Banks still vacillate as to whether they should charge the customer for checks, ATM use, safety deposit boxes, and overdrafts.

Product Mix Strategies

As more brands enter the marketplace and lock into a particular share of the market, it becomes more difficult to win and hold buyers. Other changes that occur are: 1. changes in consumer tastes and in particular, the size and characteristics of particular market segments; 2. changes in availability or cost of raw materials and other production or marketing components; and 3. the proliferation of small-share brands of factors that reduce efficiencies in production, marketing, and servicing for existing brands. Because of factors such as these, a decision is made either to identify ways of changing the product to further distinguish it from others, or to design a strategy that will eliminate the product and make way for new products. The specific strategy to accomplish these aims may be in several general categories.

Product modification: It is normal for a product to be changed several times during its life. Certainly, a product should be equal or superior to those of principal competitors. If a change can provide superior satisfaction and win more initial buyers and switchers from other brands, then a change is probably warranted.

Yet the decision should not be approached in a haphazard manner. There are definite risks. For example, a dramatic increase in product quality might price the existing target consumer out of the market, or it might cause him/her to perceive the product as being too good. Similarly, the removal of a particular product feature might be the one characteristic of the product considered most important by the market segment. A key question the marketer must answer before modifying the product is what particular attributes of the product and competing products are perceived as most important by the consumer. Factors such as quality, functions, price, services, design, packaging, and warranty may all be determinants.

This evaluative process requires the product manager to arrange for marketing research studies to learn of improvements buyers might want, evaluate the market reception given to the competitors' improvements, and evaluate improvements that have been developed within the company. Also required is a relationship with the product research and development (R&D) department.

Ideally, R&D should be able to respond quickly to the marketing department's request for product upgrading and should maintain ongoing programs of product improvement and cost reduction. Even suppliers and distributors should be encouraged to submit suggestions.

The US auto industry is a perfect example of how product modification was done correctly and incorrectly. In the early 1990s American automobile manufacturers realized that they couldn't compete with foreign competitors in quality. However, the research showed that many Americans still pined for the American dream (i.e., pack up the family, go off-road, and enjoy the outdoors). There was also the need for carpooling. Finally, gasoline was cheap ($1.18 per gallon in 1990). The result was the SUV, which prospered throughout the 1990s, and was the biggest money maker the industry ever had. This all changed in 2004 when the price of oil hit $30 per barrel and it became too expensive to drive an SUV. Ford, Toyota, Honda, and others quickly moved to doing research on hybrids and it has become a growing market as this book goes to press. Is the SUV dead? Probably.

Service products contain both intangible and tangible features. Making changes in these features should be done carefully, fully supported with sound marketing research.

Product Line Decisions: A product line can contain one product or hundreds. The number of products in a product line refers to its *depth*, while the number of separate product lines owned by a company is the product line *width*. Several decisions are related to the product line.

There are two basic strategies that deal with whether the company will attempt to carry every conceivable product needed and wanted by the consumer or whether they will carry selected items. The former is a *full-line* strategy while the latter is called a *limited-line* strategy. Few full-line manufacturers attempt to provide items for every conceivable market niche. And few limited-line manufacturers would refuse to add an item if the demand were great enough. Each strategy has its advantages and disadvantages.

Line extensions strategies involve adding products related to the initial product, whose purchase or use is keyed to the product. For example, a computer company may provide an extensive selection of software to be used with its primary hardware. This strategy will not only increase sales volume, it also strengthens the manufacturer's name associated with the owner of the basic equipment, and offers dealers a broader line. These added items tend to be similar to existing brands with no innovations. They also have certain risks. Often a company may not have a high level of expertise either producing or marketing those related products. Excessive costs, inferior products, and the loss of goodwill with distributors and customers are all possible deleterious outcomes. There is also a strong possibility that such a product decision could create conflict within the channel of distribution. In the computer example just described, this company may have entered the software business over the strong objection of their long-term supplier of software. If their venture into the software business fails, reestablishing a positive relationship with a supplier could be quite difficult.

A line extensions strategy should only be considered when the producer is certain that the capability exists to efficiently manufacture a product that compares well with the base product. The producer should also be sure of profitable competition in this new market.

Line-filling strategies occur when a void in the existing product line has not been filled or a new void has developed due to the activities of competitors or the request of consumers. Before considering such a strategy several key questions should be answered:

- Can the new product support itself?
- Will it cannibalize existing products and will existing outlets be willing to stock it?
- Will competitors fill the gap if we don't, and what will happen if we don't act?

Assuming that we decide to fill out our product line further, there are several ways of implementing this decision. Three are most common:

1. *Product proliferation:* the introduction of new varieties of the initial product or products that are similar (e.g., a ketchup manufacturer introduces hickory-flavored and pizza-flavored barbecue sauces and a special hot dog sauce).
2. *Brand extension:* strong brand preference allows the company to introduce the related product under the brand umbrella (e.g., Jell-O introduces pie filling and diet deserts under the Jell-O brand name).
3. *Private branding:* producing and distributing a related product under the brand of a distributor or other producers (e.g., Firestone producing a less expensive tire for Wall-Mart).

In addition to the demand of consumers or pressures from competitors, there are other legitimate reasons to engage in these tactics. First, the additional products may have a greater appeal and serve a greater customer base than did the original product. Second, the additional product or brand can create excitement both for the manufacturer and distributor. Third, shelf space or customer attention taken by the new product means it cannot be used by competitors. Finally, the danger of the original product becoming outmoded is hedged. Yet, there is serious risk that must be considered as well:

unless there are markets for the proliferations that will expand the brand's share, the newer forms will cannibalize the original product and depress profits.

Line-pruning strategies involve the process of getting rid of products that no longer contribute to company profits. A simple fact of marketing is that sooner or later a product will decline in demand and require pruning. Timex has stopped selling home computers. Hallmark has stopped selling talking cards.

Service products can employ these exact same product line strategies, even though much of their product is intangible and/or co-created by the customer. The Marriott Corporation is a service product manufacturer with a vast product line, containing both breadth and depth. In the last decade they have invested millions of dollars in line-extending their primary business traveler product, for example, their Residence Inns. They have added depth to this product line through Journeyplace Suites, Marriott Executive Stay and Marriott Executive Apartment.

Product Deletion

Eventually a product reaches the end of its life. This is the least understood stage of product management, because we human beings are very reluctant to think about death, even the death of a product.

There are several reasons for deleting a product. First, when a product is losing money, it is a prime deletion candidate. In regard to this indication, it is important to make sure that the loss is truly attributable to the product and not just a quirk in the company's accounting system. Similarly, these may be temporary changes in the market, such as a union strike or a road construction that has a deleterious impact on the brand for a short period of time.

Second, there are times when a company with a long product line can benefit if the weakest of these products are dropped. This thinning of the line is referred to as *product-line simplification*. Product overpopulation spreads a company's productive, financial, and marketing resources very thin. Moreover, an excess of products in the line, some of which serve overlapping markets, not only creates internal competition among the company's own products, but also creates confusion in the minds of consumers. Consequently, a company may apply several criteria to all its products and delete those that fare worst.

A third reason for deleting a product is that problem products absorb too much management attention. Many of the costs incurred by weak products are indirect: management time, inventory costs, promotion expenses, decline of company reputation, and so forth.

Missed opportunity costs reflect the final reason for product deletion. Even if a mature product is making a profit contribution and its indirect cost consequences are recognized and considered justifiable, the company might still be better off without the product because of its opportunity costs. The opportunity cost of a mature product is the profit contribution that a new and healthy product could produce if the effort and resources being devoted to the mature item were redirected.

The notion of deleting products in the nonprofit sector is often given little consideration. The general mission of most nonprofits is to provide products to their customers that by definition are not profitable. If they were, the private and government sectors would be producing them. Consequently, the criteria just discussed for product deletion determination may have to be modified or ignored. However, we offer two other criteria that apply in deleting nonprofit products. First, if the product no longer relates to the mission of the organization, it should be deleted. Examples include the many products that nonprofits sell for additional revenue, but have little to do with the core mission. Second, if the maintenance/retention of a product seriously jeopardizes the mission or life of the nonprofit, it should be considered for deletion. A cost-benefit analysis should be conducted on every product every year.

STRATEGIES FOR DEVELOPING NEW PRODUCTS

For several decades, business has come increasingly to the realization that new and improved products may hold the key to their survival and ultimate success. Consequently, professional management has become an integral part of this process. As a result, many firms develop new products based on an orderly procedure, employing comprehensive and relevant data, and intelligent decision making.

Defining the "New" in a New Product

The determination of what constitutes a "new" product remains one of the most difficult questions faced by the marketer. Does the most recent TV model introduced by Sony represent a new product even though 95 percent of the product remains the same as last year's model? Are packaged salads a new product, or is the package the only part that is really new?

Indeed, companies have often been guilty of using the word "new" in conjunction with some questionable products. For example, older products have simply been marketed in new packages or containers but have been identified as new products by the manufacturer. Flip-top cans, plastic bottles, and screw-on caps have all been used to create this image of newness. Industrial companies have been guilty of similar actions. Computer manufacturers, for instance, have slightly modified some of the basic hardware or developed some software for a particular customer (banks, churches), and have felt free to claim newness. Finally, manufacturers may add an existing product to their product line and call it new, even though it is not new to the consumer.

Does technology make a product new, or features, even the price? Is it important to understand the concept of "new" in a new product, since there is sufficient evidence that suggests that each separate category of "newness" may require a different marketing strategy.

Perhaps the best way to approach this problem is to view it from two perspectives: that of the consumer and that of the manufacturer.

The Consumer's Viewpoint

There are a variety of ways that products can be classified as new from the perspective of the consumer. *Degree of consumption modification* and *task experience* serve as two bases for classification. Robertson provides an insightful model when he suggests that new products may be classified according to how much behavioral change or new learning is required by the consumer in order to use the product.

The continuum proposed by Robertson and shown in Exhibit 8.4 depicts the three primary categories based on the disrupting influence the use of the product has on established consumption patterns. It is evident that most new products would be considered continuous innovations. Annual model changes in automobiles, appliances, and sewing machines are examples. Portable hair dryers, diet soda, and aerobic dance CDs reflect products in the middle category. True innovations are rare.

Although conceptualizing new products in terms of how they modify consumer consumption patterns is useful, there is another basis for classification. *New task experience* can also be a criteria. An individual may live in a house

Continuous Innovations	Dramatically Continuous Innovations	Discontinuous Innovations
←		→
Least disrupting influence on established consumption patterns	Some disrupting influence on established consumption patterns	Involves establishment of new consumption patterns and the creation of previously unknown products

EXHIBIT 8.4   CONTINUUM FOR CLASSIFYING NEW PRODUCTS

for several years without ever having to repair a broken window. One day a mishap occurs, and Mr. Smith is forced to go to the hardware store to buy the necessary supplies required to install a new window pane. As he has no experience at all with this task, all those products are new to Mr. Smith. The glazing compound, the new glass and molding, and metal tacks, as well as the appropriate tools, are brand new to Mr. Smith. Using the model proposed by Robertson, products can also be placed on a continuum according to degree of task experience. Clearly, a product that has existed for a great many years, such as a carpenter's level, may be perceived as totally new by the person attempting to build a straight wall. In this case, newness is in the eye of the beholder.

The obvious difficulty with this classification is that it tends to be person-specific. Just because replacing a new washer in your bathroom faucet constitutes a new product for you doesn't mean it is a new product for me. However, it is conceivable that marketing research would show that for certain types of products, large groups of people have very limited experience. Consequently, the marketing strategy for such products might include very detailed instructions, extra educational materials, and sensitivity on the part of the sales clerk to the ignorance of the customer.

Another possible facet of a new task experience is to be familiar with a particular product, but not familiar with all of its functions. For example, a homemaker may have a microwave oven that she uses primarily for heating food items and making breakfast foods. Suppose that one afternoon her conventional oven breaks and she must deliver several cakes she has donated to a church bazaar. Unfortunately, she has not baked them yet and is forced to use her microwave, a brand-new task.

The Firm's Viewpoint

Classifying products in terms of their newness from the perspective of the manufacturer is also important. There are several levels of possible newness that can be derived through changes either in production, marketing, or some combination of both.

Based on a schema developed by Eberhard Scheuing, new products, from the perspective of the business, can take the following forms:

1. *Changing the marketing mix*: One can argue that whenever some elements of the marketing mix (product planning, pricing, branding, channels of distribution, advertising, etc.) is modified, a new product emerges.

2. *Modification*: Certain features (normally product design) of an existing product are altered, and may include external changes, technological improvements, or new areas of applicability.
3. *Differentiation*: Within one product line, variations of the existing products are added.
4. *Diversification*: New product lines are added for other applications.

A final consideration in defining "new" is the legal ruling provided by the Federal Trade Commission (FTC). Since the term is so prevalent in product promotion, the FTC felt obliged to limit the use of "new" to products that are entirely new or changed in a *functionally significant* or *substantial respect*. Moreover, the term can be used for a six-month period of time. Given the limited uniqueness of most new products, this ruling appears reasonable.

Strategies for Acquiring New Products

Most large and medium-sized firms are diversified, operating in different business fields. It would be unrealistic to assume that the individual firm is either capable or willing to develop all new products internally. In fact, most companies simultaneously employ both internal and external sources for new products. Both are important to the success of a business.

Internal Sources

Most major corporations conduct research and development to some extent. However, very few companies make exclusive use of their own internal R&D. On the contrary, many companies make excellent use of specialists to supplement their own capabilities. Still, to depend extensively upon outside agencies for success is to run a business on the brink of peril. Ideally, the closer the relationship between the new business and existing product lines, the better the utilization of R&D will be. The National Science Foundation (NSF) divides R&D into three parts:

1. *Basic research*: original investigations for the advancement of scientific knowledge that do not have specific commercial objectives, although they may be in fields of present or potential interest to the reporting company
2. *Applied research*: directed toward practical applications of knowledge, specific ends concerning products and processes
3. *Development*: the systematic use of scientific knowledge directed toward the production of useful materials, devices, systems, or methods, including design and development of prototypes and processes

External Sources

External approaches to new product development range from the acquisition of entire businesses to the acquisition of a single component needed for the internal new product development effort of the firm. The following external sources for new products are available to most firms.

- *Mergers and Acquisitions.* Acquiring another company already successful in a field your company wishes to enter is an effective way of introducing products while still diversifying. Research suggests that mergers and acquisitions can take place between companies of various sizes and backgrounds, and that first experiences with this process tend to be less than satisfactory. Even large marketers such as Microsoft engage in acquisitions.

  Historically, nonprofit organizations have remained very proprietary. Experts suggest that it is too easy to become a nonprofit and that there are too many nonprofits. There are not enough dollars to support all these institutions. Mergers and resource-sharing are valuable solutions. Every nonprofit should constantly be looking for these opportunities and put aside the notion that these organization alone can solve the problem at hand.

- *Licenses and Patents.* A patent and the related license arise from legal efforts to protect property rights of investors of those who own inventions. A patent is acquired from the U.S. Patent Office and provides legal coverage for a period of seventeen years, which means all other manufacturers are excluded from making or marketing the product. However, there are no foolproof ways to prevent competition. There are two main types of patents: those for products and those for processes. The first covers only the product's physical attributes while the latter covers only a phase of a production procedure, not the product. The patent holder has the right to its assignment or license. An *assignment* is any outright sale, with the transfer of all rights of ownership conveyed to the assignee. A *license* is a right to use the patent for certain considerations in accordance with specific terms, but legal title to the patent remains with the licensor.

- *Joint Ventures.* When two or more companies create a third organization to conduct a new business, a *joint venture* exists. This organization structure emerges primarily when either the risk or capital requirements are too great for any single firm to bear. Lack of technical expertise, limited distribution networks, and unfamiliarity with certain markets are other possible reasons. Joint ventures are common in industries such as oil and gas, real estate, and chemicals, or between foreign and domestic partners.

Joint ventures have obvious applications to product development. For example, small firms with technological resources are afforded an opportunity to acquire capital or marketing expertise provided by a larger firm.

The New Product Development Process

Evidence suggests that there may be as many varieties of new product development systems as there are kinds of companies. For the most part, most companies do have a formal comprehensive new product development system, and the evolution of such systems was not necessarily the result of systematic planning. The list of activities suggested in Exhibit 8.5 illustrates the extensiveness of this process. Because of the complexity of the process, it is important that the general guidelines of effective management be applied to new product development.

Before starting our discussion of the eight-step process of new product development, a necessary caveat should be considered: a great many new products fail. Depending on definitions used for products actually introduced, failure rates range between 20 percent and 30 percent, but have been as high as 80 percent. Of more concern than the level of failure are the reasons for failure. Possibilities include technical problems, bad timing, misunderstanding the consumer, actions by competitors, and misunderstanding the environment.

Step 1: Generating New Product Ideas

Generating new product ideas is a creative task that requires a specific way of thinking. Gathering ideas is easy, but generating good ideas is another story. Examples of internal sources are:

- *Basic research:* Many companies, such as DuPont, have several scientists who are assigned the task of developing new product ideas and related technology.
- *Manufacturing:* People who manufacture products often have ideas about modifications and improvements, as well as completely new concepts.
- *Salespersons:* Company salespeople and representatives can be a most helpful source of ideas, since they not only know the customer best, but they also know the competition and the relative strengths and weaknesses of existing products.

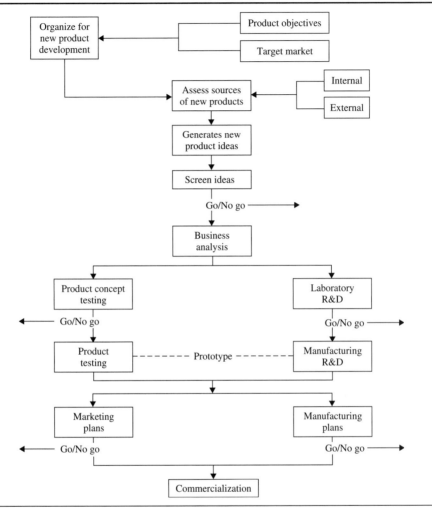

EXHIBIT 8.5   THE NEW PRODUCT DEVELOPMENT PROCESS

- *Top management:* The good top executive knows the company's needs and resources, and is a keen observer of technological trends and of competitive activity.

External sources of new product ideas are almost too numerous to mention. A few of the more useful are:

- *Secondary sources of information*: There are published lists of new products, available licenses, and ideas for new product ventures.

- *Competitors*: Good influences about competitive product development can be made on the basis of indirect evidence gained from salespeople and from other external sources, including suppliers, resellers, and customers.
- *Customers*: Frequently customers generate new product ideas, or at least relay information regarding their problems that new and improved products would help to solve.
- *Resellers*: A number of firms use councils or committees made up of representative resellers to assist in solving various problems, including product development.
- *Foreign markets*: Many companies look toward foreign markets, especially Western Europe, because they have been so active in product development.

There are probably as many approaches to collecting new product ideas as there are sources. For most companies, taking a number of approaches is preferable to a single approach. Still, coming up with viable new product ideas is rare.

Step 2: Screening Product Development Ideas

The second step in the product development process is *screening*. It is a critical part of the development activity. Product ideas that do not meet the organization's objectives should be rejected. If a poor product idea is allowed to pass the screening state, it wastes effort and money in subsequent stages until it is later abandoned. Even more serious is the possibility of screening out a worthwhile idea.

There are two common techniques for screening new product ideas; both involve the comparison of a potential product idea against criteria of acceptable new products. The first technique is a simple checklist. For example, new product ideas can be rated on a scale ranging from very good to poor, in respect to criteria such as: value added, sales volume, patent protection, affect on present products, and so forth. Unfortunately, it is quite difficult for raters to define what is fair or poor. Also, it does not address the issue of the time and expense associated with each idea, nor does it instruct with regard to the scores. A second technique goes beyond the first: the criteria are assigned importance weights and then the products are rated on a point scale measuring product compatibility. These scores are then multiplied by their respective weights and added to yield a total score for the new product idea. Exhibit 8.6 provides an example of both these techniques for screening new product ideas.

		Rating					
	Weight	Very Good (5)	Good (4)	Fair (3)	Poor (2) (1)	Unweighted Value	Weighted Value
Customer utilities							
- Amusement	.1	X				5	.6
- Comfort	.1			X		3	.3
- Convenience	.2		X			4	.8
- Satisfaction	.3		X			4	1.2
- Easy to use	.1			X		3	.3
Ability to create effective sales appeals	.3		X			4	1.2
Price	.1				X	2	.2
Product quality	.2			X		3	.6
Product profitability	.2			X		3	.6
Attractiveness of product to customers	.1		X			4	.4
Ability to produce product in large volumes	.3	X				5	l.5
Ability of new product in helping sale of other products	.1				X	1	.1
Requires low capital investment	.3		X			4	1.2
Product can be promoted through existing advertising	.2			X		3	.6
Product can be produced in existing facilities	.3		X			4	1.2
Product can be distributed through existing channels	.3				X	3	.9
Strength of competition	.2				X	3	.6
Patent situation	.1				X	2	.2
Total Score						60	12.4

EXHIBIT 8.6   SCREENING PRODUCT IDEAS

Step 3: Business Analysis

After the various product ideas survive their initial screen, very few viable proposals will remain. Before the development of prototypes can be decided upon, however, a further evaluation will be conducted to gather additional information on these remaining ideas in order to justify the enormous costs required. The focus of the business analysis is primarily on profits, but other considerations such as social responsibilities may also be involved.

The first step in the business analysis is to examine the projected demand. This would include two major sources of revenue: the sales of the product and the sales or license of the technology developed for or generated as a by-product of the given product.

A complete cost appraisal is also necessary as part of the business analysis. It is difficult to anticipate all the costs that will be involved in product development, but the following cost items are typical:

- Expected development costs, including both technical and marketing R&D
- Expected set-up costs (production, equipment, distribution)
- Operating costs that account for possible economies of scale and learning curves
- Marketing costs, especially promotion and distribution
- Management costs

Step 4: Technical and Marketing Development

A product that has passed the screen and business analysis stages is ready for technical and marketing development. Technical development involves two steps. The first is the applied laboratory research required to develop exact product specifications. The goal of this research is to construct a prototype model of the product that can be subjected to further study. Once the prototype has been created, manufacturing methods research can be undertaken to plan the best way of making the product in commercial quantities under normal manufacturing conditions. This is an extremely important step, because there is a significant distinction between what an engineer can assemble in a laboratory and what a factory worker can produce.

While the laboratory technicians are working on the prototype, the marketing department is responsible for testing the new product with its intended consumers and developing the other elements of the marketing mix. The testing process usually begins with the concept test. The *product concept* is a synthesis or a description of a product idea that reflects the core element of the proposed product. For example, a consumer group might be assembled and the interview session might begin with the question: "How about something that would do this...?"

The second aspect of market development involves consumer testing of the product idea. This activity must usually await the construction of the prototype or, preferably, limited-run production models. Various kinds of consumer preference can be conducted. The product itself can be exposed to consumer taste or use tests. Packaging, labeling, and other elements in the mix can be similarly studied. Comparison tests are also used.

Step 5: Manufacturing Planning

Assuming that the product has cleared the technical and marketing development stage, the manufacturing department is asked to prepare plans for producing it. The plan begins with an appraisal of the existing production plant and the necessary tooling required achieving the most economical production. Fancy designs and material might be hard if not impossible to accommodate on existing production equipment: new machinery is often time-consuming and costly to obtain. Compromise between attractiveness and economy is often necessary.

Finally, manufacturing planning must consider the other areas of the organization and what is required of each. More specifically, they should determine how to secure the availability of required funds, facilities, and personnel at the intended time, as well as the methods of coordinating this effort.

Step 6: Marketing Planning

It is at this point that the marketing department moves into action again. The product planner must prepare a complete marketing plan-one that starts with a statement of objectives and ends with the fusion of product, distribution, promotion, and pricing into an integrated program of marketing action.

Step 7: Test Marketing

Test marketing is the final step before commercialization: the objective is to test all the variability in the marketing plan including elements of the product. Test marketing represents an actual launching of the total marketing program. But it is done on a limited basis.

Three general questions can be answered through test marketing. First, the overall workability of the marketing plan can be assessed. Second, alternative allocations of the budget can be evaluated. Third, determining whether a new product introduction is inspiring users to switch from their previous brands to the new one and holding them there through subsequent repeat purchases is determined. In the end, the test market should include an estimate of sales, market share, and financial performance over the life of the product.

Step 8: Commercialization

At last the product is ready to go. It has survived the development process and it is now on the way to commercial success. How can it be guided to that marketing success? It is the purpose of the life cycle marketing plan to answer this question. Such a complete marketing program will, of course, involve additional decisions about distribution, promotion, and pricing.

Although this detailed new product development process appears far removed from a nonprofit organization, the process does apply. In fact, if nonprofits were willing to approach new product development in this systematic manner, they might find that fewer mistakes are made and that more of their new products would achieve their objectives.

CREATING THE EXPERIENCE FOR NONPROFIT PRODUCTS

While all the fundamental concepts and principles of product management discussed in this chapter apply to service products and nonprofit products especially, certain adjustments are necessary. Recall from an earlier chapter that service products contain several unique characteristics that distinguish them from goods products:

- Services are intangible acts;
- The customer is present during the service process;
- Production and consumption are inseparable; and
- Services cannot be inventoried.

In essence, service products comprise the interaction of people, processes, and the physical environment. If done correctly, this fragile, interconnected system produces a positive, memorable experience. This experience closely resembles a live theatrical production, consisting of actions (people), scripts (processes and procedures), and sets (physical environments). Ultimately, designing a comprehensive customer-centric superior service experience hinges on how well the service provider integrates these separate components to generate great performance and a great experience for the customer.

The following key steps should be followed in the creation and management of nonprofit products:

Step 1. *What are the objectives?* Because nonprofit organizations often have limited resources and are required via the mission statement to offer products that are often unprofitable, creating realistic and achievable product objectives is particularly important. This mandates that the nonprofit organization carefully assess the market, the competitive situation, and the resource availability. Specific questions answered through this process include: What are our resources? Are these resources being allocated effectively? Are additional resources available? What is the profile of our existing customers? Potential customers? What are the key trends in our market? Who are our competitors? What are their strengths and weaknesses? What is the reputation of our brand? What is our market position? What marketing tactics do we do well? Which ones do we do poorly? Can the organization afford to allocate the physical facilities, equipment, information technology, and human resources needed to market existing products more effectively; add enhancements designed to improve competitive appeal; or create new service offerings? Conversely, does an analysis of these operating assets suggest new opportunities to improve their utilization in the marketplace? The answers to all these questions will help the nonprofit marketer create objectives that are meaningful, clear, realistic, and doable.

Step 2. *What are the core benefits offered to customers and the costs that will be incurred?* Answering this question considers both core and augmented product elements; their characteristics in terms of both performance level and style; and where, when, and how customers will be able to have access to them. The related costs of the service product includes not only money but also defines of the amount of time, mental hassle, physical effort, and negative sensory experiences likely to be incurred by customers receiving these services.

Step 3. *What is the total nature of the service offering?* Planners of service products must take a holistic view of the entire performance they want customers to experience. As such, the product design must address and integrate three key components: the core product, the promised product, and the differentiated product. The core product supplies the central solution to the problem. It also addresses two basic questions for the marketer: 1. What business are we in? 2. What is the buyer really buying? Thus, a museum is in the business of providing historical education. Or, is it simply providing an interesting diversion? The promised product augments the core product, enhancing its value and appeal. The extent and levels of the promised product often plays a role in positioning the core product. Adding tangibility to the implied promise increases the level of perceived performance and can add value to the core product.

The third component deals with the differentiators that both the core product and the promised product possess. In its broadest sense, the design of the service offering must address how the various service components are delivered to the customer, the nature of the customer's role in these processes, how long delivery lasts, and the prescribed level and style to be offered. Each of the four categories of process—people processing, possession processing, mental stimulus processing, and information processing—has different implications for customer involvement, operational procedures, the degree of customer contact with service personnel and facilities, and requirements for supplementary services. A historical preservation organization can differentiate services via their interactive website, their education program, their annual conference, and their free site-evaluation service. Examples of differentiators are shown in Exhibit 8.7.

PRODUCTS VIEWED AS SERVICESCAPES

The servicescape model, developed by Mary Jo Bitner, provides another way of looking at the elements constituting the service product (see Exhibit 8.8). It shows that the main dimensions in the service environment include ambient conditions, space/functionality, and signs, symbols, and artifacts. Ambient conditions include those elements that are hardly noticed by the consumer, unless they are deficient. Examples include temperature, lighting, music, noise, scent, colors, and cleanliness. We all have a personal tolerance zone about many of these factors, and some are stereotypically gender-specific, for instance, women generally like their environment warmer and cleaner than men. Spatial layout refers to the ways in which machinery, equipment, friendship, and waiting areas are arranged, the size and shape of those items, and the spatial relationship among them. Functionality refers to the ability of the same items/places to facilitate the various tasks. For example, a waiting room that can't handle peak capacity may mean no one receives services. Many items in the physical environment serve as explicit or implicit signals that communicate information about the environment to its users. Poor signage confuses people, while good signage reduces crowding and stress. Certificates, furniture, artwork, floor coverings, and personal objects can all affect customer perceptions. Because individuals tend to perceive these dimensions holistically, the key to effective product design is how well each dimension fits together with everything else.

Next, the model shows that there are customer and employee response moderators. This means that the same service environment can have different effects on different customers, depending on what they like. In addition,

INFORMATION
- Directions
- Hours of Operation
- Prices
- Usage Instructions

- Warnings
- Conditions of Sale
- Notification of Changes
- Confirmation/Receipts

ORDER TAKING
- Applications
- Orders/Entry
- Reservations/Check-In

BILLING
- Periodic Statements
- Invoices
- Verbal Statements

- Machine Displays
- Self-Billing

PAYMENTS
- Self-Service
- Direct to Payee or Intermediary
- Automatic Deductions

CONSULTATION
- Advice
- Auditing
- Personal Counseling

- Tutoring/Training
- Management or Technical Consulting

HOSPITALITY
- Greeting
- Food/Beverage
- Toilets and Washrooms

- Waiting Facilities/Amenities
- Transport
- Security

EXCEPTIONS
- Special Requests

- Problem Solving

- Handling Complaints/Suggestions/
  Compliments
- Restitution

SAFEKEEPING
- Caring for Possessions Customers
  Bring with Them
- Caring for Goods Purchased
  (or Rented) by Customers

EXHIBIT 8.7 DIFFERENTIATORS

it suggests that it's important that service product designers become aware of how a particular environment enhances the productivity of frontline personnel and the quality of service they deliver. For example, patients who come into a clinic that is designed to calm and sooth their anxieties (emotional response)

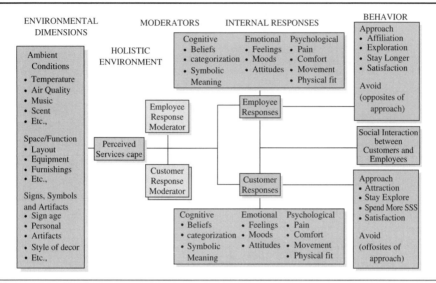

EXHIBIT 8.8   THE SERVICESCAPES MODEL

may believe as a result that the doctors and staff are caring and competent (cognitive responses). This same outcome may result for the doctors and staff. Similarly, particular environmental cues such as the type of office furniture, the apparel worn by the director, and the presence of productive/happy volunteers may connote to the potential donor that this nonprofit is client-centric and trustworthy. Therefore, both a positive cognitive and emotional outcome prevails.

Finally, the model indicates that specific behaviors should result from the creation of an experience process. In the case of the for-profit sector, desired behaviors tend to be trial, purchase, and repurchase. The desired behaviors indicated in Exhibit 8.6 tend to relate more to processes and interactions. First, there are specific individual behaviors that relate to both employees (including volunteers) and customers/clients. In general, the nonprofit marketer wants to elicit approach behaviors from both groups. Approach behaviors include all positive behaviors that might be directed toward a particular process, such as desire to stay, explore, work, affiliate, and recommend. Avoidance behaviors produce the opposite behaviors. While one might assume that approach behaviors would always be a priority, there are instances when the avoidance behavior route is necessary. An example would be a battered women's shelter where everything is done to ensure the facility remains secret from the abusive partner. Even the ability of nonprofit staff and volunteers to do their jobs effectively is influenced by all these factors. Adequate space, proper equipment, comfortable temperature and air quality all contribute to an employee's comfort and joy. Neither staff nor volunteers want to work in an environment where the executive director insists on bringing her incontinent dog to the office every day!

In addition to its effects on their individual behaviors, the servicescape influences the nature and quality of customer and employee interactions, most directly in interpersonal services. The physical environment can affect the nature of social interactions in terms of the duration of the interaction and the actual progression of events. In many nonprofit situations, a firm may want to ensure a particular progression of events and limit the duration of the service. Environmental variables such as physical proximity, seating arrangements, capacity, and flexibility can define the possibilities and limits of social episodes such as those occurring between customers and employees, or customers and other customers. The close physical proximity of staff and customers at a shelter, clinic, or church may result in dysfunctional behavior by both. Likewise, the dynamics that play out for those participating in a wilderness experience can range from creating life-long friends to life-long enemies.

The following guidelines are offered to better manage the service:

- Appreciate the importance that physical evidence can play in creating a positive experience, and think about dealing with it strategically.
- Attempt to map your service. Identify the entire process, with a focus on key contact points where problems can often occur.
- Clarify the role the servicescape plays in delivering the entire product experience. In some cases the elements of the servicescape are critical, while in other instances they are irrelevant.
- Identify opportunities that enhance physical evidence. Nonprofits sell intangibles. The more positive tangible cues that you can add to the experience the better off you will be.
- Be willing to modify the evidence on an as-needed basis. Even if the vision, goals, and objectives of the organization do not change, time and consumer expectations necessitate change and modernization.
- Physical evidence crosses functional boundaries. Creating and providing physical evidence is often the responsibility of several different functions within the organization. Human resources may provide uniforms, while IT provides technology, and public relations selects

artwork. A multifunction team approach to physical evidence is often most effective.

REFERENCE

1. This section excerpted from: Holly Hall, "What's in a Charity's Name?", *The Chronicle of Philanthropy*, August 5, 2005: pp. 31–32.

9

COMMUNICATING TO MASS MARKETS

Marketers will always strive to make things sound more impressive than they are.

—George Carlin

The center for Women in Transition, in Holland, Michigan, faced a tremendous challenge. How do you create a new brochure for donors that sensitively and accurately portrayed the hardships faced by women and children affected by domestic and sexual violence? Beth Smith interviewed several of the center's clients and discovered that the decision for a woman to leave this hostile environment is not a snap decision, it is a process. The intent of the brochures was to educate the charity's donors to a better understanding of the systematic nature of abuse.

Chris Cook, owner of Fairly Painless Advertising, recognized at the outset that the women featured were very hesitant to be identified in public as victims of abuse. It was essential that they be presented as beacons of hope and examples of success. Essentially, the center helped facilitate that accomplishment

The brochure used black-and-white photography as a key design element, portraying women of diverse ages and ethnicities, to illustrate how widespread abuse is. All the women were clients of the center, and excerpts of their life stories were the focus of the brochure. The goal was to show potential donors that the stereotypes about abuse are not true and that many profiles exist.

The brochure was considered a huge success. Attendance at the fundraising event following the mailout of the brochures raised $67,000, a 50 percent increase over the previous year. In addition, the visibility gained from the brochure helped expand the center volunteer rolls by 15 percent.[1]

INTRODUCTION

How can a nonprofit marketer clearly and effectively communicate their story (message) in a society that is so overcommunicated that the typical consumer is both overwhelmed with the vast number of messages and annoyed at the thousands of messages that have no relevance whatsoever to that person's needs and wants? The amount of sameness and the amount of communication clutter is extensive. Yet, as we have noted throughout this text, the needs and capabilities of marketers vary, and not all marketers are blessed with a creative genius. Nor do all marketers require a multimillion dollar national advertising campaign in order to reach objectives. All marketers, however, must learn to communicate their strategy to their target market. It is an especially necessary tool for nonprofits.

The concept of Integrated Marketing Communication (IMC) is offered as a general framework, which can be employed by marketers in order to design a comprehensive and effective program of communication. It acknowledges the inherent differences between marketers and builds upon the reality that "every company is cast in the role of communicator." Ultimately, it is the choice of each company whether this communication process will be performed in a haphazard, unplanned way, or whether it will be guided by stated objectives and implemented through effective strategies.

This chapter introduces the concept of IMC, a framework for organizing the persuasive communication efforts of the business. Because of its visibility, many consumers feel that they already know a great deal about IMC, or at least about advertising. Most hold either a somewhat positive or negative attitude toward advertising, aggressive salespeople, coupons, and so forth. This is a case when a little bit of information can be a dangerous thing.

This chapter also provides a discussion of four of the IMC mix elements— advertising, sales promotion, public relations, and personal selling. We begin our discussion with an explanation of the role IMC plays in the marketing strategy.

THE ROLE OF IMC

The heart of every transactional exchange is communication between parties. The buyer seeks certain basic information about product features, price, quality, support service, reputation of the seller, and so forth. All this information is intended to assess how close each alternative is to meeting desired needs and wants. We seek information to reduce possible risk associated with the transaction. Presumably, the more solid the information we have, the more secure we feel in our decision. The seller also desires information. The seller wants to know whether you qualify as a buyer (i.e., do you really need the product and can you pay for it), which product features are important to you, what other choices you are considering, are you ready to buy, how much do you know about my product, and so forth. Therefore, all the parties enter a transaction with a whole set of questions they want answers to. Some of these questions are quite explicit: "How much does it cost?" Others are quite vague and many almost are subconscious: "Will this product make me feel better about myself?" All these decisions relate to the marketer's ability to integrate marketing communications (IMC).

The primary role of IMC is to systematically evaluate the communication needs and wants of the buyer and, based on that information, design a communication strategy that will 1. provide answers to primary questions of the target audience, 2. facilitate the customer's ability to make correct decisions, and 3. increase the probability that the choice they make most often will be the brand of the information provider (i.e., the sponsor or marketer). Marketers know that if they learn to fulfill this role, a lasting relationship with the customer can be established.

Primary Tasks

If the marketer is to consistently and effectively communicate with customers, three preliminary tasks must be acknowledged and achieved. First, there must be a mechanism for collecting, storing, analyzing, and disseminating relevant information. This includes information about customers (past, present, potential), competitors, the environment, trends in the industry, and so forth. The quality of communication is closely related to the quality of information. The Red Cross, for example, constantly monitors its customers through surveys and consumer panels, and keeps track of its competitors and other changes in order to assess the relevance of all its communication vehicles.

Second, communication is not one-way; it is a dialogue. That is, all relevant parties are actually participating in the communication process. Marketers must provide a system that constantly allows the consumer to express desires, satisfactions, complaints, and disappointments about the product, the price, the message, or the way it is distributed. There is a real tendency in large-scale marketing to view the consumer as a faceless, nameless entity, without individual needs and wants. Effective marketing communication allows direct feedback (e.g., toll-free numbers, hotlines, service departments), and actively responds by making substantial changes to address customer requests.

Finally, there must be an acknowledgement that target customers may not be the same as target audiences. While the *target market* is concerned primarily with individuals who are users and potential users of the product, the *target audience* may encompass a much larger or smaller group of people. More specifically, the target audience includes all individuals, groups, and institutions that receive the marketing message and employ this information either as a basis for making the product decision or in some way employ it to evaluate the sponsoring business. Thus, the target market for E.P.T. pregnancy tests might be women between the ages of 18 and 34 with a college education; the target audience might also include parents of the youngest of these women, who either approve or disapprove of this product based on advertising messages, government agencies who assess the truthfulness of the product claim, and potential stockholders who determine the future success of the firm based on the perceived quality of the messages. IMC must identify all members of the target audience and must consider how the communication strategy must change in response to this membership.

In the end, the role of IMC is to communicate with target audiences in a manner that accurately and convincingly relays the marketing strategy of the firm.

Integrated Marketing Communication

Instead of a functional approach, IMC attempts to integrate these functions into a collective strategy. If conducted properly, IMC results in a more effective achievement of an organization's communications objectives. Although it is difficult to determine exactly what prompted the move to IMC, experts speculate as to several possible interrelated causes. Historically, mass media has been characterized as unaccountable because of its general inability to measure its results, especially sales. Recently, the availability of consumer information (especially purchase patterns) through single-source technology, such as store scanners and other related technology, has meant that marketers are now able to correlate promotional activities with consumer behavior. During this same period, companies have been downsizing their operations and task expectations have been expanded. This greater expectation has carried over into the client-advertising agency relationship. Agency employees can no longer remain specialists. Rather, they must understand all the functions performed for the client, as well as their own. In reality, IMC appears to be much the same as a promotional strategy, a concept that has been around for several years. Perhaps the term "IMC" has emerged due to the confusion with the term "sales promotion" and the failure of promotion to be adopted by the advertising industry. Only time will tell whether IMC will become a salient part of marketing communication. Yet, it is a worthwhile ideal.

THE MEANING OF MARKETING COMMUNICATION

Defining the concept of marketing communication (MC) is not an easy task, because in a real sense, everything the company does has communication potential. The price placed on a product communicates something very specific about the product. A company that chooses to distribute their products strictly through discount stores tells the consumer a great deal. Yet, if all of these things are considered communication, the following definition is offered:

> Marketing communication includes all the identifiable efforts on the part of the seller that are intended to help persuade buyers to accept the seller's message and store it in retrievable form.

Note that the central theme of the communication process is persuasion. Communication is most definitely goal-directed. It is not intended to be an arbitrary, haphazard activity. Each of the tools used in marketing communication has specific potentialities and complexities that justify managerial specialization and require directed efforts. Yet a company, even a very large one, typically does not have a specialist in each area, but only in those cases where the importance and usage frequency of the tool justify specialized competence. Historically, companies first made a separate function out of the personal selling function, later out of advertising, and still later out of public relations. The remaining tools (e.g. coupons, specials) were employed by the directors of these functional areas as needed. Although the definitions vary, the four components that make up marketing communication are as follows:

1. *Advertising*: any paid form of nonpersonal presentation of ideas, goods, or services by an identified sponsor. Although some advertising is directed to specific individuals (as, for example, in the use of direct mail), most advertising messages are tailored to a group, and employ mass media such as radio, television, newspapers, and magazines.
2. *Personal Selling*: an oral presentation in a conversation with one or more prospective purchasers for the purpose of making sales. It includes several different forms, such as sales calls by a field representative (field selling), assistance by a sales clerk (retail selling), having an Avon representative call at your home (door-to-door selling), and so forth.

3. *Public Relations*: a nonpersonal stimulation of demand for a product, service, or business unit by planting commercially significant news about it in a published medium (i.e., publicity) or obtaining favorable presentation of it through vehicles not paid for by the sponsor. Although commissions are not paid to the various media, there are salaries and other expenses that mean that public relations is not a costless form of promotion.

4. *Sales Promotion*: those marketing activities that add to the basic value of the product for a limited time period and thus directly stimulate consumer purchasing and dealer effectiveness. These activities include displays, shows and exhibitions, demonstrations, and various nonrecurring selling efforts not in the ordinary routine. As the provision for an additional incentive to buy, these tools can be directed at consumers, the trade, or the manufacturer's own sales force.

THE OBJECTIVES OF MARKETING COMMUNICATION

The basic objectives of marketing communication have been reduced to three more meaningful directives: 1. to communicate, 2. to compete, and 3. to convince. The primary purpose of MC is to communicate ideas to target audiences. This is done through advertising, personal selling, sales promotion, and/or public relations. Principles of effective communication are intended to achieve this task. Clearly, most of marketing is communications, and it is in this context that communication is included as a purpose of MC. Moreover, whatever is communicated should be accurate, truthful, and useful to the parties involved. Because of the pervasiveness of marketing communication, it has a unique responsibility to communicate with integrity.

Helping the company to compete consistently and effectively in the marketplace is the second objective. For many companies, MC may offer the company its most promising marketing opportunities. Competitors may sell essentially the same product, at the same price, in the same outlets. It is only through MC that the company may be able to appeal to certain segments, properly differentiate its product, and create a level of brand loyalty that can last for many years. In addition, the prominence of extensive communication efforts on the part of competitors means that a company that did not exhibit a strong MC program would appear dull and unconvincing to the customer. Thus, MC is employed as both a defensive and offensive weapon.

The final objective of MC is to convince. Although this goal is most often ascribed to MC, it is the most questionable. "Convince" and "persuade" are not synonymous terms. Realistically, MC does extremely well if it presents ideas in a manner that is so convincing that the consumer will be led to take the desired action. These ideas, along with a host of other factors, will help persuade the consumer to make a particular decision. Therefore, the ability of MC to present information in a convincing manner is critical. It is also necessary to "reconvince" many consumers and customers. Just because a person buys a particular brand once or a dozen times, or even for a dozen years, there is no guarantee that they won't stop using the product if not constantly reminded of the product's unique benefits.

Ultimately, MC objectives can be broken down into very specific tasks. For example, we can derive marketing communication objectives in respect to where the consumer is in the purchase process. In the case of the prepurchase phase, marketing communications can achieve the following objectives: increase brand awareness, reduce risk, increase the likelihood of purchase, develop the brand image and build its equity. There are also objectives when the consumer is in the midst of the consumption phase: increase the likelihood of repeat purchase and increase customer satisfaction. Finally, communication objectives are aligned during postpurchase: stimulate positive word-of-mouth, reduce cognitive dissonance, and increase the likelihood of repeat purchase.

In conclusion, effective marketing communication should present useful ideas (information) in a manner that makes them clearly understood (communicate), cause the consumer to believe the message is true (convince), and is as appealing or more appealing than the message delivered by competitors (compete).

HOW WE COMMUNICATE

Because communication is such an integral part of effective marketing, it is important that we provide a basic understanding of its process. Our starting point is a basic definition of human communication: a process in which two or more persons attempt to consciously or unconsciously influence each other through the use of symbols or words in order to satisfy their respective needs.

Basic Elements of Communication

The basic elements within any communication system are depicted in Exhibit 9.1. It includes two or more people or organizations called communicators. The underlying assumption of this model is that all communications (dialogue) are continuous. This factor suggests that we are constantly and simultaneously in the role of communicator and receiver. Each

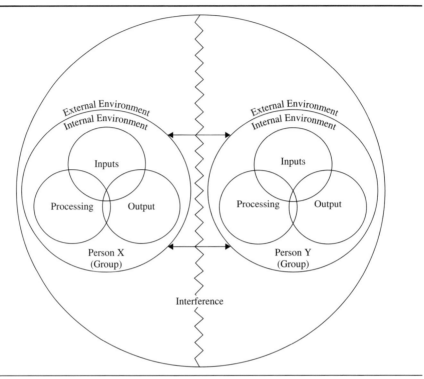

EXHIBIT 9.1 A MODEL OF HUMAN COMMUNICATION

communication is composed of a series of subsystems (i.e., inputs, outputs, processing). The input subsystem permits the communicator to receive messages and stimulus from outside as well as from the other communicator. It involves the reception of light, temperature, touch, sound, and odors via our eyes, skin, ears, nose, and tastebuds. These stimuli are intimately evaluated through a process called perception. Thus, we input and perceive advertising messages, a 50-cents-off coupon, the appearance and words of a salesperson, and so forth.

The processing subsystem of a communication includes all thought processes. As we process, we generate, organize, and reflect on ideas in response to the stimuli received. This entire process is determined not only by the stimuli just received, but also by all stimuli ever received, such as past experiences, education, health, genetics, and all other factors in our environment. Some people clearly process the humor in the Monster.com better than others.

The output subsystem includes the message and other behaviors produced by the communicator. These include nonverbal messages, verbal messages, and other physical behaviors. All of these become input (feedback) for other people and can have both intentional and unintentional effects on them.

Friend, parent, boss, client, or customers are just some of the roles we may portray in any communication process. The nature of the role directly affects the nature of communication. We communicate quite differently with our boss than we do with close friends. People who have known each other for a long time often devise their own communication system, which may include lots of nonverbal signals.

Finally, the communication system exists within an environment. The environment is everything internal and external to the communication system that can affect the system (family, school, competing advertisement, etc.). Each of the factors within the environment interacts with the communication system to a different degree. Because communication systems are open to the influence of the total environment, we can never analyze a communication event from only the point of view of the people who seem obviously involved. Everything may affect communication, positively or negatively. The latter factors may alter or distort inputs, outputs, or processing and are called interference. Interference can be generated internally (e.g., fear, love, prejudice) or externally (e.g., noise, weather, physical appearance).

Realities of Communication

The communication model just discussed is more of an ideal than the reality. Although we all have an intended message in mind, and may work very hard to formulate it just right, it is rare that the message is interpreted exactly as planned. We know for instance, the greater the number of translators, the less likely the message will be received intact. Moreover, the less control we have over the participants involved, the more likely distortion will occur.

From a strategic perspective, communication is a high-risk activity. Because there are so many uncontrollable variables, it is recommended that research should play a critical role in every facet of marketing communications. For example, every message should be pre-tested. Basic questions include: what messages (topics) are important to the receiver? What sounds, words and visuals will communicate most clearly to the identified target audience? When should the message be delivered? How often? Through which mediums? Research can also be done while the message is being delivered. Fundamental questions include. Is the message being interpreted correctly? Are there distortions that are affecting interpretation? Is the message changing the audience is some meaningful way? Finally, research done after the delivery of the message is most common: was the message interpreted correctly?

What feedback links were employed? If there is distortion, what are the sources? Can we dissect the various communication elements and determine the effectiveness of each?

Answers to questions such as these not only tell the nonprofit marketer whether the communication is working, it also suggests the best approach to doing marketing communication. If the problems and various distortions appear to be at the operational level (i.e., message design and delivery), that suggests relatively easy adjustments, and the efficiencies of mass communications are supported. If, on the other hand, the problem distortions are at the receiver level for example, poor comprehension or low media usage, then a move to more personal forms of communication, such as direct mail or personal selling, are called for.

Marketing Communication

While all communication includes the same basic components depicted in Exhibit 9.1, marketing communication differs somewhat in two respects. First, the intent of marketing communications is to present a persuasive message, which reinforces the total offer made by the marketer. Essentially, all marketing communication attempts to create uniqueness in the mind of the target audience.

Second, marketing communication can be divided into two flows (i.e., internal and external), which are directed at different target audiences. This necessitates different communication strategies, which, nevertheless, must be compatible. A company cannot be telling a customer one story and stockholders another. The flow of marketing communication is depicted in Exhibit 9.2.

DESIGNING AN IMC STRATEGY

The design of an effective IMC strategy is a very difficult and time-consuming process that requires the efforts of many members of the marketing staff. Although there has been a great deal of variety in designing this process, the steps depicted in Exhibit 9.3 are most common.

As is the case with most marketing activities, IMC is guided by a set of *objectives*. There are numerous responses that the manager may desire from his IMC effort. Although the ultimate buyer behavior desired is product purchase, several intermediate responses may prove important as well. Examples of these intermediate responses are shown in Exhibit 9.4.

If there is a marketing opportunity, there must also be a *communication opportunity*. Although the role of IMC is de-emphasized in certain marketing

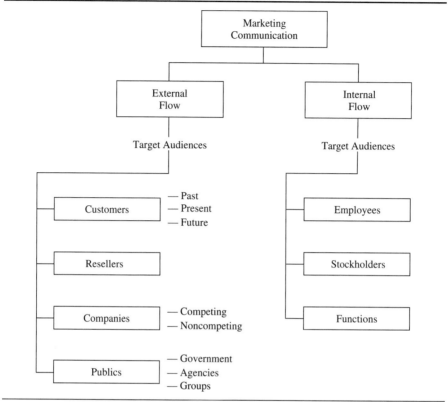

EXHIBIT 9.2   THE FLOW OF MARKETING COMMUNICATION

programs, there will also be some communicative, motivational, or competitive tasks to be performed. Whether or not the marketing programs should rely heavily on its communication ingredient to perform such tasks depends upon the mature and extent of the opportunity. There are several conditions which, if they exist, indicate a favorable opportunity to communicate: for example, it is always easier to communicate effectively when moving with the current consumer demand rather than against it. Companies such as IBM have been actively promoting their business computers, which are increasing in popularity, rather than home computers, which are not doing as well.

The third consideration is *selecting the target audience* for the IMC. This is undoubtedly the most important factor in the IMC strategy, yet it is probably the issue that many companies slight or overlook entirely. Marketing messages must be directed at the specific target for which the overall marketing program is being designed. However, very seldom is there a single group of consumers at which to direct messages. Many individuals affect the

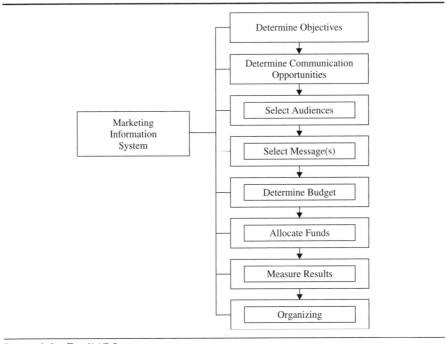

EXHIBIT 9.3   THE IMC STRATEGY

buying process, and the IMC program must be designed to reach all of them. In addition to the primary purchasers and users of the product, individuals who influence the purchase decision must also be considered. For example, consumers usually rely heavily upon the assistance and advice of others in purchasing such products as automobiles, interior decorating, major appliances, and physicians, to name but a few. Thus it is extremely important in resolving the communication issue to identify accurately not only those who consume and buy the product but also those who influence its purchase.

Determining exactly what to say to the relevant audience is the fourth consideration. The heart of IMC is the transmission of ideas of marketing significance to the seller. Whether these ideas are received and perceived as intended depends in large part on the skill used in developing the communication appeal. It also depends upon the vehicle used to deliver the message. Whether it is the message delivered by a salesperson, a newspaper, or a point-of-purchase display, the message must facilitate reaching the communication objectives.

Money is always an important factor; a typical IMC effort is extremely expensive and is becoming more expensive every day. Keeping track of

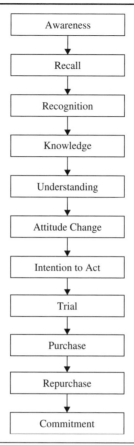

EXHIBIT 9.4   GOALS OF INTEGRATED MARKETING COMMUNICATION

these cost elements is a full-time job. The budget for a particular IMC effort can be determined through very sophisticated computer programs or through intuitive techniques such as experience, following competition, or simply spending all you can afford. Particular budgetary approaches are summarized in Exhibit 9.5.

Once you decide how much to spend, the amounts to be spent on personal selling, advertising, public relations, and sales promotion must be decided. After determining the major allocations, each of these figures must be broken down into much finer increments. For example, the advertising budget must be reallocated by media category, then by specific media, and finally, by particular dates, times, issues, and the like.

Evaluating the effectiveness of an IMC effort is very important. Three tasks must be completed when one attempts to measure the results of IMC.

Technique	General Description
Arbitrary Allocation	Management bases budget on personal experience, business philosophy, and marketing intuition
Affordability	Upper limit of budget based on available company resources
Ratio-to-Sales	Amount budgeted is based on some portion of past or forecasted sales
Competitive Comparisons	Budget based on amount being spent by major competitors
Experimental Approach	Budget based on test market results
Objective-Task Method	Determine costs of reaching specific promotional objectives and sum amounts

EXHIBIT 9.5 SUMMARY OF TECHNIQUES: SETTING THE IMC BUDGET

First, standards for IMC effectiveness, such as retention and liking, must be established. This means that the market planner must have a clear understanding of exactly what the communication is intended to accomplish. For measurement purposes, the standards should be identified in specific, quantitative terms. Second, actual IMC performance must be monitored. To do this, it is usually necessary to conduct experiments in which the efforts of other variables are either excluded or controlled. The third step in measuring IMC efficiency is to compare these performance measures against the standards. In doing so, it is theoretically possible to determine the most effective methods of marketing communication.

Finally, how a company organizes for IMC depends on the degree to which it desires to perform the communication function internally or to assign this task to outside agencies. Typically, the sales function is performed internally and the sales organization is a part of the overall standing organizational plan. Occasionally, as when manufacturer's agents are used, outside organizations are employed to perform personal selling. Advertising services might be performed internally or externally. Sales promotion activities are usually also handled internally, although it is not uncommon for advertising agencies to be consulted in connection with sales promotion plans. The same is true for public relations.

UNDERSTANDING ADVERTISING

Undoubtedly, advertising is the promotional element that most consumers feel they know the best and hold strong opinions about. This is a result of the visibility and intrusiveness of advertising. In fact, although they are exposed to it constantly, most people have little understanding of advertising.

Product/service feature	Many products have such strong technology or performance capabilities that these features can serve as a primary advertising appeal.
Product/competitive advantage	When an advertiser can determine that his or her product is superior, either in terms of features, performance, supporting services, or image, emphasizing competitive advantage has proved to be a successful appeal.
Product/service price advantage	Offering a product at a reduced price or under some special deal (e.g., buy-one-get-one-free) may be the only viable appeal in a particular ad.
News about product/service	There are times when a truly new product is developed, or when an existing product is changed or improved in a substantial manner, that highlighting this single element is the core appeal.
Product/service popularity	Although the manner varies, the notion of claiming that a product is "number one" or the most popular is an appeal that has been around for a long time.
Generic approach	In such advertising, a product or service category is promoted for its own sake, but individual makes or brands of product are not singled out.
Consumer service	A popular appeal is to illustrate through the advertisement how the product may be used to best serve the needs of the consumer.
Savings through use	An opportunity to save time, money, or energy is always very appealing to consumers.
Self-enhancement	Helping us feel better about ourselves (e.g., personal care, clothing, automobiles) is an appeal that many people can't resist.
Embarrassment or anxiety	Situations that represent a threatening situation, either physically or socially, can provide the basis for an effective appeal.
Product trial	When this appeal is used, the advertiser offers a free sample, a price reduction, or some other purchase incentive to encourage consumer use or trial.
Corporate	This type of appeal presents a company or corporation in a favorable light in order to create a favorable impression or image.

EXHIBIT 9.6 PRIMARY ADVERTISING APPEALS

The Organization of Advertising

There are within the advertising industry a wide variety of means by which advertising is created and placed in media. At one extreme, an individual might write his own classified advertisement in a newspaper in the hope of selling his daughter's canopy bed. At the other extreme, the seller employs a full-service advertising agency to create and place the advertisement, retaining only the function of final approval of plans developed by that agency. Significant specialization is developed within the full-service advertising agency to discourage clients from hiring any outside vendors or other parties to perform any of the various functions involved in planning and executing advertising programs for the various advertisers that the agency serves. Another organizational possibility is a full-scale, in-house advertising department. This department may have total responsibility for all aspects of the advertisement, or some of the tasks might be farmed out to ad agencies or other types of specialty organizations (e.g., production, talent, media placement). It is not unusual for a large corporation to employ all of these possibilities or to use different agencies for different products or in different parts of the country.

Whether or not the advertiser uses an advertising agency, does his advertising in-house, or uses some combination of the two depends upon a host of factors unique to each organization: available funds, level of expertise, expediency, and so forth. Regardless of the influencing factors, a number of basic functions must be performed by someone if creative and effective advertisements are to be placed:

- What products, institutions, or ideas are to be advertised
- Who is to prepare advertising programs
- Who in the organization engages and gives policy and other direction to the advertising agency, if any agency is used
- Who in the organization has the authority to develop advertising work and/or approves the advertising programs presented by the advertising agency
- Who pays the advertising bill
- Who determines the extent to which advertisements help reach the stated objectives

The Advertising Department

A company's advertising department can range from one person to a division that employs 500 or more people. Regardless of the size, advertising departments share similar responsibilities:

- formulating the advertising program
- implementing the program
- controlling the program
- presenting the budget
- maintaining relationships with suppliers
- establishing internal communications
- setting professional standards
- selecting an advertising agency

Developing the Creative Strategy

Once all the relevant facts are gathered and evaluated, the process of actually creating the advertisement begins. This process is very complex, and a complete description of it is well beyond the scope of this book. However, what follows are highlights of the primary parts of this process.

To begin with, the person or persons actually responsible for the complete advertisement depends upon the advertiser's organization of the advertising function and whether an advertising agency is used. More than likely, the development and approval of advertising creation is the responsibility of the senior advertising manager within the advertiser company and, when an advertising agency is used, of the agency management. In most agencies, the responsibility is that of the senior account person, in conjunction with the senior creative person assigned to the account. The advertising effort can be divided into two elements: the creative strategy and creative tactics. The *creative strategy* concerns what you are going to say to the audience. It flows from the advertising objectives and should outline what impressions the campaign should convey to the target audience. *Creative tactics* outline the means for carrying out the creative strategy. This includes all the various alternatives available, which will help reach the advertising objectives.

The place to begin the creative strategy is to ascertain the proper appeal to employ in the ad (see Exhibit 9.6). Identifying the appropriate appeal is just the first part of the advertising design process. The second part is to transform this idea into an actual advertisement. To say that there are a large variety of ways to do this would be a gross understatement. The number of techniques available to the creative strategies are not only vast, but the ability of more than one technique to successfully operationalize the same appeal makes this process even more nebulous.

Type	Strengths	Weaknesses
Television	Strong emotional impact	High costs
	Mass coverage/small cost per impression	High clutter (too many ads)
	Repeat message	Short-lived impression
	Creative flexibility	Programming quality
	Entertaining/prestigious	Schedule inflexibility
Radio	Provides immediacy	Limited national coverage
	Low cost per impression	High clutter
	Highly flexible	Less easily perceived during drive time
		Fleeting message
Newspapers	Flexibility	Short life
	Community prestige	Technical quality varies
	Market coverage	Clutter
	Offer merchandising services	Timing flexibility
	Reader involvement	Two-tiered rate structure
Magazines	Highly segmented audiences	Inflexible
	High-profile audiences	Narrow audiences
	High reproduction quality	Waste circulation
	Prestigious	High cost
	Long life	
	Extra services	
Outdoor/Transit	Inexpensive	Short/concise message
	Flexible	Negative reputation
	Reminder	Uncontrollable
	Repetition	Inflexible
	Immediacy	
Direct Mail	Flexibility	Negative image
	Develop complete/precise message	High cost per impression
	Supplements other media	High production costs
		Success dependent upon mailing list
Specialty Advertising (Directories, matchbooks, calendars, etc.)	Positive reinforcement	Wasteful
	Segmented markets	Expensive
	Flexible	
Interactive	Flexible	Hard to measure
	Repetition	Limited market coverage
	Involvement	Uncontrollable

EXHIBIT 9.7   AN APPRAISAL OF MASS MEDIA

Developing the Media Plan

Although the media plan is placed later in this process, it is in fact developed simultaneously with the creative strategy. This area of advertising has gone through tremendous changes; a critical media revolution has taken place.

The standard media plan consists of four stages: 1. stating media objectives; 2. evaluating media; 3. selecting and implementing media choices; 4. determining the media budget.

Stating Media Objectives

Media objectives are normally started in terms of three dimensions:

1. Reach—number of different persons or households exposed to a particular media vehicle or media schedule at least once during a specified time period.
2. Frequency—the number of times within a given time period that a consumer is exposed to a message.
3. Continuity—the timing of media assertions (e.g., 10 percent in September, 20 percent in October, 20 percent in November, 40 percent in December and 10 percent the rest of the year).

Evaluating Media

As noted in Exhibit 9.7, there are definite inherent strengths and weaknesses associated with each medium. In addition, it would require extensive primary research either by the sponsoring firm or their advertising agency in order to assess how a particular message and the target audience would relate to a given medium. As a result, many advertisers rely heavily on the research findings provided by the medium, by their own experience, and by subjective appraisal.

Selection and Implementation

The media planner must make media mix decisions and timing directions, both of which are restricted by the available budget. The *media mix decision* involves putting media together in the most effective manner. This is a difficult task, and necessitates quantitatively and qualitatively evaluating each medium and combination thereof.

Unfortunately, there are very few valid rules of thumb to guide this process, and the supporting research is spotty at best. For example, in attempting to compare audiences of various media, we find that A.C. Nielsen measures

Audience/Technique	Description
Consumer	
Price Discounts	Temporary reduction in price, often at point of purchases
Coupon offers	Certificates redeemable for amount specified
Combination offers	Selling two products in conjunction at a lower total price
Contests	Awarding of prizes on the basis of chance or consideration
Rebates	Refund of a fixed amount of money
Premiums	Tangible reward received for performing an act, normally a purchase
Trading stamps	Certificate awarded based on purchase amount
Sampling	Providing the product either free or for a small fee
Employee	
Orientation program	Introducing the employee to company facts
Fringe benefits	Extra incentives provided by the company to the employee
Institutional promotion	Messages portraying the company in a positive light
Motivational programs	Temporary incentives (e.g., contests, prizes, or awards)
Distributor/Dealer	
Contests	Temporary incentives offered for specific performance
Trade shows	Central location where products are displayed/sold
Push money/dealer loaders	Money offered for selling specific amounts of product
Trade deals	Dealers receive special allowances, discounts, goods, or cash

EXHIBIT 9.8 TYPES OF SALES PROMOTION TECHNIQUES

audiences based on TV viewer reports of the programs watched, while outdoor audience exposure estimates are based on counts of the number of automobile vehicles that pass particular outdoor poster locations. The *timing of media* refers to the actual placement of advertisements during the time periods that are most appropriate, given the selected media objectives. It includes not only the scheduling of advertisements, but also the size and position of the advertisement.

Determining the Media Budget

This budget is a part of the advertising budget, and the same techniques and factors that apply to the advertising budget apply to the media budget as well. However, negotiating media buys can get very complicated, requiring an expert in media buying.

Banner Advertisements and Podcasts

Before leaving the topic of advertising, both creative and media, it is important to introduce a new form of advertising—*banner advertising*. Banner ads are the dominant form of online advertising. Banner ads are graphic images in Web pages that are often animated and can include small pieces of software code to allow further interaction. Most importantly, they are "clickable," and take a viewer to another Web location when chosen.

Banner ads typically run at the top and bottom of the page, but they can be incorporated anywhere. The CASIE organization has developed a small number of standard sizes and formats. Like the Web itself, banner ads are a mixture of approaches, with elements of traditional print advertising and more targeted directed advertising. Banner ads include direct marketing capabilities. Each banner carries with it a unique identifier. This allows the Web site to track the effectiveness of the ad in generating traffic. Measurability permits ad banner pricing based on results and behavior. Click-through pricing ignores impressions and charges the advertiser based on the number of viewers that select the ad and follow it to the linking Web site.

Admittedly, the performance of banner ads to date has been less than stellar. One company, San Francisco–based Organic, has approached the problem of ineffective online advertising with a product called "expand-o." This new ad vehicle allows an advertiser to include some of its Web site's content in an expandable banner ad. At the click of a mouse, the advertisement expands to as much as five or six times its original size. For instance, an expand-o for Fort Washington, PA–based CDNow provides consumers with a sample of dynamically updated content housed on the music retailer's site. When the consumer clicks an arrow on the ad, it expands to show the top ten songs in CDNow's top 100 Billboard Chart.

Technology has introduced a vast number of new message delivery systems in the last decade. However, one system that seems to interface with nonprofits quite well is the podcast. A podcast is an Internet-based broadcast that is free to anyone with web access. Only a sliver of Americans—about six million—had downloaded audio recordings online, according to a survey taken in February 2005 by the Pew Internet & American Life Project. Podcasts earned their name because they can easily be downloaded and transferred into a portable music device, such as Apple Computer's iPod, for future listening.

However, podcasts are not just limited to those owning iPods. Other online sites, including Apple's iTunes, iPodder, Podcast Alley, and Podcast net, all offer podcasts, most of which can be downloaded free. In many cases, those who create and develop podcasts also link the programs to these Web sites.

Creating a podcast is fairly straightforward and inexpensive. Ultimately, it only takes a computer, a microphone, and some low-budget software to create an acceptable podcast. Podcasting's low cost, combined with its growing popularity, make it an appealing format for charities. Through pod-casting, nonprofit groups are only paying the cost of producing the content and making it available to people who can download the program. Readers are directed to the iTunes directory created by Apple Computers (http://www.apple.com/itunes) to check out what nonprofits are doing in this category.

In conclusion, advertising is an effective marketing communication strategy when you want to create awareness, brand recognition, and basic information. It does not do well at changing attitudes and prompting behavior. Moreover, it is very expensive and too costly for most nonprofits. Unless a nonprofit has a very large budget and/or can convince an advertising agency to take them in as a pro bono client, a nonprofit should think twice before committing to advertising. A simple directory ad and a well-done Web site may suffice.

SALES PROMOTION AND PUBLIC RELATIONS

For several years, sales promotion and public relations have been often mis-understood, mismeasured, and misused by a great many marketers. Unlike advertising and personal selling, which can claim formal structures and point to obvious accomplishments, sales promotion and PR have neither. Although this situation is changing somewhat, there is still a great deal of room for improvement. In the case of sales promotion, there exists some confusion as to which activities actually fall under this heading. Are packaging, couponing, and point-of-purchase displays all sales promotion? Because the answer to this question varies from organization to organization and across situations, sales promotion is often viewed as a catch-all category that includes every-thing that an organization does not label as advertising or public relations.

Public relations, too, is difficult to define as it deals with the ultimate intangible—creating a positive image of the company. Not only is this difficult to accomplish, but it is also virtually impossible to ascertain if you have succeeded and to what extent. An organization, for instance, might sponsor a free barbecue for a Fourth of July celebration and never really know if the money spent produced additional business. Management has a difficult time appreciating an activity that produces indirect results.

Sales Promotion: A Little Bit of Everything

As the newest member of the promotional team, sales promotion has suffered from a serious identity crisis. For example, initially the American Marketing

Association defines sales promotion as, "marketing activities, other than personal selling, advertising, and publicity, that stimulate consumer purchasing and dealer effectiveness, such as displays, shows and exhibitions, demonstrations, and various non-recurrent selling efforts not in the ordinary routine." In the AMA view, sales promotion supplements both personal selling and advertising, coordinates them, and helps make them more effective. However, this does not provide an accurate portrayal of the role played by sales promotion. A simple way of viewing sales promotion is to say that it means special offers: special in the sense that they are extra as well as specific in time or place; offers in the sense that they are direct propositions, the acceptance of which forms a deal. Simply, it increases the perceived value of the product.

As in most aspects of marketing, the rationale of sales promotion is to provide a direct stimulus to produce a desired response by customers. It is not always clear, however, what the distinctions are between sales promotion and advertising, personal selling and public relations. For example, suppose that Pillsbury decides to tape three cans of their buttermilk canned biscuits together and sell them for a price slightly cheaper than the three sold individually. Is that a branded multipack special offer and therefore promotional? Or is it just an example of a giant-sized economy pack, and therefore a product or packaging tactic? In order to sort out which it is, the question has to be asked, is it intended to be a permanent feature of the manufacturer's product policy to have the family pack as a component of the product? If it is not, it is a sales promotion scheme.

The same sort of problem comes up when studying strategies run by firms in service industries. If a hotel offers cut-price accommodations at off-peak times of the years, is it a feature of the hotel management's pricing policy or is it a promotional tactic? If the hotel management provides price reductions on tickets to local theaters for their guests, is it part of the product or is it a device to attract customers for a limited period only? Again, the answer can only be given once the question about permanence is asked. Even then, there still tend to be elements of advertising, personal selling, public relations and sales promotion in many promotional vehicles, and this may be the right approach. A manufacturer, for instance, has made substantial contributions of both cash and products to the local heart fund telethon. Immediately following the telethon, they run a full-page ad in several magazines describing their contributions, and describing a special rebate of 5 cents for every candy wrapper mailed in. The 5 cents can be donated to the heart fund if the customer wishes. The sales reps also have copies of this promotion to show their customers. Clearly, this strategy has all four components of the IMC mix.

Types of Sales Promotion

There are a great many techniques that are considered sales promotion. One way of organizing this myriad of techniques is in terms of audience. As shown in Exhibit 9.8, sales promotions are directed at consumers, employees, and distributors, and dealers. While consumers attract the greatest number of sales promotion devices, the other two audiences are growing in importance. While space does not permit a discussion of these strategies, some generalizations apply to all. Specifically, the value of a sales promotion is especially prominent when a marketer is introducing a new product, especially a product with high perceived risk; is interested in creating a repeat purchase pattern for the customer; is attempting to create movement of large amounts of products quickly; is attempting to counter the strategy of a competitor; and is trying to move marginal customers to make a choice. Sales promotion cannot compensate for a poor product or ineffective advertising. Nor can it create strong brand loyalty or reverse a declining sales trend. Be aware that once a type of sales promotion is expected by the customer, you risk not ever being able to eliminate it without diminishing the perceived value of the product.

Public Relations: The Art of Maintaining Goodwill

Every organization engages in some form of public relations (PR). In essence, every form of communication emitted by an organization both internally and externally is perceived by various publics. In turn, these publics form attitudes and opinions about that organization, which affect their behaviors. These behaviors range from low morale on the part of the employees to product purchase on the part of consumers.

Nevertheless, public relations looms as one of the most misunderstood and mistrusted elements in marketing. Consequently, management may provide marketing in general with full support, ample scope, and time for planning, but often does not establish a role for public relations. Public relations may be brought in belatedly at advanced stages of the marketing process as a peripheral area with no real purpose.

Obtaining a good working definition of public relations requires an acknowledgement of the concept's core elements. Four such elements emerge. First, the ultimate objective of PR is to retain as well as create goodwill. Second, the successful procedure to follow in public relations is to first do good, and then take credit for it. Third, the publics addressed by the PR program must be described completely and precisely. In most instances, PR programs are aimed at multiple publics that have varying points of view and needs. Consequently, the publics served should be researched just as carefully as the target audiences for an advertising campaign. Finally, public relations is a planned activity. There is an intelligence behind it.

The definition that encompasses all these considerations, and was coined at the First Assembly of Public Relations Associations in 1987, follows:

> Public relations practice is the art of social science in analyzing trends, predicting their consequences, counseling organization leaders, and implementing planned programs of action, which serve both the organizations and the public interest.

Public Relations' Publics

A public may be said to exist whenever a group of people is drawn together by definite interests in certain areas and has definite opinions upon matters within those areas. There are many publics, and individuals are frequently members of several that may sometimes have conflicting interests. For example, in the case of a school bond vote, a voter might be torn between feelings as a parent and as a member of a conservative economic group opposed to higher taxes, or an elderly couple with no children now in school, and feeling no obligation to support children.

Public relations must be sensitive to two general types of publics: internal and external. *Internal publics* are the people who are already connected with an organization, and with whom the organization normally communicates in the ordinary routine of work. Typical internal publics in an industry are the employees, stockholders, suppliers, dealers, customers, and plant neighbors. For example, employees want good wages and working conditions, opportunities for advancement, and a secure retirement. Customers want a dependable supply of quality products provided at a fair price and supported by convenient services. Stakeholders want dividends, growth, and a fair return on their investments. How does PR communicate to these publics about these issues?

External publics are composed of people who are not necessarily closely connected with a particular organization. For example, members of the press, educators, government officials, or the clergy may or may not have an interest in an industry. The leaders of the industry cannot assume any automatic interest and, to some extent, must choose whether to communicate with these groups.

There is, of course, interaction between internal and external publics. Yet it cannot be assumed that good relations with insiders will ever be translated to outsiders without effort. An employee who is quite happy on the job may be much more interested in bowling than in the fact that the firm has just opened a new branch in Phoenix. The firm must think of what interests the external public and not what interests the firm. With employees and other internal publics, there is a fair chance that all interests may coincide because all are connected with the same organization; with an external audience, the assumption should be that the chance of such accidental coincidence of interest is slight.

Public Relations Techniques

The public relations process is quite complex and involves a wide variety of techniques. Public relations is different than any other type of promotion, because a great deal of the communication provided by a PR person must be screened and reprocessed through a third party that is not employed by the company. Therefore, if I wished for the local newspaper and television station to carry a story detailing the grand opening of my new store, I have no guarantee that either will send a representative to cover the store opening or that they will cover it the way I would have liked. Even if I were to write the story myself and send it to the newspaper, including appropriate photographs, the editor might choose not to print it or modify it. The fact that PR is characterized by a low level of control necessitates that PR people establish a positive relationship with the various media. Without first accomplishing this goal, the tools employed by the PR person are usually doomed to failure. Various public relations techniques are described as follows:

Company Publications

Brochures: Every nonprofit should have a brochure that contains the organization's name, address, telephone number, email address, web-site address, mission, purpose and primary interests, affiliations, tax-exempt status, ways of making contributions/volunteering, and key contact person(s).

Print and Electronic Newsletters: Nonprofits should publish a newsletter at least quarterly. It should be sent free-of-charge to all board members, members, political leaders, media, potential/current donors, and other influencers. It should be well designed and maintain that design as well as an ascribed name and familiar name. It should contain current and relevant news.

News Releases: This is a prepared statement sent to the media. News releases are distributed to media who are most likely to print or broadcast them. Therefore, it is critical that you understand how each medium wishes to receive the news releases. The rules vary, but all releases should contain an importance designation, a date for the releases, and contact information. Most releases will be edited before final publication/broadcast, although many neighborhood newspapers will print releases word-for-word.

Often, publicity photographs/videos are sent to complement news releases. Both should be sent in a format acceptable to the media. In addition, the media may decide to only run the visual, so provide a caption.

Finally, public service announcements (PSAs) represent another type of news release. It is provided free-of-charge by the broadcast medium and serves as an excellent and cost-effective way to get the organization's key messages and its name delivered to thousands of viewers and listeners. The 30-second message can tell about a free service, health risk, or how to join. It concludes with "this message is brought to you by (the name of the organization) and this station as a public service."

Annual Report: All nonprofits must provide an annual report that supplements the financial information provided to stakeholders. Its level of sophistication is really up to the nonprofit. However, it should be accurate, readable, and communicate the key results and proposed initiatives.

Press Conferences

If a nonprofit organization has a story of major interest to the public or needs to respond to negative news, they may want to hold a press conference. To do so, a media advisory is distributed in the same manner as a press release, indicating the time, place, subject, and speakers. At the press conference, written materials (a press kit) should be distributed, along with a photo of the speaker(s). There should also be a podium draped with the organization's logo. Most importantly, the topics to be discussed should be relevant to the reporters, and the spokesperson should be trained and prepared to answer the appropriate questions.

Meetings, Conferences, and Workshops

Running an event where other stakeholders attend is fraught with risks and includes hundreds of decisions. Choosing topics and speakers that will resonate with participants is the first critical decision. It is also necessary to clearly delineate the goals and objectives of the event. Date(s), location, time, costs, prices, exhibits, and a host of other factors must be considered. A poorly planned event can destroy all the positives created by marketing.

Open houses/tours are a quasi-event. Essentially, the decision to do this depends on the objectives and the appropriateness of the open house/tour. Unless it leads to measurable benefits to the organization, it should be avoided.

Participation

This includes decisions to participate in community activities (e.g., clubs, charities). Again, there should be measurable benefits.

PERSONAL SELLING AND THE MARKETING COMMUNICATION MIX

Personal selling is an element of marketing that most nonprofit organizations either reject or do poorly. Presumably, the causes supported by nonprofits are so profound that there is little need to sell them to stakeholders. Yet, convincing a client to accept treatment, a board member to work harder, a donor to give more, or a consumer to buy a product, all could benefit from a fundamental understanding of personal selling. In respect to affecting behavior, personal selling is the most effective communication tool. While nonprofits may have a very small sales organization, and these people may not have the title of salesperson, the benefits are apparent.

Few companies coordinate marketing communication efforts in support of the sales force. Salespeople are often separated from marketing communications specialists because of both the structure of the business and difference in perspective. Most salespeople view other marketing communication activities strictly as a means to help sell a product or company. Advertisers, sales promotion managers, and public relations experts rarely consider the needs and suggestions of salespeople, and salespeople seldom pay attention to information about a marketing communication campaign.

Integrating personal selling with other marketing communication elements may seriously affect that salesperson's job. Regis McKenna, international consultant, contends that although marketing technology has made salespeople more effective, it may also decrease the need for traditional salespeople who convince people to buy. As we move closer to "real-time" marketing, he believes customers and suppliers will be linked directly, so that customers can design their own products, negotiate price with suppliers, and discuss delivery and other miscellaneous concerns with producers rather than salespeople. McKenna suggests that the main role of salespeople will no longer be to "close" the sale. Instead it will be to carry detailed design, quality, and reliability information, and to educate and train clients.

Don Schultz, Northwestern University professor of marketing and proponent of IMC, supports this notion of the modern salesperson. "If you create long-term affiliations, then you don't sell. You form relationships that help people buy." He observes that because products have become more sophisticated, the businesses that buy are often smaller than those that sell. "Today, I think the sales force is primarily focused on learning about the product and not about the market. We're talking about flipping that around," he concludes. In short, effective personal selling must focus on customer relationships.

To integrate personal selling with other marketing communication tools to forge strong customer relationships, top management should lead the integration effort. Unless managers understand what salespeople do, however, integration may not be successful. Before considering how to combine selling efforts with other marketing communication tools, we first examine the job of personal selling.

The underlying rationale for personal selling is facilitating exchange. As suggested by a personal selling expert, it is "the art of successfully persuading prospects or customers to buy products or services from which they can derive suitable benefits, thereby increasing their total satisfaction." A professional salesperson recognizes that the long-term success for the organization depends on consistently satisfying the needs of a significant segment of its target market. This modern view of selling has been called "nonmanipulative selling," and the emphasis of this view is that selling should build mutual trust and respect between buyer and seller. Benefit must come to both parties (see Exhibit 9.9).

The Selling Process

To better understand the job of a salesperson and how it should be managed, the selling process can be broken into a series of steps. Each step in the process may not be required to make every sale, but the salesperson should become skilled in each area in case it is needed. The steps are shown in Exhibit 9.10.

Factor	Personal Selling	Mass Selling
Speed in a Large Audience	Slow	Fast
Cost per Individual Reached	High	Low
Ability to Attract Attention	High	Low
Clarity of Communications	High	Moderate
Chance of Selective Screening	Moderate	High
Direction of Message Flow	Two Way	One Way
Speed of Feedback	Fast	Slow
Accuracy of Feedback	High	Low
Ability to Affect Behavior	High	Low

EXHIBIT 9.9   DIFFERENCES IN PERSONAL SELLING AND MASS SELLING

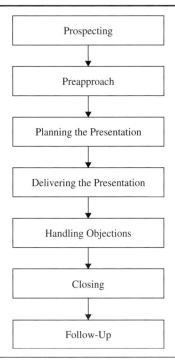

EXHIBIT 9.10   THE SELLING PROCESS: STEPS INVOLVED

Prospecting

Prospecting is defined as the seller's search for, and identification of, qualified potential buyers of the product or service. Prospecting can be thought of as a two-stage process: 1. identifying the individuals and/or the organizations that might be prospects, and 2. screening potential prospects against evaluative qualifying criteria. Potential prospects that compare favorably to the evaluative criteria can then be classified as qualified prospects.

Preapproach

After the prospect has been qualified, the salesperson continues to gather information about the prospect. This process is called the preapproach. The preapproach can be defined as obtaining as much relevant information as possible regarding the prospect prior to making a sales presentation. The knowledge gained during the preapproach allows the tailoring of the sales presentation to the particular prospect. In many cases, salespeople make a preliminary call on the prospect for the purpose of conducting the preapproach.

This is perfectly acceptable, and most professional buyers understand that such a call may be necessary before a sales presentation can be made.

Planning the Presentation

Regardless of the sales situation, some planning should be done before the sales presentation is attempted. The amount of planning that will be necessary and the nature of the planning depend on many factors, including: 1. the objective or objectives of the presentation, 2. how much knowledge the salesperson has regarding the buyer, buyer needs, and the buying situation, 3. the type of presentation to be planned and delivered, and 4. the involvement of other people assisting the salesperson in the sales presentation.

Careful planning offers advantages for both the salesperson and the buyer. By carefully planning the presentation, a salesperson can: 1. focus on important customer needs and communicate the relevant benefits to the buyer, 2. address potential problem areas prior to the sales presentation, and 3. enjoy self-confidence, which generally increases with the amount of planning done by the salesperson. In planning the presentation, the salesperson must select the relevant parts of their knowledge base and integrate the selected parts into a unified sales message. For any given sales situation, some of the facts concerning the salesperson's company, product, and market will be irrelevant. The challenge to the salesperson is in the task of distilling relevant facts from the total knowledge base. The key question here is, "What information will the prospect require before they will choose to buy my offering?"

Delivering the Presentation

All sales presentations are not designed to secure an immediate sale. Whether the objective is an immediate sale or a future sale, the chances of getting a positive response from a prospect are increased when the salesperson: 1. makes the presentation in the proper climate, 2. establishes credibility with the prospect, 3. ensures clarity of content in the presentation, and 4. controls the presentation within reasonable bounds.

Handling Objections

During the course of the sales presentation, the salesperson can expect the prospect to one or more points made by the salesperson. Sales objections raised by the prospect can be defined as statements or questions by the prospect, which can indicate an unwillingness to buy. Salespeople can learn to handle customer's objections by becoming aware of the reasons for the objections. The objections of customers include objections to prices, products, service, the company, time, or competition. The reasons for objections include that customers have gotten into the habit of raising objections, customers have a desire for more information, and customers have no need for the product or service being marketed. Salespeople can overcome objections by following certain guidelines including viewing objections as selling tools, being aware of the benefits of their products, and creating a list of possible objections and the best answers to those objections.

Closing

To a large degree, the evaluation of salespeoples' performance is based on their ability to close sales. Certainly, other factors are considered in evaluating performance, but the bottom line for most salespeople is their ability to consistently produce profitable sales volume. Individuals who perform as salespeople occupy a unique role: they are the only individuals in their companies who bring revenue into the company.

There may be several opportunities to attempt to close during a presentation, or opportunity may knock only once. In fact, sometimes opportunities to close may not present themselves at all and the salesperson must create an opportunity to close. Situations where a closing attempt is logical include:

- When a presentation has been completed without any objective from the prospect.
- When the presentation has been completed and all objections and questions have been answered.
- When the buyer indicates an interest in the product by giving a closing signal, such as a nod of the head.

Follow-up

To ensure customer satisfaction and maximize long-term sales volume, salespeople often engage in sales follow-up activities and the provision for post-sale service. If a sale is not made, a follow-up may eventually lead to a sale.

Strengths and Weaknesses of Personal Selling

Personal selling has several important advantages and disadvantages compared with the other elements of marketing communication mix (see Exhibit 9.5). Undoubtedly, the most significant strength of personal selling is its flexibility. Salespeople can tailor their presentations to fit the needs, motives, and behavior of individual customers. As salespeople see the prospect's reaction to a sales approach, they can immediately adjust as needed.

Personal selling also minimizes wasted effort. Advertisers typically expend time and money to send a mass message about a product to many people outside the target market. In personal selling, the sales force pinpoints the target market, makes a contact, and expends effort that has a strong probability of leading to a sale. Consequently, an additional strength of personal selling is that measuring effectiveness and determining the return on investment are far more straightforward for personal selling than for other marketing communication tools, where recall or attitude change is often the only measurable effect.

Another benefit of personal selling is that a salesperson is in an excellent position to encourage the customer to act. The one-on-one interaction of personal selling means that a salesperson can effectively respond to and overcome objections (customers' concerns or reservations about the product) so that the customer is more likely to buy. Salespeople can also offer many specific reasons to persuade a customer to buy, in contrast to the general reasons that an ad may urge customers to take immediate action.

A final strength of personal selling is the multiple tasks the sales force can perform. For instance, in addition to selling, a salesperson can collect payment service or repair products, return products, and collect product and marketing information. In fact, salespeople are often best at disseminating negative and positive word-of-mouth product information.

High cost is the primary disadvantage of personal selling. With increased competition, higher travel and lodging costs, and higher salaries, the cost per sales contract continues to increase. Many companies try to control sales costs by compensating sales representatives based on commission only, thereby guaranteeing that salespeople get paid only if they generate sales. However, commission-only salespeople may become risk-averse and only call on clients who have the highest potential return. These salespeople, then, may miss opportunities to develop a broad base of potential customers that could generate higher sales revenues in the long run.

Companies can also reduce sales costs by using complementary techniques, such as telemarketing, direct mail, toll-free numbers for interested customers, and online communication with qualified prospects. Telemarketing and online communication can further reduce costs by serving as an actual selling vehicle. Both technologies can deliver sales messages, respond to questions, take payment, and follow up.

Another disadvantage of personal selling is the problem of finding and retaining high-quality people. First, experienced salespeople sometimes realize that the only way their income can outpace their cost-of-living increase is to change jobs. Second, because of the push for profitability, businesses try to hire experienced salespeople away from competitors rather than hiring college graduates, who take three to five years to reach the level of productivity of more experienced salespeople. These two staffing issues have caused high turnover in many sales forces.

Another weakness of personal selling is message inconsistency. Many salespeople view themselves as independent from the organization, so they design their own sales techniques, use their own message strategies, and engage in questionable ploys to create a sale. Consequently, it is difficult to find a unified company or product message within a sales force, or between the sales force and the rest of the marketing communication mix.

A final weakness is that sales force members have different levels of motivation. Salespeople may vary in their willingness to make the desired sales calls each day; to make service calls that do not lead directly to sales; or to use new technology, such as a laptop, e-mail, or the company's Web site. Finally, overzealous sales representatives may tread a thin line between ethical and unethical sales techniques. The difference between a friendly lunch and commercial bribery is sometimes blurred.

THE IMC MIX

The manner in which the four components of IMC (i.e., advertising, personal selling, sales promotion, public relations) are combined into an effective whole is called the *IMC mix*. The IMC mix tends to be highly customized. While, in general, we can conclude that business-to-business marketers tend to emphasize personal selling and sales promotion over advertising and public relations, and that mass marketers are just the opposite, there are many exceptions. However, the following four factors tend to have an impact on the particular IMC mix a company might select:

1. *Marketing/IMC objectives*: Companies that desire broad market coverage or quick growth in market share, for example, must emphasize mass advertising in order to create a dramatic and simultaneous impact.
2. *Nature of the product*: The basic characteristics of a product (highly technical) suggest the need for demonstration and explanation through personal selling, or mass advertising in the case of a product with emotional appeal (perfume).
3. *Place in the product life cycle*: Products in the introductory stage in the life cycle often need mass advertising and sales promotion, those

in maturity need personal selling, and those in decline employ sales promotion.

4. *Available resources*: Companies with limited financial and human resources are often restricted to sales promotion and public relations while those with plenty of both opt for mass advertising and personal selling.

The most striking fact about IMC techniques is their cross-substitutability. They represent alternate ways to influence buyers to increase their purchases. It is possible to achieve a given sales level by increasing advertising expenditures or personal selling, or by offering a deal to the trade or a deal to customers. This substitutability calls for treating the various IMC tools in a joint-decision framework.

The Campaign

Determining what particular devices to use and how to combine them in order to achieve IMC objectives is one of the greatest challenges facing the communication planner. Ordinarily, management makes use of the campaign concept. A campaign is a planned, coordinated series of marketing communication efforts built around a single theme or idea and designed to reach a predetermined goal. Although the term "campaign" is probably thought of most often in connection with advertising, it seems appropriate to apply the concept of a campaign to the entire IMC program.

Many types of IMC campaigns may be conducted by a company, and several may be run concurrently. Geographically, a firm may have a local, regional, or national campaign, depending upon the available funds, objectives, and market scope. One campaign may be aimed at consumers and another at wholesalers and retailers.

A campaign revolves around a theme, a central idea or focal point. This theme permeates all IMC efforts and tends to unify the campaign. A theme is simply the appeals developed in a manner considered unique and effective. As such, it is related to the campaign's objectives and the customer's behavior. It expresses the product's benefits. Frequently the theme takes the form of a slogan, such as De Beers "A diamond is forever." Some campaigns use the same theme for several campaigns; others develop a different theme for each new campaign.

In a successfully operated campaign, the efforts of all groups concerned will be meshed effectively. The advertising program will consist of a series of related, well-timed, carefully placed ads. The personal selling effort can be tied in by having the salesperson explain and demonstrate the product benefits stressed in ads. Also, the sales force will be fully informed about the advertising part of the campaign—the theme, media used, schedule of appearance of ads, appeals used, and so on. The sales force will also inform the middlemen, the wholesalers and retailers, about this campaign, and convince them to incorporate it into their total marketing effort. Sales promotional devices will be coordinated with the other aspects of the campaign. For each campaign, new display materials must be prepared, reflecting the ads and appeals used in the current campaign, in order to maximize the campaign's impact at the point of sale. Personnel responsible for the physical distribution activities must ensure that adequate stocks of the product are available in all outlets prior to the start of the campaign. Finally, people working in public relations must be constantly kept aware of new products, product demonstrations, new product applications, and so forth. Of course, it is extremely important to provide enough lead time so that the public relations effort can take advantage of optimum timing.

CONCLUSIONS

Like all marketing organizations, nonprofits must engage in strategic communications. All the same communication tools are available to both for-profits and nonprofits. Yet, tradition and limited resources suggest that many of these communication tools are not part of the nonprofits arsenal. Mass advertising, for example, requires a heavy investment of cash and talent. The normal 2 percent effectiveness rate, combined with the necessary critical mass, makes this choice less than optimal for nonprofit organizations. Likewise, public relations is thought of as free by many nonprofits. Nothing could be further from the truth. The dollars and time needed to create effective public relations can be enormous. Sales promotion tactics are often employed by nonprofits. Price discounts and other special deals are common. Without understanding the real benefits and consequences of sales promotion, it can be a risky strategic alternative. Finally, personal selling is rarely considered. Again, the traditions of nonprofits purport that such aggressive marketing is inappropriate. Still, in a nonprofit, everyone is selling. Ultimately, all employees and volunteers should be trained to sell even if very passively.

All communication tactics should emerge from the marketing strategy and should not be based on tradition or what is easiest to do. They should be integrated and responsible personnel should be held accountable. Whether you like it or not, everything your organization does communicates to target audiences and beyond. It just makes sense to control this marketing element.

REFERENCE

1. This section adapted from Candie Jones, "Designers Take Creative Approaches to Promoting Charitable Causes", *The Chronicle of Philanthropy*, April 6, 2006, p. 49.

10

PRICING THE PRODUCT

Price is the only element of the marketing mix that produces revenue;
all the other elements produce costs

—*Philip Kotler*

Marja Hilfiker, a native of Finland, helped start the Academy of Hope as part of her church, the Church of the Savior, in Washington. The Academy is an adult-literacy charity that has offered basic education and career assistance for the past 20 years to low-income Washington residents. The program began with one person and helped 400 in 2005.

There are statistics that clearly show a need for these services. A study published by the federal government in 2004 shows that 30 million adults have serious shortcomings in their ability to read, write, and calculate.

The Academy's approach is very caring and no badgering to participate is allowed. It offers students help in small math, science, and English classes, as well as providing a lot of support, including help with resumes and job-interviewing skills, individual tutoring, and computer skills. Words of motivation also appear in short biographies of academy graduates posted by the group's front door. When a student misses a class, the teacher tracks him or her down with a phone call.

The budget, which now tops $660,000 annually, was supported early-on with bake sales. Today, students are expected to pay tuition of $10 per month. This gives them a sense of investment in the work and helps to offset costs. No one is ever turned away. Donations from individuals account for another third of the budget, with grants accounting for 20 percent. The remainder comes from corporations and the tuition fees.[1]

INTRODUCTION

From a customer's point of view, value is the sole justification for price. Many times customers lack an understanding of the cost of materials and other costs that go into the marketing of a product. But those customers can understand what that product does for them in terms of providing value. It is on this basis that customers make decisions about the purchase of a product. Creating value is also what the Academy of Hope does every day.

Effective pricing meets the needs of consumers and facilitates the exchange process. It requires that marketers understand that not all buyers want to pay the same price for products, just as they do not all want the same products, the same distribution outlets, or the same promotional messages. Therefore, in order to effectively price products, markets must distinguish among various market segments. The key to effective pricing is the same as the key to effective product, distribution, and promotion strategies. Marketers must understand buyers and price their products according to buyer needs if exchanges are to occur. However, one cannot overlook the fact that the price must be sufficient to support the plans of the organization, including satisfying stakeholders. The price charged for the good or service sold remains the primary source of revenue for most business.

This is just as true for nonprofit organizations as it is for for-profit companies. Nonprofits may use synonyms for price, such as charge, donation, tuition, fee, or contribution, but in the end, they all help cover costs, and allow the organization to survive. Unlike for-profits, nonprofits face some unique pricing problems. Most notably, the price charged may be less than costs, or price may not exist at all. As the designation suggests, nonprofits are not in business to make profits and satisfy stockholders. They often offer their services for free or on a sliding scale. They hope to make up the deficit through grants, donations, government's supplements, selling merchandise, and so forth. The uncertainty associated with these funding sources remains a major problem faced by virtually all nonprofits. Yet, it does not diminish the need for nonprofit marketers to understand the principles of setting price, despite the fact that many nonprofit organizations operate in nonprice markets. As will be discussed later, in the nonprofit sector it may make more sense to think about "value" rather than traditional price.

In this chapter we decipher the elements of pricing and value creation as employed by for-profit organizations. We then suggest adjustments in understanding and application that will enhance the ability of nonprofits to price their products.

PRICE DEFINED: THREE DIFFERENT PERSPECTIVES

Although setting the price is usually a marketing decision, setting it correctly requires an understanding of both the customer and society's view of price. In some respects, price setting is the most important decision made by a business. A price set too low may result in a deficiency in revenues and the demise of the business. A price set too high may result in poor response from customers and, unsurprisingly, the demise of the business. The consequences of a poor pricing decision, therefore, can be dire. We begin our discussion of pricing by considering the perspective of the customer.

The Customer's View of Price

As discussed in an earlier chapter, a customer can be either the ultimate user of the finished product or a business that purchases components of the finished product. It is the customer that seeks to satisfy a need or set of needs through the purchase of a particular product or set of products. Consequently, the customer uses several criteria to determine how much they are willing to expend in order to satisfy these needs. Ideally, the customer would like to pay as little as possible. This perspective is summarized in Exhibit 10.1.

Therefore, for the business to increase value (i.e., create the competitive advantage), it can either increase the perceived benefits or reduce the perceived costs. Both of these elements should be considered elements of price.

To a certain extent, perceived benefits are the mirror image of perceived costs. For example, paying a premium price—e.g., $650 for a piece of Lalique crystal—is compensated for by having this exquisite work of art displayed in one's home. Other possible perceived benefits are directly related to the price—value equation elements such as status, convenience, the deal, brand, quality, choice, and so forth. Many of these benefits tend to overlap. For instance, a Mercedes Benz E 750 is a very high-status brand name and possesses superb quality. This makes it worth the $100,000 price tag. Further, if Mr. Smith can negotiate a deal reducing the price by $15,000, that would be his incentive to purchase. Likewise, someone living in an isolated mountain

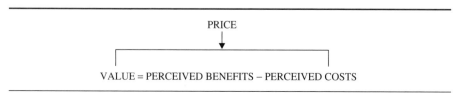

EXHIBIT 10.1   THE CUSTOMER'S VIEW OF PRICE

community is willing to pay substantially more for groceries at a local store rather than drive 78 miles to the nearest Safeway. That person is also willing to sacrifice choice for greater convenience. Increasing these perceived benefits is represented by a recently coined term—*value-added*. Thus, providing value-added elements to the product has become a popular strategic alternative. Computer manufacturers now compete on value-added components such as free delivery setup, training, a 24-hour help line, trade-in, and upgrades.

Perceived costs include the actual dollar amount printed on the product, plus a host of additional factors, both real and perceived. As noted, these perceived costs are the mirror-opposite of the benefits. When finding a gas station that is selling its highest grade for 6 cents less per gallon, the customer must consider the 16-mile drive to get there, the long line, the fact that the middle grade is not available, and heavy traffic. Therefore, inconvenience, limited choice, and poor service are possible perceived costs. Other common perceived costs include risk of making a mistake, related costs, lost opportunity, and unexpected consequences, to name but a few. A new cruise traveler discovers she really doesn't enjoy that venue for several reasons—she is given a bill for incidentals when she leaves the ship, she has used up her vacation time and money, and she receives unwanted materials from this company for years to come.

In the end, viewing price from the customer's perspective pays off in many ways. Most notably, it helps define value—the most important basis for creating a competitive advantage.

What counts to the marketer, therefore, is how stakeholders perceive prices. If the customer does not understand the true costs paid by the marketer, the marketer may have to base his price recommendations on the customer's perceived costs and benefits.

Price from a Societal Perspective

Price, at least in dollars and cents, has been the historical view of value. Derived from a bartering system—exchanging goods of equal value—the monetary system of each society provides a more convenient way to purchase goods and accumulate wealth. Price has also become a variable society employs to control its economic health. Price can be inclusive or exclusive. In many countries, such as Russia, China, and South Africa, high prices for products such as food, health care, housing, and automobiles means that most of the population is excluded from purchase. In contrast, countries such as Denmark, Germany, and Great Britain charge little for health care and consequently make it available to all. Yet, the tax burden in these countries may make living there prohibitive.

The Marketer's View of Price

Price is important to marketers because it represents marketers' assessment of the value customers see in the product or service and are willing to pay for it. A number of factors have changed the way marketers undertake the pricing of their products and services.

1. Foreign competition has put considerable pressure on U.S. firms' pricing strategies. Many foreign-made products are high in quality and compete in U.S. markets on the basis of lower price for good value.

2. Competitors often try to gain market share by reducing their prices. The price reduction is intended to increase demand from customers who are judged to be sensitive to changes in price.

3. New products are far more prevalent today than in the past. Pricing a new product can represent a challenge, as there is often no historical basis for pricing new products. If a new product is priced incorrectly, the marketplace will react unfavorably and the "wrong" price can do long-term damage to a product's chances for marketplace success.

4. Technology has led to existing products having shorter marketplace lives. New products are introduced to the market more frequently, reducing the "shelf life" of existing products. As a result, marketers face pressures to price products to recover costs more quickly. Prices must be set for early successes including fast sales growth, quick market penetration, and fast recovery of research and development costs.

PRICING OBJECTIVES

Firms rely on price to cover the cost of production, to pay expenses, and to provide the profit incentive necessary to continue to operate the business. We might think of these factors as helping organizations to: 1. survive, 2. earn a profit, 3. generate sales, 4. secure an adequate share of the market, and 5. gain an appropriate image.

1. *Survival*: it is apparent that most managers wish to pursue strategies that enable their organizations to continue in operation for the long term. So survival is one major objective pursued by most executives. For a commercial firm, the price paid by the buyer generates the firm's revenue. If revenue falls below cost for a long period of time, the firm cannot survive.

2. *Profit*: survival is closely linked to profitability. Making a $500,000 profit during the next year might be a pricing objective for a firm. Anything less will ensure failure. All business enterprises must earn a long-term profit. For many businesses, long-term profitability also allows the business to satisfy their most important constituents—stockholders. Lower-than-expected or no profits will drive down stock prices and may prove disastrous for the company.

3. *Sales*: just as survival requires a long-term profit for a business enterprise, profit requires sales. As you will recall from earlier in the text, the task of marketing management relates to managing demand. Demand must be managed in order to regulate exchanges or sales. Thus marketing management's aim is to alter sales patterns in some desirable way.

4. *Market Share*: if the sales of Safeway Supermarkets in the Dallas–Fort Worth metropolitan area account for 30 percent of all food sales in that area, we say that Safeway has a 30 percent market share. Management of all firms, large and small, are concerned with maintaining an adequate share of the market so that their sales volume will enable the firm to survive and prosper. Again, pricing strategy is one of the tools that is significant in creating and sustaining market share. Prices must be set to attract the appropriate market segment in significant numbers.

5. *Image*: price policies play an important role in affecting a firm's position of respect and esteem in its community. Price is a highly visible communicator. It must convey the message to the community that the firm offers good value, that it is fair in its dealings with the public, that it is a reliable place to patronize, and that it stands behind its products and services.

DEVELOPING A PRICING STRATEGY

Good pricing strategy is usually based on sound assumptions made by marketers. It is also based on an understanding of the two other perspectives discussed earlier. Clearly, sale pricing may prove unsuccessful unless the marketer adopts the consumer's perspective toward price. Similarly, a company should not charge high prices if it hurts society's health.

A pricing decision that must be made by all organizations concerns their competitive position within their industry. This concern manifests itself in either a competitive pricing strategy or a nonprice competitive strategy. Let's look at the latter first.

Nonprice Competition

Nonprice competition means that organizations use strategies other than price to attract customers. Advertising, credit, delivery, displays, private brands, and convenience are all example of tools used in nonprice competition. Businesspeople prefer to use nonprice competition rather than price competition, because it is more difficult to match nonprice characteristics. Competing on the basis of price may also have a deleterious impact on company profitability. Unfortunately, when most businesses think about price competition, they view it as matching the lower price of a competitor, rather than pricing smarter. In fact, it may be wiser not to engage in price competition for other reasons. Price may simply not offer the business a competitive advantage (employing the value equation).

Competitive Pricing

Once a business decides to use price as a primary competitive strategy, there are many well-established tools and techniques that can be employed. The pricing process normally begins with a decision about the company's pricing approach to the market.

Approaches to the Market

Price is a very important decision criteria that customers use to compare alternatives. It also contributes to the company's position. In general, a business can price itself to match its competition, price higher, or price lower. Each has its pros and cons.

Pricing to Meet Competition

Many organizations attempt to establish prices that, on average, are the same as those set by their more important competitors. Automobiles of the same size and having equivalent equipment tend to have similar prices. This strategy means that the organization uses price as an indicator or baseline. Quality in production, better service, creativity in advertising, or some other elements of the marketing mix are used to attract customers who are interested in products in a particular price category.

The keys to implementing a strategy of meeting competitive prices are an accurate definition of competition and knowledge of competitor's prices. A maker of hand-crafted leather shoes is not in competition with mass producers. If that firm attempts to compete with mass producers on price, higher production costs will make the business unprofitable. A more realistic definition of competition for this purpose would be other makers of hand-crafted leather shoes. Such a definition, along with knowledge of the competition's prices, would allow a manager to put the strategy into effect. Banks shop competitive banks every day to check their prices.

Pricing above Competitors

Pricing above competitors can be rewarding to organizations, provided that the objectives of the policy are clearly understood and that the marketing mix is used to develop a strategy to enable management to implement the policy successfully.

Pricing above competition generally requires a clear advantage on some nonprice element of the marketing mix. In some cases, it is possible due to a high price-quality association on the part of potential buyers. But such an assumption is increasingly dangerous in today's information-rich environment. *Consumer Reports* and other similar publications make objective product comparisons much simpler for the consumer. There are also hundreds of dot.com companies that provide objective price comparisons. The key is to prove to customers that your product justifies a premium price.

Pricing below Competitors

While some firms are positioned to price above competition, others wish to carve out a market niche by pricing below competitors. The goal of such a policy is to realize a large sales volume through a lower price and profit margins. By controlling costs and reducing services, these firms are able to earn an acceptable profit, even though profit per unit is usually less.

Such a strategy can be effective if a significant segment of the market is price-sensitive and/or the organization's cost structure is lower than competitors. Costs can be reduced by increasing efficiency, employing economies of scale, or by reducing or eliminating such things as credit, delivery, and advertising. For example, if a firm could replace its field sales force with telemarketing or online access, this function might be performed at lower cost. Such reductions often involve some loss in effectiveness, so the trade-off must be considered carefully.

Historically, one of the worst outcomes that can result from pricing lower than a competitor is a "price war." Price wars usually occur when a business believes that price-cutting produces increased market share, but does not have a true cost advantage. Price wars are often caused by companies misreading or misunderstanding competitors. Typically, price wars are overreactions to threats that either aren't there at all or are not as big as they seem.

Another possible drawback when pricing below competition is the company's inability to raise price or image. A retailer such as K-mart, known as a discount chain, found it impossible to reposition itself as a provider of designer women's clothes. Can you image Swatch selling a $3,000 watch?

How can companies cope with the pressure created by reduced prices? Some are redesigning products for ease and speed of manufacturing or reducing costly features that their customers do not value. Other companies are reducing rebates and discounts in favor of stable, everyday low prices (ELP). In all cases, these companies are seeking shelter from pricing pressures that come from the discount mania that has been common in the United States for the last two decades.

NEW PRODUCT PRICING

A somewhat different pricing situation relates to new product pricing. With a totally new product, competition does not exist or is minimal. What price level should be set in such cases? Two general strategies are most common— penetration and skimming. *Penetration pricing* in the introductory stage of a new product's lifecycle means accepting a lower profit margin and to price relatively low. Such a strategy should generate greater sales and establish the new product in the market more quickly. *Price skimming* involves the top part of the demand curve. Price is set relatively high to generate a high profit margin and sales are limited to those buyers willing to pay a premium to get the new product (see Exhibit 10.2).

Which strategy is best depends on a number of factors. A penetration strategy would generally be supported by the following conditions: price-sensitive consumers, opportunity to keep costs low, the anticipation of quick market entry by competitors, a high likelihood for rapid acceptance by potential buyers, and an adequate resource base for the firm to meet the new demand and sales.

A skimming strategy is most appropriate when the opposite conditions exist. A premium product generally supports a skimming strategy. In this case, "premium" doesn't just denote high cost of production and materials; it also suggests that the product may be rare or that the demand is unusually high. An example would be a $500 ticket for the World Series or an $80,000 price tag for a limited-production sports car. Having legal protection via a patent or copyright may also allow for an excessively high price. Intel and their Pentium chip possessed this advantage for a long period of time. In most cases, the initial high price is gradually reduced to match new competition and allow new customers access to the product.

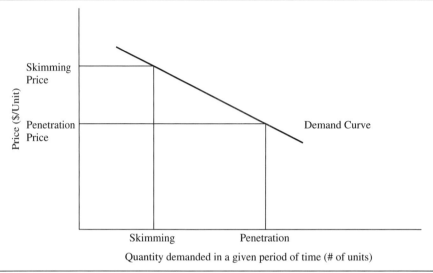

EXHIBIT 10.2 PENETRATION AND SKIMMING: PRICING STRATEGIES

PRICING LINES

You are already familiar with price lines. Ties may be priced at $15, $17, $20, and $22.50; jeans may be priced at $30, $32.95, $37.95, and $45. Each price must be far enough apart so that buyers can see definite quality differences among products. Price lines tend to be associated with consumer shopping goods such as apparel, appliances, and carpeting rather than product lines such as groceries. Customers do very little comparison-shopping on the latter.

Price lining serves several purposes that benefit both buyers and sellers. Customers want and expect a wide assortment of goods, particularly shopping goods. Many small price differences for a given item can be confusing. If ties were priced at $15, $15.35, $15.75, and so on, selection would be more difficult; the customer could not judge quality differences as reflected by such small increments in price. So, having relatively few prices reduces the confusion.

From the seller's point of view, price lining holds several benefits. First, it is simpler and more efficient to use relatively fewer prices. The product/service mix can then be tailored to selected price points. *Price points* are simply the different prices that make up the line. Second, it can result in a smaller inventory than would otherwise be the case. It might increase stock turnover and make inventory control simpler. Third, as costs change, either increasing or decreasing the prices can remain the same, but the quality in the line can be changed. For example, you may have bought a $20 tie 15 years ago. You can buy a $20 tie today, but it is unlikely that today's $20 tie is of the same fine quality as it was in the past. While customers are likely to be aware of the differences, they are nevertheless still able to purchase a $20 tie. During inflationary periods, the quality/price point relationship changes. From the point of view of salespeople, offering price lines will make selling easier. Salespeople can easily learn a small number of prices. This reduces the likelihood that they will misquote prices or make other pricing errors. Their selling effort is therefore more relaxed, and this atmosphere will influence customers positively. It also gives the salesperson flexibility. If a customer can't afford a $2,800 Dell system, the $2,200 system is suggested.

PRICE FLEXIBILITY

Another pricing decision relates to the extent of *price flexibility*. A flexible pricing policy means that the price is bid or negotiated separately for each exchange. This is a common practice when selling to organizational markets where each transaction is typically quite large. In such cases, the buyer may initiate the process by asking for bidding on a product or service that meets certain specifications. Alternatively, a buyer may select a supplier and attempt to negotiate the best possible price. Marketing effectiveness in many industrial markets requires a certain amount of price flexibility.

Discounts and Allowances

In addition to decisions related to the base price of products and services, marketing managers must also set policies related to the use of discounts and allowances. There are many different types of reductions—each designed to accomplish a specific purpose.

Quantity discounts are reductions in base price given as the result of a buyer purchasing some predetermined quantity of merchandise. A *noncumulative quantity discount* applies to each purchase and is intended to encourage buyers to make larger purchases. This means that the buyer holds the excess merchandise until it is used, possibly cutting the inventory cost of the seller and preventing the buyer from switching to a competitor at least until the stock is used. A *cumulative quantity discount* applies to the total bought over a period of time. The buyer adds to the potential discount with each additional purchase. Such a policy helps to build repeat purchases. Building material dealers, for example, find such a policy quite useful in encouraging builders to concentrate their purchase with one dealer and to continue with the same dealer over time. It should be noted that such cumulative quantity discounts are extremely difficult to defend if attacked in the courts.

Seasonal discounts are price reductions given on out-of-season merchandise. An example would be a discount on snowmobiles during the summer. The intention of such discounts is to spread demand over the year. This can allow fuller use of production facilities and improved cash flow during the year. Electric power companies use the logic of seasonal discounts to encourage customers to shift consumption to off-peak periods. Since these companies must have production capacity to meet peak demands, the lowering of the peak can lessen the generating capacity required.

Cash discounts are reductions on base price given to customers for paying cash or within some short time period. For example, a 2-percent discount on bills paid within ten days is a cash discount. The purpose is generally to accelerate the cash flow of the organization.

Trade discounts are price reductions given to middlemen (e.g., wholesalers, industrial distributors, retailers) to encourage them to stock and give preferred treatments to an organization's products. For example, a consumer goods company may give a retailer a 20 percent discount to place a larger order for soap. Such a discount might also be used to gain shelf space or a preferred position in the store.

Personal allowances are similar devices aimed at middlemen. Their purpose is to encourage middlemen to aggressively promote the organization's products. For example, a furniture manufacturer may offer to pay some specific amount toward a retailer's advertising expenses if the retailer agrees to include the manufacturer's brand name in the ads.

Some manufacturers or wholesalers also give prize money called spiffs for retailers to pass on to the retailer's sales clerks for aggressively selling certain items. This is especially common in the electronics and clothing industries, where it is used primarily with new products, slow movers, or high margin items.

Trade-in allowances also reduce the base price of a product or service. These are often used to allow the seller to negotiate the best price with a buyer. The trade-in may, of course, be of value if it can be resold. Accepting trade-ins is necessary in marketing many types of products. A construction company with a used grader worth $70,000 would not likely buy a new model from an equipment company that did not accept trade-ins, particularly when other companies do accept them.

PRICE BUNDLING

A very popular pricing strategy, *price bundling*, is to group similar or complementary products and to charge a total price that is lower if they were sold separately. Dell Computers and Gateway Computers follow this strategy by combining different components for a set price. Customers assume that these computer experts are putting together an effective product package and they are paying less. The underlying assumption of this pricing strategy is that the increased sales generated will more than compensate for a lower profit margin. It may also be a way of selling a less popular product by combining it with popular ones. Clearly, industries such as financial services and telecommunications are big users of this.

PSYCHOLOGICAL ASPECTS OF PRICING

Price, as is the case with certain other elements in the marketing mix, appears to have meaning to many buyers that goes beyond a simple utilitarian statement. Such meaning is often referred to as the *psychological aspect* of pricing. Inferring quality from price is a common example of the psychological aspect. A buyer may assume that a suit priced at $500 is of higher quality than one priced at $300. From a cost-of-production, raw material, or workmanship perspective, this may or may not be the case. The seller may be able to secure the higher price by nonprice means such as offering alterations and credit or the benefit to the buyer may be in meeting some psychological need such as ego enhancement. In some situations, the higher price may be paid simply due to lack of information or lack of comparative shopping skills. For some products or services, the quantity demanded may actually rise to some extent as price is increased. This might be the case with an item such as a fur coat. Such a pricing strategy is called *prestige pricing*.

Products and services frequently have *customary prices* in the minds of consumers. A customary price is one that customers identify with particular items. For example, for many decades a five-stick package of chewing gum cost five cents and a six-ounce bottle of Coca-Cola cost five cents. Candy bars now cost 60 cents or more, a customary price for a standard-sized bar. Manufacturers tend to adjust their wholesale prices to permit retailers in using customary pricing. However, as we have witnessed during the past decade, prices have changed so often that customary prices are weakened.

Another manifestation of the psychological aspects of pricing is the use of *odd prices*. We call prices that end in such digits as 5, 7, 8, and 9 "odd prices" (e.g., $2.95, $15.98, or $299.99); even prices are $3, $16, or $300. For a long time marketing people have attempted to explain why odd prices are used. It seems to make little difference whether one pays $29.95 or $30 for an item. Perhaps one of the most often heard explanations concerns the psychological impact of odd prices on customers. The explanation is that customers perceive even prices such as $5 or $10 as regular prices. Odd prices, on the other hand, appear to represent bargains or savings and therefore encourage buying. There seems to be some movement toward even pricing: however, odd pricing is still very common. A somewhat related pricing strategy is *combination pricing*. Examples are two-for-one or buy-one-get-one-free. Consumers tend to react very positively to these pricing techniques.

ALTERNATIVE APPROACHES TO DETERMINING PRICE

Price determination decisions can be based on a number of factors, including cost, demand, competition, value, or some combination of factors. However, while many marketers are aware that they should consider these factors, pricing remains somewhat of an art. For purposes of discussion, we categorize the alternative approaches to determining price as follows: 1. cost-oriented pricing; 2. demand-oriented pricing; and 3. value-based approaches.

Cost-oriented Pricing

The *cost-plus method*, sometimes called gross margin pricing, is perhaps most widely used by marketers to set price. The manager selects as a goal a particular gross margin that will produce a desirable profit level. Gross margin is the difference between how much the goods cost and the actual price for which it sells. This gross margin is designated by a percent of net sales. The percent selected varies among types of merchandise. That means that one product may have a goal of 48 percent gross margin while another has a target of 33 1/3 percent or 2 percent.

The cost-based pricing approach begins with a discussion of costs into variable and fixed. *Variable costs* change with demand; by customer, location, season, and so forth. For example, food and fuel costs for United Airlines are variable costs, and they will vary for each scheduled flight. *Fixed costs* do not change with the quantity demanded although demand may have some impact on them. The cost of an airplane and utilities is fixed for United. Demand does not directly affect these costs; however, demand will determine whether they need more airplanes or add more gates. Determining whether labor is a fixed or variable cost remains one of the most difficult calculations. While there may be a set number of employees working at a restaurant under normal conditions, extra employees are often brought in during a special holiday or event. In this example, the level of demand has an impact on labor costs and can be treated as variable costs.

A primary reason that the cost-plus method is attractive to marketers is that they do not have to forecast general business conditions or customer demand. If sales volume projections are reasonably accurate, profits will be on target. Consumers may also view this method as fair, since the price they pay is related to the cost of producing the item. Likewise, the marketer is sure that costs are covered.

A major disadvantage of cost-plus pricing is its inherent inflexibility. For example, department stores have often found difficulty in meeting competition from discount stores, catalog retailers, or furniture warehouses because of their commitment to cost-plus pricing. Another disadvantage is that it does not take into account consumer's perceptions of a product's value. Finally, a company's cost may fluctuate so constant price changing is not a viable strategy.

Although this pricing approach may seem overly simplified, it has definite merit. The problem facing managers of certain types of business such as retail food stores is that they must price a very large number of items and change many of those prices frequently. The standard mark-up usually reflects historically profitable margins and provides good guideline for pricing.

Exhibit 10.3 illustrates Harper's Landscaping Service's bid for maintaining the trees, shrubs, flower beds, and lawn adjacent to a federal building. Based on past experiences and cost forecasts, four different time estimates are derived for four related tasks.

Labor costs will vary since different levels of expertise are required. The total cost of labor is estimated at $26,976.00. Payroll taxes, insurance, and employee benefits cost approximately 30 percent of payroll or $8,650.00. Materials are estimated at $45,000.00. Equipment costing $6,200.00 will be needed if the contract extends into two years and is not included in this bid. Finally, the price that is set will depend on the pricing objective of the company and what type of return they need to cover fixed costs. The 20 percent contribution margin covers all their fixed costs (relative to this contract) and an actual profit margin of 7.5 percent, normal for this industry.

Certainly costs are an important component of pricing. No firm can make a profit until it covers its costs. However, the process determining costs and then setting a price based on costs does not take into consideration what the customer is willing to pay at the marketplace. As a result, many companies that have set out to develop a product have fallen victim to the desire to

Harper's Landscape			Bid: Agriculture Building
Labor	(A) Lawn mowing		10 × 4 × 25 = 1000 hours
	(B) Planting/Maintaining, beds		6 × 4 × 25 = 600 hours
	(C) Shrub/Tree Maintenance		4 × 4 × 25 = 400 hours
	(D) Winter Maintenance		4 × 2 × 27 = 216 hours
Labor costs	A	$10.00/Hr	
	B	$11.00/Hr	
	C	$20.00/Hr	
	D	$11.00/Hr	
Bid	Total Labor Costs		$26,976.00
	Payroll taxes, Ins. Benefits		$8,650.00
	Materials		$45,000.00
	Total Costs		$90,626.00
	20% Contribution Margin		$19,300.00
	Bid Price		$109,926.00

Exhibit 10.3   Sample Cost-Based Bid for Landscaping

continuously add features to the product, thus adding cost. When the product is finished, these companies add some percentage to the cost and expect customers to pay the resulting price. These companies are often disappointed, as customers are not willing to pay this cost-based price.

Break-even Analysis

A somewhat more sophisticated approach to cost-based pricing is the *break-even analysis*. The information required for the formula for break-even analysis is available from accounting records in most firms. The break-even analysis is the price that will produce enough revenue to cover all costs at a given level of production. Total cost can be divided into fixed and variable (total cost = fixed cost + variable cost). Recall that *fixed cost* does not change as the level of production goes up or down. The rent paid for the building to house the operation might be an example. No cost is fixed in the long run, but in the short run, many expenses cannot realistically be changed. *Variable cost* does change as production is increased or decreased. For example, the cost of raw material to make the product will vary with production (see Exhibit 10.4).

To illustrate how break-even analysis works, let's suppose you are the director of a museum that is about to bring in an exhibit called Body Works 2. You want to determine how many customers you can expect to purchase

Revenue and costs (in $000)

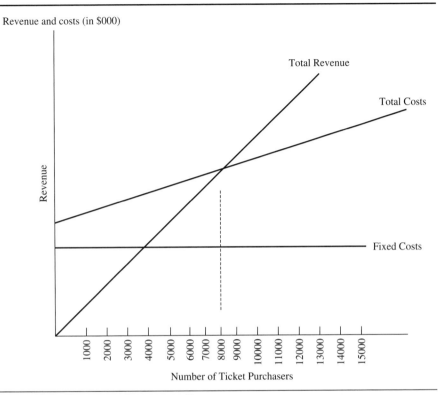

EXHIBIT 10.4   BREAK-EVEN ANALYSIS FOR BODYWORKS

tickets at various price points. Ultimately, you want to set a ticket fee (for nonmembers) during this three-month exhibit. First, you have decided that you must cover all your fixed costs during this period, which include real estate taxes, utilities, building maintenance, labor, and so forth. The estimated fixed costs are $175,000 and are represented on the break-even chart as a horizontal line. The variable cost for each ticket purchased—cost of exhibit, extra labor, room set-up, and so on—is $8.00 per ticket buyer.

Finally, you have decided to charge $30.00 per ticket. This is shown on the total revenue line, which begins at $0 and rises $30 per ticket sold. The number of tickets needed to break even is 7,955, and is determined by the intersection of the total revenue and total cost curves. If fewer than 7,955 tickets are sold at $30 each, the event will lose money, and ticket sales of 7,956 and above will generate a profit. Of course, this whole scenario is contingent upon whether $30 will be an attractive price for potential customers.

By using the following break-even formula, any price can be considered:

$$\text{BREAK-EVEN VOLUME} = \frac{\text{FIXED COSTS}}{\text{PRICE-VARIABLE COSTS}}$$

If we wanted to consider a $40 ticket price, we would derive the following results:

$$\text{BREAK-EVEN VOLUME} = \frac{\$175,000}{\$40 - \$8} = 5,470$$

There are several reasons why cost-based pricing is so popular. First, it is relatively simple to calculate cost, but quite difficult to estimate demand. This is particularly important for a business that has many items to price, such as a museum's gift shop. Second, in many industries this technique is most prevalent, which makes it easy to compare costs and prices. Finally, cost-based pricing seems inherently fair to customers, who don't mind a marketer making a fair profit. They assume that price-gauging is not part of the calculation.

There are some shortcomings as well. First, there is an assumption that fixed costs don't change at all and that variable costs are relatively constant. Both of these assumptions can prove false. A related problem is the difficulty in correctly assigning costs as fixed or variable. Labor, for example, can often be placed in both categories. Most importantly, the price selected may have very little to do with the price the consumer is willing to pay or should pay. Experience and guesswork may not be reliable predictors of a realistic price.

Target Rates of Return

Break-even pricing is a reasonable approach when there is a limit on the quantity that a firm can provide and particularly when a target return objective is sought. Assume, for example, that the firm with the costs illustrated in the previous example, Bodyworks 2 determines that it can provide no more than 10,000 units of the product in the next period of operation. Furthermore, the firm has set a target for profit of 20 percent above total costs. Referring again to internal accounting records and the changing cost of production at near capacity levels, a new total cost curve is calculated. From the cost curve profile, management sets the desirable level of production at 80 percent of capacity or 8,000 units. From the total cost curve, it is determined that the cost for producing 8,000 units is $18,000. Twenty percent of $18,000 is $3,600. Adding this to the total cost at 8,000 units yields the point at that quantity through which the total revenue curve must pass. Finally, $21,600 divided by

8,000 units yields the price of $2.70 per unit; here the $3,600 in profit would be realized. The obvious shortcoming of the target return approach to pricing is the absence of any information concerning the demand for the product at the desired price. It is assumed that all of the units will be sold at the price that provides the desired return.

It would be necessary, therefore, to determine whether the desired price is in fact attractive to potential customers in the marketplace. If break-even pricing is to be used, it should be supplemented by additional information concerning customer perceptions of the relevant range of prices for the product. The source of this information would most commonly be survey research, as well as a thorough review of pricing practices by competitors in the industry. In spite of their shortcomings, break-even pricing and target return pricing are very common business practices.

Demand-oriented Pricing

Demand-oriented pricing focuses on the nature of the demand curve for the product or service being priced. The nature of the demand curve is influenced largely by the structure of the industry in which a firm competes. That is, if a firm operates in an industry that is extremely competitive, price may be used to some strategic advantage in acquiring and maintaining market share. One the other hand, if the firm operates in an environment with a few dominant players, the range in which price can vary may be minimal.

The process begins with the creation of a demand/price schedule. Generally speaking, it shows the demand for a service at various prices, based on historical data or survey data. Exhibit 10.5 illustrates the demand for the classical music festival at six different prices. Demand increases as the price declines until the price reaches $60.

At that pricing point, demand starts declining. It appears that the price is too low and expected quality is too low as well. If the firm's pricing objective is market share maximization, the $60 price will yield the highest demand. To determine sales and profit maximization prices, it will be necessary to calculate total revenue, total variable costs, and gross margins. If we assume a variable cost of $20 per unit, then the $60 price would yield the highest total revenue at $480,000, as well as the highest gross margin of $360,000.

Value-based Pricing

If we consider the three approaches to setting price, cost-based is focused entirely on the perspective of the company with very little concern for the customer; demand-based is focused on the customer, but only as a predictor

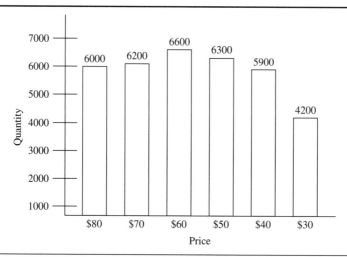

EXHIBIT 10.5　DEMAND/PRICE SCHEDULE

of sales; and value-based focuses entirely on the customer as a determinant of the total price/value package. Marketers who employ value-based pricing might use the following definition: "It is what you think your product is worth to that customer at that time." Moreover, it acknowledges several marketing/price truths:

- To the customer, price is the only unpleasant part of buying.
- Price is the easiest marketing tool to copy.
- Price represents everything about the product.

Still, value-based pricing is not altruistic. It asks and answers two questions: 1. what is the highest price I can charge and still make the sale? and 2. am I willing to sell at that price? The first question must take two primary factors into account; customers and competitors. The second question is influenced by two more: costs and constraints. Let's discuss each briefly.

Many customer-related factors are important in value-based pricing. For example, it is critical to understand the customer buying process. How important is price? When is it considered? How is it used? Another factor is the cost of switching. Have you ever watched the TV program *The Price is Right*? If you have, you know that most consumers have poor price knowledge. Moreover, their knowledge of comparable prices within a product category—e.g. ketchup—is typically worse. So price knowledge is a relevant factor. Finally, the marketer must assess the customers' price expectations. How much do you expect to pay for a large pizza? Color TV? DVD? Newspaper? Swimming pool? These expectations create a phenomenon called "sticker shock" as exhibited by gasoline, automobiles, and ATM fees.

A second factor influencing value-based pricing is competitors. As noted in earlier chapters, defining competition is not always easy. Of course there are like-category competitors such as Toyota and Nissan. We have already discussed the notion of pricing above, below, and at the same level of these direct competitors. However, there are also indirect competitors that consumers may use to base price comparisons. For instance, we may use the price of a vacation as a basis for buying vacation clothes. The cost of eating out is compared to the cost of groceries. There are also instances when a competitor, especially a market leader, dictates the price for everyone else. Coca-Cola determines the price for soft drinks. Kellogg's establishes the price for cereal.

If you're building a picnic table, it is fairly easy to add up your receipts and calculate costs. For a global corporation, determining costs is a great deal more complex. For example, calculating incremental costs and identifying avoidable costs are valuable tasks. *Incremental cost* is the cost of producing each additional unit. If the incremental cost begins to exceed the incremental revenue, it is a clear sign to quit producing. *Avoidable costs* are those that are unnecessary or can be passed onto some other institution in the marketing channel. Adding costly features to a product that the customer cannot use is an example of the former. As to the latter, the banking industry has been passing certain costs on to customers for decades.

Another consideration is opportunity costs. Because the company spent money on store remodeling, they are not able to take advantage of a discounted product purchase. Finally, costs vary from market to market as well as from quantities sold. Research should be conducted to assess these differences.

Although it would be nice to assume that a business has the freedom to set any price it chooses, this is not always the case. There are a variety of constraints that prohibit such freedom. Some constraints are formal, such as government restrictions in respect to strategies like collusion and price-fixing. This occurs when two or more companies agree to charge the same or very similar prices. Other constraints tend to be informal. Examples include matching the price of competitors, the traditional price charged for a particular product, and charging a price that covers expected costs.

Ultimately, value-based pricing offers the following three tactical recommendations:

- Employ a segmented approach toward price based on such criteria as customer type, location, and order size.
- Establish highest possible price level and justify it with comparable value.
- Use price as a basis for establishing strong customer relationship.

PRICING IN NONPROFITS

Nonprofit organizations are faced with two unique challenges in respect to pricing. First, nonprofits normally sell service products, which are intangible and inseparable from the consumers. How does a nonprofit place a price on an idea or delivered service that is co-produced by the customer? Second, the missions of nonprofits often mean that one or more of the stakeholders are not charged a price. Each of these questions will be addressed next.

Pricing Service Products

While consumers can approximate the cost of building an automobile or a computer, research indicates that this knowledge level is much lower for service products. There are several reasons for this difference. First, because service products are very difficult to standardize, there is no baseline for cost comparisons. Take the example of a physical check-up. Not every doctor defines it in the same way and the charge may vary as well. A second difference relates to the tendency of service providers to be unwilling to estimate price in advance. Often this is a tradition. Or, the provider may not know the answer since there are so many unknowns. Third, because of the special needs of service recipients, prices may vary as well. Every divorce has different components, resulting in dramatic differences in fees charged by the same lawyer. Fourth, the customer may be required to gather cost information from several disparate sources in the case of service products. This process has been simplified thanks to the Internet, but it is still more difficult than for goods products. Finally, prices are not very visible for service products. Consider your bank statement or your telephone bill. How many of the cost items listed do you understand? Although prices for service may not be hidden, they often are obscure.

For all the reasons cited, many customers do not see the price at all until after they receive certain services. Consequently, price is often not a key criterion for a purchase, as it often is for goods. Price is likely to be an important criterion in repurchase, however. Furthermore, monetary price in repurchase may be an even more important criterion than in initial purchase.

In addition to the monetary price placed on the service product or sent via an invoice, there are other costs as well. Nonmonetary costs represent other sources of sacrifice perceived by consumers when buying and using a service. Customers may view these costs as more important. They include psychological costs, search costs, and time costs. Psychological costs can be fraught with anxiety and risk. Fear of not understanding your bank loan or fear of the outcome of medical tests constitute psychological costs that customers experience as sacrifice when they are purchasing and using services. This tends to be especially true for new service products, such as banking online. Search costs—the efforts invested to identify and select among services you desire—tend to be higher for services than for goods. Service prices are not displayed on shelves and prices are known only when a customer has decided to experience the service. As noted, in some industries (travel and hotels), search costs have been reduced through the Internet. Most services require direct participation of the consumer and these consume real time: time waiting as well as time spent when the customer interacts with the service provider. Consider the time invested with a typical visit to your physician— average waiting time of 21.6 minutes.

In addition to the options available to cut monetary costs and reduce that price to the consumer, the ability to reduce nonmonetary costs may be as important. For example, a services marketer can reduce the perceptions of time when use of the service is embedded in other activities. Clinics can do weigh-ins and blood pressure checks, instead of letting the patient sit in the waiting area. Also, customers may be willing to pay to avoid other costs. Paying a premium for fast check-in and check-out are part of frequent flyer or miles programs offered by airlines and car rentals. There are also programs that allow customers to "buy" time. Babysitting, lawn care, cleaning services, personal shoppers, and carpet cleaning, represent net gains in the discretionary time of consumers. Finally, reducing psychological costs can be facilitated through guarantees, customer training, product education, and reliable response times, to name but a few possibilities.

One of the accepted truths in services marketing is that buyers use price (both monetary and nonmonetary) as an indicator of service quality. To the extent this assessment is valid depends on several factors, one of which is the other information available to them. When service attributes are accessible, when a brand name fairly represents the company's reputation, or when the level of marketing communication clearly relays the company's beliefs, customers may choose to use these cues rather than price. In other cases, where cues are intangible and it is difficult to judge quality, price is an acceptable surrogate. Another factor that increases the dependence on price as a quality indicator is the risk associated with the service purchase. In high-risk situations, such as medical treatment or a legal case, the customer will look to price as an indicator of quality. In the end, setting the total price for services is a decision of great importance. Not only does it cover costs or match competitors, it also facilitates the decision-making process.

There are also adjustments at the tactical level in pricing services:

- Costs are difficult to locate, track, and estimate and require an input system of measurement, such as time, and a contingency amount.
- Leading competitors often establish the baseline within a category, requiring other competitors to match such prices (possibly having higher costs), or to use a different price point (and risk being perceived as being too high or low).
- Nonmonetary costs must be factored into the calculation of perceived value to the customer.
- Because many customers do not possess accurate reference prices for services, services marketers are more likely than product marketers to organize price information for customers so they know how to view it.
- Customers find that price bundling simplifies their purchase and payment, and enhances perceived quality.
- In service industries in which outcome is very important but uncertainty is high, price may be a contingency based on outcome.

Nonprofits and Pricing

All the issues discussed for service product pricing apply to nonprofit pricing as well, with some additions. Most notably, many nonprofit organizations operate in a nonprice market, which means that clients/recipients are not charged for services received. Historically, there are valid reasons for giving nonprofit products away to consumers. First, there is the purely economic rationale that it makes no sense to spend more to collect a fee than it is worth. Trying to collect $1.00 from a homeless person for a hot meal may cost more than the initial fee. Second, there are instances when charging a fee for a service rendered is either politically or socially deplorable. Imagine Katrina survivors paying rent for their stay at the Superdome. Third, some nonprofits, such as foundations, have the necessary resources so that they do not charge for their services or publications. Finally, prices are not called for when there is no intent to influence consumer behavior.

There are several reasons why nonprofits should charge for their goods and services, especially if we include nonmonetary pricing. Most notably, pricing a product generates cash. Given the dire straits of many nonprofits, it is appropriate to charge a fair price for products in order to remain a viable organization. A second reason to charge a price (both monetary and nonmonetary) is to influence the clients'/stakeholders' attitudes, beliefs, opinions, and behavior. Unless the price is high enough, the wait long enough, and the risk high enough, clients will not place value on the service offered. Nonprofit services that are too easy to come by are sometimes viewed as not worth the effort. A final reason to charge a price is to keep track. Unless a nonprofit knows how many units have been sold, it does not know how many to order next time or whether the product is a success.

REFERENCE

1. This section adapted from: Nicole Lewis, "How One Grass-Roots Literacy Charity Keeps Hope Alive", *The Chronicle of Philanthropy*, August 20, 2006; p. 7

11

THE CHANNELS OF DISTRIBUTION

In every instance, we found that the best run companies stay as close
to their customers as humanly possible.

—Tom Peters

The American Museum of Natural History (AMNH) is one of the world's
great museums. Since 1869, the AMNH has pursued two missions: to explore
the world and to educate learners of all ages about the extraordinary diversity
of nature, the cosmos, and human culture. Every year, the museum sends
top-caliber researchers in the fields of anthropology and the natural sciences to
the ends of the earth, and they return with additions to its extensive collection
of over 32 million objects and specimens.

In addition to its 45 exhibition halls, the AMNH has created a number
of different ways to deliver their products to their various customers. For
example, the Web site for the AMNH (www.amnh.org) provides access to all
the educational resources of the museum by going to the "kids & families"
and "education" sections of the home page. *Resource for Learning (RFL)*
is an online catalog that serves as the gateway to the museum's extensive
collection of scientific and cultural educational materials. *RFL* is geared to
K through 12 educators and anyone interested in teaching or learning about
science. "Ology" is a favorite destination for 7- to 12-year-olds. The suf-
fix of "ology" means the study of something. Seminars on science are the
museum's online professional development program and a key component
of its educational outreach. The Web site for Science Bulletins (sciencebul-
letins.amnh.org) features current research in astrophysics and biodiversity.

The AMNH also has physically extended its channels into the neighborhoods. They converted a recreational vehicle and take it on the road to

tour schools. The RV varies exhibits periodically, and covers areas such as global warming, the environment, the science of water, and the science of perceptions.

INTRODUCTION

The opening vignette points to the importance of distribution in the nonprofit sector. Because of the intangibility of service products, one might conclude that a mechanism for delivering such products is irrelevant. In fact, the opposite is true. The channel of distribution, and the processes it encompasses, often becomes the key tangible elements of a service product. Service products, like goods products, must be delivered to customers. However, services require looking at the channel of distribution somewhat differently. In this chapter we consider the traditional channel management process as well as the necessary adjustments to it that nonprofits must make. Effective channel management may be the best way to save money and the most effective way to compete.

Just as with the other elements of the firm's marketing program, distribution activities are undertaken to facilitate the exchange between marketer and consumers. There are two basic functions performed between the marketer and the ultimate consumer (see Exhibit 11.1). The first, called the exchange function, involves sales of the product to the various members of the channel of distribution. The second, the physical distribution function, moves products through the exchange channel, simultaneously with title and ownership. Decisions concerning both of these sets of activities are made in conjunction with the firm's overall marketing plan and are designed so that the firm can best serve its customers in the marketplace. In actuality, without a channel of distribution the exchange process would be far more difficult and ineffective.

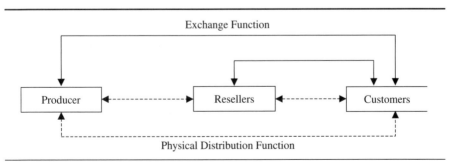

EXHIBIT 11.1   DUAL-FLOW SYSTEM IN MARKETING CHANNELS

The key role that distribution plays is satisfying a firm's customers and achieving a profit for the firm. From a distribution perspective, customer satisfaction involves maximizing time and place utility to the organization's suppliers, intermediate customers, and final customers. In short, organizations attempt to get their products to their customers in the most effective ways. Further, as stakeholders find their needs satisfied by an increased quantity and variety of goods, the mechanism of exchange (i.e., the channel) increases in importance.

The two basic utilities provided by the distribution system are availability and accessibility. Availability denotes that the service product is available for purchase where and when the consumer wants it. Traditionally, hours of operation provided availability via brick and mortar outlets. Supermarkets are now open seven days a week and 24 hours each day, because over 50 percent today's consumers grocery shop between 5 P.M. and 12 A.M. Direct mail or Internet shopping means there are no restrictions to availability, although these purchases are somewhat restricted by delivery alternatives. Catalogs and Web sites mean the store is always open.

Accessibility suggests that the exchange is relatively easy for the customer. Banks have created greater accessibility by providing ATMs and electronic banking. Consumers can now conduct numerous financial transactions at home or at work with very little effort. Advances in telecommunications have made many service products more accessible. For example, travel agents can now do much of their business over the phone. Faxes allow them to send reservations forms to customers and online forms allow travelers to complete applications at their leisure.

THE EVOLUTION OF THE MARKETING CHANNEL

As consumers, we Americans have clearly taken for granted that when we go to a supermarket the shelves will be filled with products we want; when we are thirsty there will be a Coke machine or bar around the corner; and when we don't have time to shop, we can pick up the telephone and order from the L.L. Bean catalog or through the Internet. Of course, if we give it some thought, we realize that this magic is not a given, and that hundreds of thousands of people plan, organize, and labor long hours so that this modern convenience is available to you, the customer. It hasn't always been this way, and it is still not this way in many other countries. Perhaps a little anthropological discussion will help our understanding.

The channel structure in a primitive culture is virtually nonexistent. The family of a tribal group is almost entirely self-sufficient. The group is composed of individuals who are both communal producers and consumers of whatever goods and services can be made available. As economies evolve, people begin to specialize in some aspect of economic activity. They engage in farming, hunting, or fishing, or some other basic craft. Eventually, this specialized skill produces excess products, which they exchange or trade for needed goods that have been produced by others. This exchange process or barter marks the beginning of formal channels of distribution. These early channels involve a series of exchanges between two parties who are producers of one product and consumers of the other.

With the growth of specialization, particularly industrial specialization, and with improvements in methods of transportation and communication, channels of distribution become longer and more complex. Thus, corn grown in Illinois may be processed into corn chips in West Texas, which are then distributed throughout the United States. Or, turkeys grown in Virginia are sent to New York so that they can be shipped to supermarkets in Virginia. Channels don't always make sense.

The channel mechanism also operates for service products. In the case of medical care, the channel mechanism may consist of a local physician, specialists, hospitals, ambulances, laboratories, insurance companies, physical therapists, home care professionals, and so forth. All of these individuals are interdependent, and could not operate successfully without the cooperation and capabilities of all the others.

Based on this relationship, we define a *marketing channel* as "sets of interdependent organizations involved in the process of making a product or service available for use or consumption, as well as providing a payment mechanism for the provider."

This definition implies several important characteristics of the channel. First, the channel consists of *institutions*, some under the control of the producer and some outside the producer's control. Yet all must be recognized, selected, and integrated into an efficient channel arrangement.

Second, the channel management *process* is continuous and requires constant monitoring and reappraisal. The channel operates 24 hours a day and exists in an environment where change is the norm.

Finally, channels should have certain distribution *objectives* guiding their activities. The structure and management of the marketing channel is, thus, in part, a function of a firm's distribution objective. It is also a part of the marketing objectives, especially the need to make an acceptable profit. Channels usually represent the largest costs in marketing a product.

One traditional framework that has been used to express the channel mechanism is the *concept of flow*. These flows, touched upon in Exhibit 11.2,

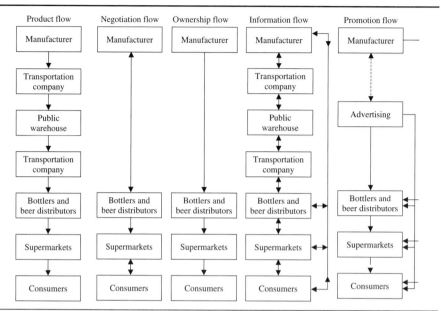

EXHIBIT 11.2 FIVE FLOWS IN THE MARKETING CHANNEL FOR PERRIER WATER

Source: Bart Rosenbloom, *Marketing Channels: A Management View*, Chicago: Dryden Press, 1983

reflect the many linkages that tie channel members and other agencies together in the distribution of goods and services. From the perspective of the channel manager, there are five important flows.

1. Product flow
2. Negotiation flow
3. Ownership flow
4. Information flow
5. Promotion flow

These flows are illustrated for Perrier water in Exhibit 11.2. The *product flow* refers to the movement of the physical product from the manufacturer through all the parties who take physical possession of the product until it reaches the ultimate consumer. The *negotiation flow* encompasses the institutions that are associated with the actual exchange processes. The *ownership flow* shows the movement of title through the channel. *Information flow* identifies the individuals who participate in the flow of information either up or down the channel. Finally, the *promotion flow* refers to the flow of persuasive communication in the form of advertising, personal selling, sales promotion, and public relations.

FUNCTIONS OF THE CHANNEL

The primary purpose of any channel of distribution is to bridge the gap between the producer of a product and the user of it, whether the parties are located in the same community or in different countries thousands of miles apart. The channel is composed of different institutions that facilitate the transaction and the physical exchange. Institutions in channels fall into three categories: 1. the producer of the product—a craftsman, manufacturer, farmer, or other extractive industry producer; 2. the user of the product—an individual, household, business buyer, institution, or government; 3. certain middlemen at the wholesale and/or retail level. Not all channel members perform the same function.

A channel performs three important functions:

1. *Transactional functions* —buying, pricing, selling, providing credit and risk assumption.
2. *Logistical functions* —assembly, storage, sorting, and transportation.
3. *Facilitating functions* —post-purchase service and maintenance, financing, information dissemination, and channel coordination or leadership.

These functions are necessary for the effective flow of product and title to the customer and payment back to the producer. Certain characteristics are implied in every channel. First, although you can eliminate or substitute channel institutions, the functions that these institutions perform cannot be eliminated. Typically, if a wholesaler or a retailer is removed from the channel, the function they perform will be either shifted forward to a retailer or the consumer, or shifted backward to a wholesaler or the manufacturer. For example, a producer of custom hunting knives might decide to sell through direct mail instead of retail outlets. The producer absorbs the sorting, storage, and risk functions; the post office absorbs the transportation function; and the consumer assumes more risk in not being able to touch or try the product before purchase.

Second, all channel institutional members are part of many channel transactions at any given point in time. From the customer's perspective, the complexity may be quite overwhelming. Consider for the moment how many different products you purchase in a single year, and the vast number of channel mechanisms you use. From the marketer's point of view, the use of a multichannel strategy allows the use of two or more channels to reach one or more market segments. In addition to increasing market coverage, this strategy often lowers costs of distribution.

Third, the fact that you are able to complete all these transactions to your satisfaction, as well as to the satisfaction of the other channel members, is due to the *routinization* benefits provided through the channel. Routinization means that the right products are most always found in places (catalogs or stores) where the consumer expects to find them, comparisons are possible, prices are marked, and methods of payment are available. Routinization aids the producers as well as the consumer, in that the producer knows what to make, when to make it, and how many units to make.

Fourth, there are instances when the best channel arrangement is *direct*, from the producer to the ultimate user. This is particularly true when available middlemen are incompetent, unavailable, or the producer feels he can perform the tasks better. Similarly, it may be important for the producer to maintain direct contact with customers so that quick and accurate adjustments can be made. Direct-to-user channels are common in industrial settings, as are door-to-door selling and catalog sales. Indirect channels are more typical and result, for the most part, because producers are not able to perform the tasks provided by middlemen.

Finally, although the notion of a channel of distribution may sound unlikely for a service product, such as health care or air travel, service marketers also face the problem of delivering their product in the form and at the place and time their customer demands. Banks have responded by developing bank-by-mail, Automatic Teller Machines (ATMs), and other distribution systems. The medical community provides emergency medical vehicles, outpatient clinics, 24-hour clinics, and home-care providers. As noted in Exhibit 11.3, even performing arts employ distribution channels. In all three

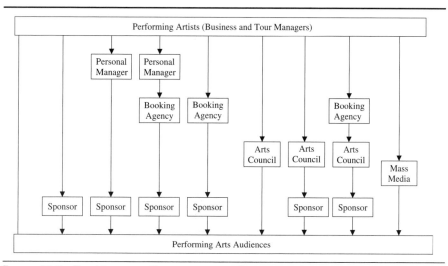

Exhibit 11.3 The Marketing Channels for the Performing Arts

cases, the industries are attempting to meet the special needs of their target markets while differentiating their product from that of their competition. A channel strategy is evident.

CHANNEL INSTITUTIONS: CAPABILITIES AND LIMITATIONS

There are several different types of parties participating in the marketing channel. Some are members, while others are nonmembers. The former perform negotiation functions and participate in negotiation and/or ownership while the latter participants do not.

Producer and Manufacturer

These firms extract, grow, or make products. A wide array of products is included, and firms vary in size from a one-person operation to those that employ several thousand people and generate billions in sales. Despite these differences, all are in business to satisfy the needs of markets. In order to do this, these firms must be assured that their products are distributed to their intended markets. Most producing and manufacturing firms are not in a favorable position to perform all the tasks that would be necessary to distribute their products directly to their final user markers. A computer manufacturer many know everything about designing the finest personal computer, but know absolutely nothing about making sure the customer has access to the product.

In many instances, it is the expertise and availability of other channel institutions that make it possible for a producer/manufacturer to even participate in a particular market. Imagine the leverage that a company like Frito-Lay has with various supermarket chains. Suppose you developed a super-tasting new snack chip. What are your chances of taking shelf-facings away from Frito-Lay? Zero. Thankfully, a specialty catalog retailer is able to include your product for a prescribed fee. Likewise, other channel members can be useful to the producer in designing the product, packaging it, pricing it, promoting it, and distributing it through the most effective channels. It is rare that a manufacturer has the expertise found with other channel institutions.

Retailing

Retailing involves all activities required to market consumer goods and services to ultimate consumers who are motivated to buy in order to satisfy individual or family needs in contrast to business, institutional, or industrial use. Thus, when an individual buys a computer at Circuit City, groceries at Safeway, or a purse at Ebags.com, a retail sale has been made.

We typically think of a store when we think of a retail sale. However, retail sales are made in ways other than through stores. For example, retail sales are made by a door-to-door salesperson, such as an Avon representative; by mail order through a company such as Lillian Vernon; by automatic vending machines; and by hotels and motels. Nevertheless, most retail sales are still made in brick-and-mortar stores.

Nonstore Retailing

Nonstore retailing describes sales made to ultimate consumers outside of a traditional retail store setting. In total, nonstore retailing accounts for a relatively small percentage of total retail sales, but it is growing and very important with certain types of merchandise, such as life insurance, cigarettes, magazines, books, CDs, and clothing.

One type of nonstore retailing used by such companies as Avon, Electrolux, and many insurance agencies is *in-home selling*. Such sales calls may be made to preselected prospects or in some cases on a cold call basis. A variation of door-to-door selling is the *demonstration party*. Here one customer acts as a host and invites friends. Tupperware has been very successful with this approach.

Vending machines are another type of nonstore retailing. *Automated vending* uses coin-operated, self-service machines to make a wide variety of products and services available to shoppers in convenient locations. Cigarettes, soft drinks, hosiery, and banking transactions are but a few of the items distributed in this way. This method of retailing is an efficient way to provide continuous service. It is particularly useful with convenience goods.

Mail order is a form of nonstore retailing that relies on product description to sell merchandise. The communication with the customer can be by flyer or catalog. Magazines, CDs, clothing, and assorted household items are often sold in this fashion. As with vending machines, mail order offers convenience but limited service. It is an efficient way to cover a very large geographical area when shoppers are not concentrated in one location. Many retailers are moving toward the use of newer communications and computer technology in catalog shopping.

Service marketers often use a type of hybrid nonstore retailer known as agents. *Agents* perform tasks that the producer cannot or chooses not to do. Two service industries that use agents extensively are insurance companies and airlines. Allstate insurance uses agents to provide product information to customers, write policies, collect payments, and service the account. The agent will turn the client over to an adjuster when an accident occurs. Similarly, travel agents represent several airlines. They provide information, make reservations, collect payment, and maintain the account. The Internet has reduced the need for both kinds of agents. Over 34,000 travel agents have lost their positions during the last decade.

Online marketing has emerged during the last decade; it requires that both the retailer and the consumer have computer and modem. A modem connects the computer to a telephone line so that the computer user can reach various online information services. There are two types of online channels: 1. commercial online channels—various companies have set up online information and marketing services that can be accessed by those who have signed up and paid a monthly fee, and 2. Internet—a goal web of some 45,000 computer networks that is making instantaneous and decentralized global communication possible. Users can send e-mail, exchange views, shop for products, and access real-time news.

Wholesaling

Another important channel member in many distribution systems is the wholesaler. *Wholesaling* includes all activities required to market goods and services to businesses, institutions, or industrial users who are motivated to buy for resale or to produce and market other products and services. When a bank buys a new computer for data processing, a school buys audio-visual equipment for classroom use, or a dress shop buys dresses for resale, a wholesale transaction has taken place.

The vast majority of all goods produced in an advanced economy have wholesaling involved in their marketing. This includes manufacturers, who operate sales offices to perform wholesale functions, and retailers, who operate warehouses or otherwise engage in wholesale activities. Even a centrally planned socialist economy needs a structure to handle the movement of goods from the point of production to other product activities or to retailers who distribute to ultimate consumers. Note that many establishments that perform wholesale functions also engage in manufacturing or retailing. This makes it very difficult to produce accurate measures of the extent of wholesale activity. For the purpose of keeping statistics, the Bureau of the Census of the United States Department of Commerce defines wholesaling in terms of the percent of business done by establishments who are primary wholesalers. It is estimated that only about 60 percent of all wholesale activity is accounted for in this way.

Physical Distribution

In a society such as ours, the task of physically moving, handling and storing products has become the responsibility of marketing. In fact, to an individual firm operating in a high-level economy, these logistical activities are critical. They often represent the only cost-saving area open to the firm. Likewise, in markets where product distinctiveness has been reduced greatly, the ability to excel in physical distribution activities may provide a true competitive advantage. Ultimately, physical distribution activities provide the bridge between the production activities and the markets that are spatially and temporally separated.

Physical distribution management may be defined as the process of strategically managing the movement and storage of materials, parts, and finished inventory from suppliers, between enterprise facilities, and to customers. Physical distribution activities include those undertaken to move finished products from the end of the production line to the final consumer. They also include the movement of raw materials from a source of supply to the beginning of the production line, and the movement of parts and the like to maintain the existing product. Finally, it may include a network for moving the product back to the producer or reseller, as in the case of recalls or repair.

Before discussing physical distribution, it is important to recognize that physical distribution and the channel of distribution are not independent decision areas. They must be considered together in order to achieve the organization's goal of satisfied customers. Several relationships exist between physical distribution and channels, including the following:

1. Defining the physical distribution standards that channel members want
2. Making sure the proposed physical distribution program designed by an organization meets the standards of channel members
3. Selling channel members on physical distribution programs
4. Monitoring the results of the physical distribution program once it has been implemented

CHANNEL STRUCTURE

In deciding what type of channel structure to use, service companies have three alternatives: exclusive distribution, selective distribution, and intensive distribution. When a service marketer wants to maintain a high level of control over the third party or agent, they might opt for *exclusive distribution*. For example, State Farm would select one agent to operate in a geographic region. In turn, that agent could only sell State Farm products. Or, the Louvre in Paris would allow only one retailer in each American city to sell its reproductions.

Selective distribution means that a selected group of distributors would be allowed to sell the marketers' products. Strong control would not be critical, but it would still be important. Thus, the independent insurance agent might sell several complementary brands. Agents would be selected very carefully, as would the insurance companies sold.

Intensive distribution attempts to saturate the market by selecting as many outlets as possible. This makes sense when the brand has a strong position in the market and outlets have a minimal impact on the brand's success. Major credit card companies would be an example. The Muscular Dystrophy Association employs this strategy during their annual pledge drive.

Push versus Pull

Another strategic option available through channels is the notion of push versus pull. In the case of a push strategy (see Exhibit 11.4) the producer sells to the wholesaler, who then sells to the retailer, who in turn sells to the consumer. In this arrangement, each institution in the channel assumes responsibility for specific tasks, and is rewarded accordingly. Likewise, each channel member must market the product to the next in line. In the pull strategy, the manufacturer/producer takes primary responsibility for marketing to the ultimate consumer. This is done primarily through marketing communication functions such as advertising, sales promotion, and personnel selling. Ideally, the consumer is so highly motivated that he demands that the retailer

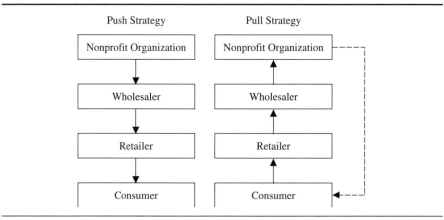

EXHIBIT 11.4   PUSH VERSUS PULL

shelve the product, which in turn prompts the retailer to ask the wholesaler to carry the product. Thus, the product is pulled through the channel. Both options have their pros and cons. Consequently, most marketers use some combination of push and pull. Push asks more from middlemen and drives up costs and the final price. Pull works better when the brand is strong and little is needed from middlemen.

THE CHANNEL MANAGEMENT PROCESS

Evidence suggests that a channel should be managed just like the product, promotion, and pricing functions. This channel management process contains four steps: 1. analyze the customer, 2. establish the channel objectives, 3. specify distribution tasks, and 4. evaluate and select from channel alternatives.

Analyze the Customer

We begin the process of channel management by answering two questions. First, to whom shall we sell this merchandise immediately? Second, who are our ultimate users and buyers? Depending upon a host of factors, including the type of product, functions performed in the channel, and location in the channel, the immediate and ultimate customers may be identical or they may be quite separate. In both cases, some fundamental questions would apply. There is a need to know what the customer needs, where they buy, when they buy, why they buy from certain outlets, and how they buy.

It is best that we first identify the traits of the ultimate user, since the results of this evaluation might determine the other channel institutions we would use to meet these needs. For example, the buying characteristics of the purchase of a high-quality VCR might be as follows:

- Purchased only from a well-established, reputable dealer
- Purchased only after considerable shopping to compare prices and merchandise characteristics
- Purchaser willing to go to some inconvenience (time and distance) to locate the most acceptable brand
- Purchased only after extended conversations involving all interested parties, including dealer, users, and purchases
- Purchase may be postponed
- Purchased only from a dealer equipped to render prompt and reasonable product service

These buying specifications illustrate the kinds of requirements that the manufacturer must discover. In most cases, purchase specifications are fairly obvious and can be unearthed without great difficulty. On the other hand, some are difficult to determine. For example, certain consumers will not dine at restaurants that serve alcohol; others will patronize only supermarkets that exhibit definite ethnic characteristics in their merchandising. Nonetheless, by careful and imaginative research, most of the critical factors that bear on consumer buying specifications can be determined.

Knowing the buying specifications of consumers, the channel planner can decide on the type or types of wholesaler and/or retailer/agent through which a product should be sold. This requires that a manufacturer contemplating distribution through particular types of retailers become intimately familiar with the precise location and performance characteristics of those he or she is considering.

In much the same way that buying specifications of ultimate users are determined, the manufacturers must also discover buying specifications of resellers. Of particular importance is the question, "from whom do my retail outlets prefer to buy?" The answer to this question determines the types of wholesalers (if any) that the manufacturer should use. Although many retailers prefer to buy directly from the manufacturers, this is not always the case. Often, the exchange requirements of manufacturers (e.g., infrequent visits, large order requirements, and stringent credit terms) are the opposite of those desired by retailers. Such retailers would rather buy from local distributors who have lenient credit terms and offer a wide assortment of merchandise.

Establish the Channel Objectives

The channel plan is derived from channel objectives. They are based on the requirements of the purchasers and users, the overall marketing strategy, and the long-run goals of the corporation. However, in cases when a company is just getting started or an older company is trying to carve out a new market niche, the channel objectives may be the dominant objectives. For example, a small manufacturer wants to expand outside the local market. An immediate obstacle is the limited shelf space available to this manufacturer. The addition of a new product to the shelves generally means that space previously assigned to competitive products must be obtained. Without this exposure, the product is doomed.

As one would expect, there is wide diversity of forms that channel objectives can take. The following areas encompass the major categories:

- Growth in sales—by reaching new markets, and/or increasing sales in existing markets.

- Maintenance or improvement of market share—educate or assist channel components in their efforts to increase the amount of product they handle.
- Achieve a pattern of distribution—structure the channel in order to achieve certain time, place, and form utilities.
- Create an efficient channel—improve channel performance by modifying various flow mechanisms.

Specify Distribution Tasks

After the distribution objectives are set, it is appropriate to determine the specific distribution tasks (functions) to be performed in that channel system. The channel manager must be far more specific in describing the tasks, and must define how these tasks will change depending upon the situation. An ability to do this requires the channel manager to evaluate all phases of the distribution network. Tasks must be identified fully, and costs must be assigned to these tasks. For example, a manufacturer might delineate the following tasks as being necessary in order to profitably reach the target market:

- Provide delivery within 48 hours after order placement.
- Offer adequate storage space.
- Provide credit to other intermediaries.
- Facilitate a product return network.
- Provide readily available inventory (quantity and type).
- Provide for absorption of size and grade obsolescence.

Evaluate and Select from Channel Alternatives

Determining the specific channel tasks is a prerequisite for the evaluation and selection process. There are three bases for channel alternatives: 1. number of levels, 2. intensity at the various levels, 3. types of intermediaries at each level.

Number of Levels

Channels can range in levels from two to several (five being typical). The two-level channel (producer to consumer) is a direct channel and is possible only if the producer or customers are willing to perform several of the tasks performed by intermediaries. The number of levels in a particular industry might be the same for all the companies simply because of tradition. In other industries, this dimension is more flexible and subject to rapid change.

Intensity at Each Level

Once the number of levels has been decided, the channel manager needs to determine the actual number of channel components involved at each level. How many retailers in a particular market should be included in the distribution network? How many wholesalers? The intensity decision is extremely critical, because it is an important part of the firm's overall marketing strategy. Companies such as Coca-Cola and Timex watches have achieved high levels of success through their intensive distribution strategy.

Types of Intermediaries

As discussed earlier, there are several types of intermediaries that operate in a particular channel system. The objective is to gather enough information to have a general understanding of the distribution tasks these intermediaries perform. Based on this background information, several alternatives will be eliminated.

EXPANDING THROUGH DISTRIBUTION

In addition to the channel management process just outlined, expanding the distribution network can be an effective strategy for growing the organization. There are a number of options available to accomplish this objective:

- Expansion of service to another location. Opening another office is fairly inexpensive as long as the potential market is justified.
- Adding another service product. An existing counseling organization offers online registration process.
- Adding a new market segment. A health club that expands its swimming lessons from children to include senior citizens is employing this strategy.

These three primary strategies can be combined in a variety of ways to increase sales, cut costs, and serve a larger constituency. There are several possible risks when growing channels (i.e., finding good locations, expenditures exceed benefits, quality control, inadequate human resources, customer confusion, effective management, and too-rapid growth).

CHANNEL DECISIONS FOR NONPROFITS

Every channel concept and ensuing strategies discussed have important potential payoffs for the nonprofit. Unfortunately, most nonprofits do not have the necessary resources to operationalize a traditional channel mechanism. Often partnerships are required, assuming that such partnerships reflect the mission of the nonprofit. The Brain Injury Association of Iowa's awareness program, for example, was able to meet its objectives for very low costs by asking emergency room physicians to distribute materials explaining symptoms following a traumatic brain injury. Further, they were asked to "sell" patients on the need to keep track of symptoms and come back to the emergency room if any symptoms appear. Iowa corporations were also asked to post marketing materials in all their buildings.

More prevalent is the assumption made by many nonprofits that they have no channel problems because they have no channels. Many churches aren't convinced that the pastor and office staff are producers or that the church itself is a type of retailer, delivering products to customers. Imagine First Baptist Church being compared to Wal-Mart. Yet, if you are convinced by now that nonprofits must be run as businesses and that marketing is the primary driver, then adopting a channel perspective must follow.

The following questions must be addressed if a nonprofit is to employ channel management that is both effective and efficient:

Should a nonprofit employ a direct or indirect channel strategy?

The answer to this question is quite complex and is dependent on the interplay of a number of factors, including the size of the market, the target market(s), the nature of the product, available middlemen, and financial capabilities. If the market is geographically concentrated, for example, there is a single target market, the product is complex, there are few high quality middlemen, and the nonprofit has limited resources, direct distribution makes the most sense. Middlemen are more useful when the market is widely dispersed, the product needs little technical support, and the nonprofit has neither a sales force nor the financial resources to build one.

An exception to this tendency is when nonprofits establish a channel linking them to donors and potential donors. In such instances, the nonprofit does not want the donor to establish a relationship with an intermediary. Having a direct connection is vital. However, there are instances when another nonprofit agency facilitates the donation process. An example is the United Way or the United Negro College Fund. In both cases, lower costs and reduced competition serve as reasons why their member agencies look to them to fundraise.

There are also situations where the nonprofit channel closely resembles the channel of a for-profit organization. For example, the Boy Scouts owns its own retail outlets, but also distributes its equipment through some 3,000 retail outlets. There is also the case of many blood banks that not only collect blood through a central location, where the inconvenience and other costs are borne by the donor, but also sends out mobile units where they bear most of the costs. In fact, most nonprofits tend to use some combination of direct and indirect channels. Since nonprofits sell services that are co-produced and cannot be stored, most such services must be distributed directly. This does not mean the nonprofit organization cannot take all or part of its services on the road and make them more accessible. The benefit of using intermediaries is their superior efficiency and effectiveness in the performance of many marketing tasks and functions. Unless the nonprofit can do them as well, at a level they can afford, indirect channels may be the best solution.

What is the optimal site and time?

When the nonprofit considers the best site for its channel institutions they must examine two factors: where and when. As is true with all good businesses, nonprofits should select sites that provide optimal convenience and exposure to all their stakeholders, especially customers. The easier the outlet is to find and use, the more likely customers will return. Yet, the old adage assigned to the success of retailers—location, location, location!—is not as critical for nonprofits. Plus, there is the possibility that a nonprofit will have a space donated for free or at a greatly reduced rent. Even in these cases the organization still must consider convenience and visibility. Likewise, if the customer must come in contact with middlemen employed by the nonprofit, convenience and visibility must also be selection criteria. It would make little sense for a customer to deal with a producer on one side of town and the middleman on the opposite side.

The *when* is just as important. When should the outlet open for the day and when should it close? Nonprofit clients are notorious for wanting services when they want them, regardless of how much it might inconvenience staff. Services cannot be stored and nonprofits must often accommodate these requests.

The demands of clients must be balanced with the operational capacity of the nonprofit. That is, it does not depend on the number of clients but on the maximum number of clients for which the system is designed. For many nonprofits, such as colleges, for a system designed to service 5,000 students during the day and 2,000 students at night, costs won't differ much up to a certain point. However, if enrollment rises to 8,000, the total costs may exceed total revenue. In a similar example, an emergency medical clinic may determine that being open 24 hours a day, seven days a week makes no sense from an operational and service perspective. There is an example in Lexington, Kentucky where two such clinics coordinated hours and directed clients to the other clinic when they were closed. In the end, the nonprofit must decide who will bear the various costs, the customer or them. What is the optimal level of distribution intensity? Recall from our earlier discussion that intensity refers to the amount of the market covered by the nonprofit's distribution network—the greater the intensity, the larger the percentage of potential customers (clients, donors) exposed to the nonprofit products. Traditionally, this decision is determined by the type of service product being offered. Military recruiting offices are found in every city of any noteworthy size, but government-run bookstores are concentrated in Washington, D.C., with only 19 outlets in other states. This dispersion could even vary within an industry. The number of state lottery offices differs dramatically from state to state. If we start with the option of exclusive distribution (one outlet per geographic area) we can suggest possible guidelines. First, this approach tends to work best for products that are purchased infrequently. Adopting a pet represents a product that is purchased infrequently. Second, it should be a product that is consumed over a long period of time. An adopted pet can live for many years. Finally, a great many choices are available to the customer. Animal shelters certainly offer many alternatives for people to donate and adopt dogs and cats.

Should We Use Intensive or Selective Distribution?

Intensive distribution represents the antithesis of selective distribution in that the goal is to have the product available in as many outlets as possible. The intent is to provide the customer with as much convenience as possible. The retail outlets have no interest in promoting one brand over another, and their responsibility is to simply shelve the product and collect payment. For example, contraceptives in poor countries are distributed through medical channels such as health centers, clinics, and hospitals, but also through commercial outlets such as retailers on-the-street vendors, and churches.

Most nonprofits opt for a selective distribution strategy. This in-between approach suggests that only some of the available outlets are selected to distribute the product. In the world of nonprofits, this is often a compromise position rather than a true distribution strategy. The YMCA would like to have a facility in every city with a population of more than 25,000 citizens, but that is not feasible. Still, the word "selective" should be taken as a guideline, and outlets should be chosen in light of the overall marketing strategy.

CONCLUSIONS

It is hard for nonprofit marketers to imagine how the channel management concept applies to them. Thinking of a nonprofit as a manufacturer or a retailer doesn't sound right. Yet, taken in the context that a nonprofit sells service products, a channel does exist. Applying the principles of channel management can mean that a nonprofit understands that a convenient location is important for their clients, volunteers, and potential donors. Realizing that a Web site is part of the channel places additional focus on this tool and expands its functions. The notion of creating satellite locations can create an important competitive advantage. The channel is usually the most expensive part of marketing, and a nonprofit marketer would be wise to know how to create and manage it cost effectively.

12

RAISING FUNDS AND ACQUIRING VOLUNTEERS

Not-for-profit organizations need strong boards of directors, loyal supporters, and a keen sense of mission; not-for-profit organizations also need cash.

—Stanley Weinstein, professional fundraiser

Leo Grillo has a passion. His goal is to rescue every abandoned dog or cat outside his backyard, but especially in the Los Angeles National Forest. He then provides the animals with a permanent home at a 125-acre shelter. The shelter has 960 dogs and 600 cats, all of which Mr. Grillo has rescued personally.

Although maintaining the shelter is an expensive proposition, Mr. Grillo has proven to be a gifted fundraiser. The shelter, known as Dedication and Everlasting Home to Animals, or Delta Rescue, survives solely on private donations of more than $5.5 million per year, and enough cash flows in to finance another of Mr. Grillo's passions—creating documentary and feature films about animals.

The shelter spares no expense in providing a good life for the animals. Most of the dogs live in straw bale and stucco houses in relatively large pens that each contain two animals. The cats live in dozens of "catteries," including one that has an elaborate Wild West theme. At any given time, the shelter hospital is providing chemotherapy to 10 to 15 dogs.

Mr. Grillo's success in fundraising appears to rest on two elements. First, the recognition that there are pet lovers everywhere who want to "make sure that animals get a fair shake." Delta is a "no-kill" shelter. The second is the "power of a good story." The latter actually helps the former self-select. In a typical letter to donors, which he drafts with a fountain pen, Mr. Grillo tells an emotional story about rescuing an animal. He will spend hours photographing the animal he is talking about in the letter, trying to capture the emotion that prompted him to write about it in the first place. He closes each letter with a plea for financial support. "Please send your best gift today. We have over 1,500 animals to feed, care for, and love." Notes retired fundraising consultant, Jerry Huntsinger, "People don't really care about the organization...they care about who the charity helps, whether it is animals, feeding refugees, or fighting disease."

INTRODUCTION

Leo Grillo is a very successful nonprofit marketer. Despite the fact that he hasn't had the opportunity to read this book, he appears to have a fundamental understanding of services marketing—the way you make a nonprofit more tangible is through personalization. Connect potential donors and volunteers with examples they can identify with in a real way and you are more likely to be successful—you will get a lot of people to care about what your organization does and how it does it. You want the donor and volunteer to take ownership in your program. This means that you want to acquaint donors with what you are as an organization (via a clear mission), what you are trying to get accomplished (via clear objectives), so that they can identify with both. Everything has to be tied back to the benefits to the community.

There are literally thousands of consultants you can hire, books you can read, and software you can install that will help you raise money and/or attract volunteers. In many cases, a nonprofit's dire need to create programs or find a new location drives the entire organization and leads to the tactics discussed in earlier chapters. Fundraising and volunteer acquisition must be part of the marketing plan rather than the only element that resembles marketing.

In this chapter, we will look at both of these challenges from a strategic perspective. It should be noted that both are also unique to the United States. They also provide greater benefits than those provided to the individual nonprofit. First of all, campaigns such as the American Heart Association or the Salvation Army or the Girl Scouts let people get involved and that becomes important because they do become advocates. In addition, in the United States charitable giving is as much a force in the freedom of democracy as the right of assemblage, right to vote, or freedom of the press. It's another way of expressing ourselves. Someone who pays taxes does not think of himself or herself as getting involved in the welfare program. But if they invest in a Salvation Army activity or the Visiting Nurses program, they do feel involved. They are involved spiritually and they are involved monetarily. That makes a difference.

SOURCES OF REVENUE AND RELATED TRENDS

A simple rule-of-thumb in the charitable institutions sector is to divide the sources of revenues into three equal parts:

- 1/3 from fundraising
- 1/3 from membership dues
- 1/3 from program revenue

Yet, the fact is, these numbers are the equivalent of the Census reporting that the average American family has 1.78 children—it's a meaningless number. Often, averages or industry norms represent nobody. The reality is that each 501(c)3 has its own set of unique needs. To illustrate this point, consider the basic needs of a sample of nonprofits in Wichita, Kansas:

- Caring Hearts—needs 30 medium-sized frozen turkeys, packages of socks and underwear for children ages 2 to 18, and 100 plain cardboard boxes for canned donations.
- Forever Crowned—needs a building 4,000 square feet or larger; four portable classrooms and a moving company to move them; monetary donations; men's suits, shoes, and accessories. Volunteers—grant writer, GED instructor.
- Salvation Army—needs hygiene items, nonperishable food, infant items, supplies for middle/high school students, bed and bath linens, plastic dishware, winter items, etc. Volunteers—holiday bell ringers.
- Quivira Council Boy Scouts of America—needs white copy paper, Adobe software, ready-to-eat snacks, new hand and power tools for camps, 80 psi compressor, and black top repaired.

Admittedly, many of these items will be purchased through cash donations, but the cost of having a volunteer blacktop your parking lot is far less expensive than hiring someone to do it. The point is that every nonprofit has its own set of basic needs and using national figures as a reference point can be misleading. Perhaps the information displayed in Exhibit 12.1 describes the needs of nonprofits a bit better.

Viewing needs in this manner provides a better match between specific needs identified, individuals providing these needs, and a strategy for meeting

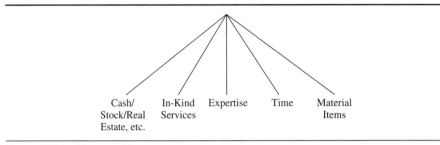

Exhibit 12.1   Needs of Nonprofits

each type of need. This will take the nonprofit marketer away from the generalization that fundraising is the only prospect for sustaining and growing the organization and appreciate all the other possible sources of support.

Where the Money Comes From

For most nonprofits the primary need is to acquire money. There are three traditional revenue streams for nonprofits. 1. Earned income: fees for service, enrollments or sales; 2. Government: from local municipalities to federal agencies; and 3. Contributed income: foundations, corporations, and individuals. According to a recent report published by *Giving USA*, the annual tally of philanthropy in the United States was $260.3 billion in 2005, an increase of 27 percent after inflation. About half of 2005's $15 billion increase in donations over 2004 was given in response to three natural disasters: the Indonesian tsunamis, the Gulf Coast hurricanes, and the earthquake in Pakistan. Nearly 60 percent of 803 charities that were surveyed by *Giving USA* reported that they had raised more money in 2005 than in 2004, and 28 percent said they had raised less. The pie chart in Exhibit 12.2 displays the sources of the $260 billion. Historically, individual donors are the dominant source of dollars, representing 77 percent of the 2005 total. Other relevant facts include the following:

- While donations from living Americans grew by 2.9 percent bequests dropped by 8.6 percent, reflecting a decline in death rate.
- Corporate giving increased by 18.5 percent, prompted by higher profits and contributions to disaster relief.
- Grants from private, community, and operating foundations rose by 2.1 percent.
- The role of the government as the provider of safety net services and core community benefits has significantly diminished.

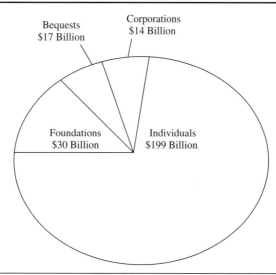

Corporations
$14 Billion

Bequests
$17 Billion

Foundations
$30 Billion

Individuals
$199 Billion

EXHIBIT 12.2 CHARITABLE GIVING: 2005

- Globalization of markets has resulted in fewer "home town" companies.

The distribution of these funds to the various recipients is as follows:

Religion	$93.18 B
Education	38.56 B
Human Services	25.36 B
Health	22.54 B
Public/Society benefits	14.03 B
Arts, culture, humanities	13.51 B
Environment, animals	8.86 B
Other	44.24 B

While donations to human-services organizations rose by 28 percent, since 2005, not all types of charities fared well. Churches and other religious organizations failed to keep up with inflation, while health charities and cultural groups suffered a decline.

The report also identifies several possible challenges. For example, rising gas prices might deter donors, since they will have less disposable income.

There is also evidence that despite the fact that foundations have increased their giving, the grants are smaller and the duration has been shorter. These is also evidence that there will be a decline in bequests, due in part to low birth rates from 1924 to 1935. In addition, if Congress abolishes the estate tax or changes it in some meaningful way, fewer people will have to pay—and those who do will pay lower rates. This could produce fewer bequests.

While all the sources of revenue are important to most nonprofits, we will focus on raising money from individuals in the form of donations. It represents the primary source of income, and nonprofits that are dependent on the other methods are referred to the many specialized references.

Guidelines for Fundraising

Smart businesspeople try to make the most money over a long period of time. There is no reason why a nonprofit marketer can not do the same. Since 80 percent of the money derived for nonprofits comes from individuals, it makes sense to spend 80 percent of your fund raisingfundraising resources asking individuals for money. Train your staff, board, and volunteers to be constantly collecting fund raising-relevant information. In one recent survey, nearly 90 percent of people said they would give "if they were asked."

The following principles have evolved over centuries to produce the best results from fundraising.

- *Make the Most Money in the Least Amount of Time*. You want to make a lot of money quickly, so that the staff and volunteers can spend more of their time and effort on the nonprofit's programs. It is much easier and more efficient to ask for a $75 donation than to sell twenty $5 raffle tickets. This doesn't preclude careful planning. It includes doing research on the market and target donors, as well as a realization that you will only be successful if you have a product line that is deemed valuable to these individuals.
- *Think Long-Range*. There is no reason to reinvent yourself every year. Instead, the fundraising process should employ a long time perspective. An event this year should be viewed as training for next year. This not only imposes learning to the activity, but it also improves the likehood that each ensuing year will be more successful. Finally, it denotes that the process will be strategic in its underpinnings.
- *Accurate Record-Keeping is Critical*. The best way to make sure you have control over your fund raisingfundraising is to maintain clear and

complete records. Clarity is desirable in all fundraising efforts; it is indispensable in your record keeping. Reports that only the treasurer or your CPA can decode or records written on the back of last weeks' agenda are confusing in the short run and lead to disaster in the long run. In addition, the legal and ethical needs to be both accountable and transparent make this a mandate rather than a choice.

- *Identify the Donors' Personal Interest*. While the activity of asking people for money sounds simple enough, the fun comes when we try to identify the reasons why each person donates. Why do they give? Why do they want to return? What is their self-interest? Do they want to be contacted directly or indirectly? There are no general surveys that will provide you with this information. The need is for personal research, since giving is an individualized activity. If you want to find a prospective donor's self-interest, all you really need to do is ask.

- *Make it Enjoyable*. Fundraising is stressful for all those involved. Therefore, it is important to include fun into the process. If done correctly, fundraising can facilitate the personal growth of all those involved and increase the budget at the same time. Each person will feel more and more self-confident, closer to the other members and provider of the organization as the fundraising effort goes on. All these pleasant outcomes are only possible if there is good training, the right people are assigned to the right tasks, and the process is effectively managed.

There is one more preliminary consideration before engaging in the fundraising process. *Fundraising must align with the mission of the nonprofit*. External considerations are many. A nonprofit must be very careful to not accept donations with "strings attached." These "strings" may take the organization away from its primary mission or they may even be in conflict with the mission. The mission cannot be compromised because of conditions prescribed by donors. Likewise, the mere association of the nonprofit and the donor or donor organization may reflect badly on the reputation of the nonprofit. This occurred recently with charities that were sponsored by United Way. There are also internal considerations. Most notably, nonprofit must seek funding that safely and reliably provides for the health of the nonprofit. Grants, for example, are very unpredictable, as is heavy reliance on an individual or organization. If this attitude of "putting all your eggs in one basket" jeopardizes the mission, it should be reconsidered. We begin with a review of why people donate.

UNDERSTANDING WHY PEOPLE DONATE

The reasons why people donate money to charities and other nonprofit organizations are complex and somewhat varied. A rule-of-thumb in the fundraising industry is that "people give to people...to help people." And, as our opening vignette suggests, they also "give to animals...to help animals." They don't give to institutions. Still, it's not that simple. A tremendous amount of research has been conducted on better understanding "why people donate." A recent national survey sponsored by Public Agenda offered the following findings:

- Most donors are enthusiastic and positive about the organizations they give to and about the charitable sector in general.
- Most donors were aware of highly-publicized scandals at some charities, and their recollections were specific and clear-cut. In most cases, these scandals had led them to avoid giving to the organization in the future.
- Most donors appear to base their giving on a gut-level interest in a cause and a faith in the people involved. Very few carefully researched their giving decisions.
- People give in relation to their means and in relation to what others give.
- Although well aware of problems and scandals in the sector, very few donors called for more government oversight and regulation.
- Most donors seemed to admire and trust local nonprofits more than the government and more than "far away" national charities.
- Donors did complain about some fundraising techniques used by charities to raise money, and often volunteered examples of what they saw as "slick," inappropriate, or wasteful practices.
- Highly-polished direct mail campaigns, telemarketing, unsolicited premiums, multiple or duplicate appeals in a short period of time were often cited as examples of charities acting like "businesses."

We appear to know little about this donation process per se. In part this is due to the typical nature of the donation exchange process. Unlike a normal exchange where both parties give and receive something of tangible and immediate value, the donation exchange process provides no such guarantee to the donor and in some cases the recipient. In fact, in many instances there is no direct reward, or the reward is intangible or delayed. Clearly, it is difficult to understand what prompts an individual to engage in such an unbalanced relationship.

At least part of the confusion about the donation process is the lack of clarity about the concept itself. Clearly, the most general construct is prosocial behavior, behavior that is valued by the individual's society. *Helping behavior* can be considered to be a subcategory of prosocial behavior-defined as "voluntary acts performed with the intent to provide some benefit to another person, that may or may not require personal contact with the recipient and may or may not involve anticipation of external rewards."

Donation appears to differ from general helping behavior in respect to two specific dimensions: 1. the typical participants in the exchange, and 2. the characteristics of the resources donated. In regard to the former, the donor is an individual and the recipient may be an individual group, or institution. In regard to the latter parameter, personal donation includes the giving of resources that are tangible and have some economic value. This would include money, assets, and blood and body parts. These two characteristics not only distinguish donation behavior from other types of helping behavior but also bring it within the realm of consumer behavior.

Exhibit 12.3 displays a simple model of donation behavior. We will try to explain the elements as completely as possible. We begin with a discussion of giver characteristics.

Giver Characteristics

As indicated, there are several personal and demographic characteristics associated with people who donate. These variables tend to vary from study-to-

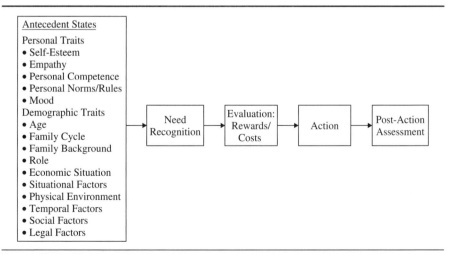

EXHIBIT 12.3 DONATION DECISION MODEL

study, and it is difficult to identify consistent characteristics. Fortunately, there appears to be a framework that offers a way of synthesizing and better understanding the characteristics of the giver: the altruistic personality. An *altruistic personality* tends to be more empathetic to the feelings and needs of others and sees the world from an emotional perspective. He or she has internalized personal rules of justice, social responsibility, and modes of moral reasoning, judgment, and knowledge. Moreover, the consistently altruistic person is likely to have an integrated personality, strong feelings of personal efficacy and well-being, and what might generally be called "integrity." We also know that these characteristics, while somewhat stable during a persons' life, do increase or decrease based on the age, life-situation, mood, and so forth, of the individual. Finally, altruism is on a continuum rather than a dichotomy, with people moving up and down on this continuum throughout their life. As such, altruism is a valid touchstone in identifying donors as well. The following five personal characteristics have consistently correlated with the altruistic personality.

Self-Esteem. Self-esteem is a feeling of general competence. Evidence exists that self-esteem is correlated with positive character traits. Self-esteem bears a significant relationship both to volunteering to help and to helping. Furthermore, successful helping serves to reinforce one's self-esteem.

Personal Competence. An individual whose goal is to help and/or enhance the self-concept, and who is also competent and self-confident engages in helping behavior. In general, both actual competence (e.g., physical prowess, financial resources) and perceived competence (e.g., experience, feedback from others) have been found to be related to helping.

Empathy. Empathy may be defined as experiencing the emotional state of another. This matching of emotion can result from either, 1. cues given off directly by the other person, or 2. one person's conscious knowledge of the other person's situation. Several studies have found a relationship between empathy and altruistic or helping behavior.

Personal Norms/Roles. In every society, individuals develop behaviors that they feel reflect their own personalities, experience, and value. One part of this behavioral pattern is referred to as our personal norms. Social psychologists define social norms as a set of social do's and don'ts—shared expectations about how we should act, backed by the threat of group sanctions or the promise of rewards. A *rule* may be defined as a standard by which events are judged and on that basis, approved or disapproved. Those that are held strongly enough to be considered "oughts" are called moral principles. Those held more abstractly are referred to as "values." There is evidence that there is a link between internalized values and helping behavior.

Mood State. Mood is a condition of latent affective tone that is subject to change through the intervention of relatively weak situational events. It excludes deep or chronic states such as clinical depression. In general, the relationship between mood state and altruism tends to be U-shaped. That is, both positive and negative moods produce more benevolence than a neutral mood. The relationship between negative mood state and altruism has been somewhat inconsistent, while the relationship between a positive mood state and donation behavior has been consistently positive.

In a recent study, Marc Barasch surveyed and observed individuals living in Canada in respect to their altruistic tendencies. He concluded that 1.5 percent (1 out of 70) were dyed-in-the-wool altruistic. Some of the characteristics that were noted included: tender-minded, an insatiable intellectual curiosity and a willingness to think outside the box, a tendency to question authority, a highly integrated spiritual belief system (not necessarily based on an organized religion), a high level of trust (in others, in the future, in fate, in the heart).

In summary, understanding these traits that correlate with altruism is an excellent starting point in generating donations. If one consistently and authentically appeals to these characteristics, success should follow.

Demographic characteristics have been the focus of most of the research conducted on donor characteristics. The information is relatively easy to collect and match with type and level of giving. For example, a partial list of demographic traits associated with charitable giving include the following: occupation, children (number and age), home ownership, age, income, education, sex, and race. In respect to specific studies: seniors (age 75 +) are the most likely to have contributed to health causes, as well as most likely to give to religious, social services, and political nonprofits; significantly fewer GenY's (7 to 27 years old) have given money to a charity; 70 percent of both Gen X (ages 28 to 42) and Baby Bloomers (ages 42-60) plan to give to charities; a higher number of New Englanders give to charity than do residents of any other region of the country; individuals in the $75,000 to $99,999 are the most generous income group. Worth noting is the fact that these reported results are not always consistent, nor do they distinguish the various recipients of these donations. The demographics listed in Exhibit 12.3 are those that appear most reliable.

Age has clearly been a reliable characteristic. The elderly do donate at the highest level. Next, individuals who are "empty nesters" or further along in their family life cycle give more. There is also evidence that individuals who come from a family of givers are more likely to give themselves. Closely related is the role the individual played growing up. The eldest child, often the caregiver, turns out to care for people throughout his life. Finally, a person who has a healthy economic situation is prompted to donate at a higher level than a person who is struggling economically. Recall from our earlier discussion that donors are responsible and would not jeopardize their family's well-being by donating money they don't have.

All this demographic information is easy to collect and would create a reliable profile of a potential donor. Combine this with the altruistic-related information discussed earlier, and a comprehensive target market emerges.

Situational Variables

Identifying and better understanding the role of situational variables accounts for exceptions and for motivations related to giving behavior. Several situational variables have been identified that may impact an individual's willingness to give:

- Physical environment—location, decor, sounds, and similar physical stimuli
- Temporal factors—the time of the day, the interpurchase interval, time pressure, and so on
- Social—presence of other people, interpersonal interaction, and so on
- Legal—laws and physical restrictions

The research findings connecting situational variables with giving behavior are marginal. Still, the nonprofit marketer should be cognizant that these situational variables may be important, and do the personal research to see how they impact their situation.

Need Recognition

The actual decision to donate begins with an awareness of a need. Unlike a personal unfulfilled need to buy more milk, replace a car, or take a much needed vacation, the need, in this case, is someone else's. While the donor may have an internal need to feel better about themselves, or a practical need to get a tax deduction, the focus is on the need of the charity's recipients.

Creating need awareness for a nonprofit may be quite different than that employed for a for-profit. For instance, the need request may be quite explicit, such as a request from the recipient or through an agent of the recipient, such as a fellow worker, advertisement, or a letter from a board member; or implicit, such as a general awareness that there are poor people who need help or watching your alma mater win a football game.

An anomaly associated with recognizing a need in a nonprofit setting is the role played by the recipient. Potential donors evaluate the behavior of recipients as part of their determination that there is a "real" need. Anything that a donor reads, sees, or hears about the behavior of a recipient that is perceived as disingenuous, will reduce the validity of the need and the behavior of a donor. The many scandals attached to nonprofits, along with outrageous salaries paid to some nonprofit executives, are examples of negative recipient behavior.

In general, if the appearance, behavior, and response of the recipient is viewed favorably by the potential donor, then personal contact is a positive strategy. In contrast, recipients who are not grateful enough or are too grateful, behave rudely, or don't appear worthy of the donation, are unlikely to receive further benefits.

In addition, while we normally think of donation as one individual helping a lesser one, the donation of resources to an institution may prompt an entirely different interpretation of the role played by the recipient. In the case of donating money to a church, museum, or university, for example, it may be important that the recipient be positioned as having a role somewhat equivalent to the donor. Perhaps this is due, at least partly, to the fact the donor expects to eventually recoup part of his or her donation.

Evaluation of Rewards and Costs

Once a potential donor determines there is a legitimate need, they next assess the possible rewards and costs if they are to pursue a donation. At least part of the assessment entails what is referred to as *obligation salience*. A variety of factors enter into this consideration. Societal norms can be quite important, particularly if the donation phenomenon has received some sort of affirmation from a particular society or culture. For example, giving money to the church, synagogue, mosque, or other religious institution is considered quite appropriate in the United States in general, even more appropriate in the Mormon culture, and less appropriate in France. Personal norms reflect our tendency to evaluate behaviors and requests in a unique manner. The notion of being a giving, caring person may mean we always react favorably to requests for help. Of course, the opposite may also be true. We also evaluate the relative seriousness of the request. Research suggests that people have giving priorities, with their religious organization being most important and nonobligatory commitments, such as the United Way, being lowest. Seriousness might also vary depending on who delivers the message, and whether this request is delivered in person or through an impersonal medium. Finally, compliance factors are considered. What are we really being asked to do? Is the request reasonable? If compliance involves possible discomfort, the process may stop there.

Having completed the obligation assessment, the individual will next engage in an evaluation of possible costs and rewards. Inhibitory factors would probably be considered first. Can I really afford to donate? Am I qualified? How do I really feel about the recipient? Are there any comparable donating experiences that provide positive or negative feedback? How much personal control do I have? What is the true nature of the request? What is the time of commitment? Will I be asked to give again?

Possible rewards can be both tangible and intangible. An alumni donates $5,000 to his college so that he has season tickets and receives certain privilege when he is on campus. However, he also expects to enhance his self-esteem. This is an area where the marketer should consider the characteristics exhibited by the altruistic giver. The challenge is to tangibilize these intangible benefits. Clearly, there needs to be a tangible metric that verifies that the money donated produced the promised benefits.

Making the Decision

The decision related to donation parallels the same set of options we employ as consumers: delay, no action, action. As noted in earlier discussions, habit may play a prominent role. Many people write a check to their church every Sunday morning. Automatic bank drafts or other automatic deduction systems place habit into the realm of technology. In a broader sense, habit may be a reflection of one's general predilection to donate or not donate, given certain factors. The result being the mental reference point—"I always donate when asked."

This is a point in the donation process where the marketer must play a prominent role. Once again, solid marketing research is very helpful. You should understand how the potential donor arrived at this point in the process. What positive and negative criteria have been employed? Is there a deal-breaker? Is there a factor that will promote action? Are they long-standing givers? If so, what have been their giving patterns? Are they bored? If the person is a new giver, we need to know if they give to other nonprofits? What donation process are they comfortable with? How do we deal with objections for both groups?

As is evident, this is not a time for the marketer to sit back and allow the potential donor to act independently. Rather, it is a time when the marketer can make a big difference by both understanding the donor and facilitating positive action, again and again.

Evaluation

The final stage in the donation decision process is to evaluate the outcome. Now that we have made the donation, how do we feel about the results? Are the rewards as great as we thought they would be? Are the costs as bad? Was the recipient grateful? Helped? Since this final assessment involves mostly intangibles and is mostly subjective, it remains an area misunderstood. While donation agencies have attempted a great deal of tangibalization (children's agencies provide a bio of a child, charities announce the names of donors, universities honor donors at award dinners), the actual results are difficult to appraise. The better we understand the donor, what motivates her, and what her expectations are, the more likely the evaluation will be in our favor.

ARE YOU READY TO RAISE MONEY?

Too many nonprofits assume that raising money, via donors, memberships, sales of products, or fees, is simply a decision the executive director and board members make whenever they gauge there's a need. This ad hoc approach to fundraising is a terrible mistake. Fundraising is a tactical alternative that is derived from the marketing plan and the ensuing strategies. Therefore, we offer the following checklist that you can employ to determine if you are prepared for fundraising.

1. An understandable mission statement that encompasses:
   o What issue/need/problem we work on
   o Who we serve
   o How?
   o To what end? Why?
2. Clearly delineated objectives that are derived from:
   o A comprehensive situation analysis
   o Strengths, weaknesses, opportunities, and threats (S.W.O.T)
   o Identification of the key target markets
   o Assurance that the services offered are of high quality
3. Identification of strategies that will be employed to achieve objectives, along with projected costs
4. Financial assessment of your organization for the last five years, including a delineation of actual revenue sources/amounts and costs
   o Determine the areas of success and failures in respect to past fundraising efforts.
   o Identify trends in fundraising for your sector

5. Identify the structure of your organization, along with its capacity to grow or change directions. Make sure the board is strong. Develop an active volunteer pool.
6. Determine the amount of funds available for fundraising.

STEPS IN FUNDRAISING

There are many different suggested paths for successful fundraising. The following steps reflect a compilation. Several sources are referenced at the end of this chapter for those who want more detail.

Step 1. *Gather information.* Schedule an initial fundraising planning meeting with the board, key staff, and individuals who have participated in past fundraising efforts. Review the mission statement/vision statement, as well as the proposed marketing plan. Identify relevant marketing research information: both information already collected and that which still needs to be collected. Identify all fundraising assets (i.e. talents, connections, access). Determine how much the organization has netted from the following: personal major gift solicitation, mail, telephone, special events, grants, bequests, and other planned gifts. What are your human resources? What is your equipment and facilities status? What is your budget?

Step 2. *Identify target donor prospects.* Understand that the assessment of target donor prospects should be from the point-of-view of the donor, not the needs of the organization. Find out what each target prospect wants and then show them how the prescribed action, i.e. donating, meets their needs. Identify the altruism-related traits, demographics, and situational variables that prompt them to give. Finally, determine whether they are the right donors, given the mission statement.

Step 3. *Set Goals and Objectives.* Setting appropriate goals and objectives is one of the most important tasks in fundraising. This process can be very detailed and should include the following:

   o Review income history over the last few years (income statement, major donor giving histories, reasons for successes/failures).
   o Assess the competitive situation.
   o Identify patterns in income.
   o Project potential income and set objectives for each source.
   o Match these with projected expenses.

Step 4. *Devise strategies for reaching each objective.* Begin with an appraisal of your overall fundraising plan, delineating how important each source of revenue (i.e. grants, corporate support, contributed income, earned income, etc.), will be. Depending upon this assessment, possible strategic alternatives might include segmentation, product focus, direct marketing, cost-cutting, outspending, and so forth.

Step 5. *Implement strategic alternatives.* The specific tactics, or actions, selected as the detailed part of each strategy represents the broadest area of fundraising. Before discussing some of these tactics, there are some preliminary considerations:

  ○ Consider how to train your staff and indicate the number of staff employed to fundraise and time they will spend on this task.

  ○ Consider how to train your board members and indicate the number of board members employed to fundraise and time they will spend on this task.

  ○ Devise a timetable that characterizes the annual efforts by short/intermediate/or long-term activities; give a preview of the activities in a summary that allows participants, upon reading, to know what to expect throughout the year(s).

Tactical Considerations

There are many tactics employed to raise money. The following represent the most often used, along with a brief description. There are many excellent references that discuss these tactics in detail. It is critical that these tactics be tied to a comprehensive marketing plan and not be considered in isolation.

  • *Direct Mail:* one of the most utilized methods for raising operational monies; also one of the most expensive. A 2 percent response rate is normal. A shotgun approach is often used, making it necessary to carefully identify the market you are mailing to, and to carefully consider the cost of mailing. Direct mail is still considered the most successful fundraising tactic.

  • *Special Events:* an exciting way to raise funds, which can also result in exposure and good public relations for your organization. There are very good ways and very bad ways to run special events. You should expect to make a 5 to 10 percent profit the first year (assuming you keep accurate cost records) and 25 to 35 percent the second year.

- *Planned Giving:* an extremely visible means of adding additional revenue, particularly as your constituents grow older. This can include bequests, uni-trusts, reverse mortgages, as well as many other giving instruments that can be used in planned giving.
- *Board of Directors Giving:* an accepted and necessary form of giving. Corporations and foundations want to know what percentage of the board actually gives. This giving is often put on a sliding scale.
- *Telemarketing:* a select way to raise money for certain projects. Some people in the field have misused this method, so you must be sure your process is a secure one. Door-to-door canvassing can be included in this category.
- *Fee for Service:* the fee that is generated from clients. It is a way to give clients more of a vested interest in the organization. It also gives the donor another criteria when looking at your organization.
- *In-Kind Donations:* an invaluable source of support. This can meet needs in virtually all phases of the organization, from obtaining bed linens from a hospital that has disposed of them after a set period, to securing the pro bono services of a corporate executive to work on a long-range marketing plan.
- *Capital Campaign:* not just bricks and mortar, but a campaign at generating an influx of money. This is usually a major effort that requires an expanded board, a timeline, a definite goal, and perhaps an outside consultant. Most capital campaigns bring in new donors due to the new or renewed excitement around this type of fund drive.
- *Annual Campaign:* sometimes referred to as the membership campaign; this is your annual appeal for support and should include: 1. a letter asking for the money and 2. another letter to act as a memory trigger.
- *Matching Gift Program:* you can determine if your staff, volunteers, or board members and their families work for companies that have matching gift programs by conducting a careful inventory. This means that the organization will match any commitment made by that contact within your organization. This is a consideration when seeking both volunteers and board members.
- *Volunteer Giving:* this doesn't sound promising, but it is extremely viable. Volunteers are often your most reliable source of donations. Since they are insiders, you must be sure that you are using monies effectively, and that there is an overt appreciation of their volunteer efforts.

- *Shared Services:* one of the most overlooked forms of income. Any way that you can reduce the outlay of your organization is worth exploring. By sharing the expense of administration or sharing a van with another organization, you are both benefiting.
- *Speaker's Bureau:* a speaker's bureau takes advantage of the fact that you have an exciting organization with something to say and someone to say it to. Begin with a publicity campaign to make your nonprofit the "source of expertise" on your issue and make your leader the authority. Contact the program chairman of all the civic organizations, professional organizations, houses of worship, and schools in your area. Creating a sliding scale fee, schedule based on the number of people in the audience and length of the presentation.
- *Selling Products:* selling good products can provide a dependable source of income for the group as well as provide a satisfying form of involvement for volunteers. You want to sell something that appeals to the general public but still connects with the focus of the organization.
- *Online Fund Raising:* the Internet has now become an immediate, convenient, and safe way for donors to give; online donations increased by 50 percent from 2005 to 2006 (mostly because of donations to Katrina) and are expected to continue to grow in the future. Currently, a nonprofit must have a Web site, e-mail, newsletter, and online stores. Individual donors are giving 31 percent more online than offline: $116.65 online versus $89.25 offline. The only reason to use the Internet is to build better relationships: relationships with current supporters/members and donors, relationships with people you serve, and relationships with prospective supporters and donors. The expected response rate is 6 percent. Combine offline and online donation efforts for an even better percentage rate.

Step 6. *Create a budget.* It is important to create and accurate and realistic budget and related worksheet. In addition, individual "gift solicitation" trading documents should feed into the overall budgetary document. Ultimately, the nonprofit's staff and board members have two concerns related to the organization's budget: the nonprofit institution's overall budget and fiscal health, and the budget and cost-effectiveness of the fundraising program. With careful monitoring of the budget process, management can determine in advance to what extent contributed income is especially urgent or when financing might be needed. Budgeting is imperative for the board and management to anticipate unfavorable situations and to take timely corrective action. Budgeting also allows the board and management to identify unexpected favorable variance. Unanticipated positive cash results can signal a fundraising or earned income opportunity on which to build.

Step 7. *Evaluate results and make changes.* Accountability remains one of the major weaknesses in nonprofit fundraising. Specific metrics should be created at the same time that objectives are delineated. Often the total actual costs of fundraising are not identified, meaning that the return-on-investment measure is inflated. Should former donors be separated from new donors? There must be an efficient and systematic process for tracking gifts, collecting money, and providing acknowledgments. Likewise, frequent reports, meetings and other information should be shared with appropriate stakeholders. Finally, share results. If you were successful, celebrate. If you fell short of expectations, ascertain errors so that you may correct them next time.

THE CASE STATEMENT

A document that states the major reasons for supporting the nonprofit organization is the comprehensive formal case statement. It serves as the touch point for all outgoing communication. It addresses the following questions:

- What is the organization's history?
  - Founding dates and founders
  - Primary accomplishments
  - Crucial points in its evolution
- Whom does the organization serve?
  - Demographic characteristics
  - Behavioral descriptions-anecdotes
- What needs are being served?
  - The primary challenges
  - Status of the problem
- What are the solutions offered by the organization?
  - Description of programs
  - Additional services
- What is the reputation of the nonprofit as a business?
  - Evidence that the organization is stable
  - Evidence that the organization is fiscally secure

- How is the planning process described?
  - ○ Identify the participants
  - ○ Indicate broadness level
  - ○ Indicate thoroughness
- What are the goals for the future?
  - ○ Indicate areas where goals are applied
  - ○ Identify how goals will benefit the various stakeholders
- How will the donors' contribution be used?
  - ○ Reasons for fundraising
  - ○ Identify budget items
  - ○ Relevance to company's mission
- How will the donor be acknowledged?
  - ○ Identify tangible elements
  - ○ Identify intangible elements

Development planners who answer all these questions will have created a comprehensive formal case for support. This written document should be shared with all those participating in fundraising. It clarifies the organization's thinking. It gets everyone moving in the same direction and provides a common language to address questions and concerns.

RECRUITING AND MANAGING VOLUNTEERS

Volunteers can play a vital role in the success of many nonprofit organizations. These individuals, because of their dedication and belief in the organization, can lower the costs of the nonprofit as well as serve as a primary source of consistent support. Volunteers differ from donors in that the former give intangibles such as time and/or expertise, while the latter give tangibles. Although no one knows the exact number of volunteers at any point in time, it would be safe to say volunteer's number in the millions.

Recent statistics indicate the following:

- Volunteers spent an average of 134 hours on volunteer activities from September 2004 to September 2005.
- Approximately 30 percent of the total U.S.adult population volunteered at least once (66 million people).
- Donation of time was applied as follows: Religious, 34.8 percent; Educational/Youth Services, 26.2 percent; Social/Community Services, 13.4 percent; Hospital/Health, 7.7 percent; other, 18.7 percent.

- Volunteerism by age is as follows: 16 to 24 years, 24.4 percent; 25 to 34 years, 25.3 percent 35 to 44 years, 34.5 percent; 45 to 54 years, 32.7 percent; 55 to 64 years, 30.2 percent; 65 years and older, 24.8 percent.
- At an estimated value of $18.04 per hour of volunteer work, that equates to about $2,417 given per volunteer.
- The areas of volunteer application are: fundraising, 30 percent; food preparation/serving, 26 percent; labor/transportation, 23 percent; teaching, 21 percent.
- Over 62 percent of charity leaders said they do not rely on any companies to provide volunteers.
- Only 12 percent of nonprofit groups report that they regularly give their volunteers a chance to work on projects that match their skills.
- Over 68 percent of volunteers were college graduates, and 62 percent had income of at least $75,000.
- African Americans, Latinos, and Asian Americans remain less likely to volunteer than the total population.
- Among workers who volunteer, 40 percent said they actively look for opportunities to use the skills they have in their jobs.

The opportunities for volunteers can range from small nonprofits, where every staff member is a volunteer and the process tends to be informal; to more formal areas such as serving as a board member; to very structured volunteering, such as the Peace Corps and Teach for America. It should be noted that applications to the formal groups are at record numbers. This growth is coming from recent college graduates.

The range of activities assigned to volunteers is vast. Some clerical duties and mass mailings don't involve volunteer interface with recipients. There are also volunteers that interact with recipients, ranging from serving food to offering counseling. At the other extreme, volunteers can be called upon to perform critical specialized duties, including doctors and other health care providers who render medical care, finance experts, attorneys, CPAs, and marketers. The line between voluntarism, in-kind services, and pro bono services is muddled. However, there is no doubt that people who share the organization's values can be asked to donate their personal and professional time to the cause.

Why People Volunteer

Since volunteering is the other side of the helping coin, we assume that the decision model describing donation behavior applies to volunteer behavior as well. However, there are some key characteristics that suggest that volunteering is somewhat unique. Most notably, volunteering requires more from the individual than making a donation. The latter may require a few minutes of effort (i.e., writing a check, once or twice each year). Volunteering, in comparison, may require hundreds of hours of the volunteer's time, a variety of inconveniences, and perhaps financial costs. One can safely assume that these costs must be matched with a variety of rewards. If the rewards were not greater, it is unlikely that volunteering would continue.

A second difference is the possible role that donation behavior has on volunteering. For example, it is possible that an individual may volunteer because they either do not have dollars to donate or they are assessing the worthiness of the organization, via volunteering, before they donate. Both possibilities indicate that volunteers should be viewed as potential donors.

A final difference associated with volunteering versus donating relates to the social benefits offered to volunteers. While we mention returning Baby Boomers as a vast pool of volunteers, it may also be a potential cesspool of lonely people looking to gossip and waste time. Nonprofits must be prepared to either screen out or manage volunteers who are there for the wrong reasons.

Beyond these differences, people volunteer for many of the same reasons associated with donating; volunteers have an interest and empathy for the problems addressed by the nonprofit; they feel needed and that their efforts will make a difference; they need to do their civic duty; they have personal interest or experience with the problem the nonprofit seeks to solve; and so forth. Surprisingly, one of the most consistent reasons identified over many years is that the volunteer: "was asked"; and, asking is most effective when the request comes from a friend or current volunteer. The most common reason given for not volunteering is "lack of time."

Managing the Volunteer Product

Offering a person an opportunity to volunteer is just one of the products offered by the nonprofit. As such, it must treated as part of the product line. Key questions should be addressed. Do we need to have volunteers? At what level? For what purposes? How do they interface with the other things we do? Is the program effective? At the base of all this is the need to make sure that someone competent is assigned to managing the volunteer program. Having an effective volunteer program reflects well on the origins of nonprofits discussed in Chapter 1. For most nonprofits, volunteers offer a positive strategic marketing alternative.

REFERENCES

1. "Volunteering in the United States: A Snapshot", *Corporation for National and Community Services*, Reported in *The Chronicle of Philanthropy*, June 29, 2006, p. 39.

2. Beth Walton, "Volunteer Rates Hit Record Numbers", *USA Today*, July 7–9, 2006: p. A1.

3. *GIVING USA 2006: The Annual Report on Philanthropy for the Year 2005*, (New York: Giving the USA Foundation™, 2006).

4. "The Charitable Impulse", *A Report from the Public Agenda for the Kettering Foundation and Independent Sector*, www.publicagenda.org 2006.

5. Marc Ian Barsch, "Extreme Altruists", *Psychology Today*, March–April, 2005: pp. 77–82.

SUGGESTED READINGS

Stanley Weinstein, *The Complete Guide to Fundraising Management*, Second ed. Hoboken, NJ: John Wiley & Sons, 2002.

Joan Flanagan, *The Grassroots Fundraising Book*, Contemporary Books (New York: McGraw-Hill), 1982.

INDEX